Luminos is the Open Access monograph publishing program
from UC Press. Luminos provides a framework for preserving and
reinvigorating monograph publishing for the future and increases
the reach and visibility of important scholarly work. Titles published
in the UC Press Luminos model are published with the same high
standards for selection, peer review, production, and marketing as
those in our traditional program. www.luminosoa.org

Feminist Cyberlaw

Feminist Cyberlaw

Edited by

Meg Leta Jones and Amanda Levendowski

UNIVERSITY OF CALIFORNIA PRESS

University of California Press
Oakland, California

Suggested citation: Jones, M. L. and Levendowski, A. (eds.) *Feminist Cyberlaw*.
Oakland: University of California Press, 2024.
DOI: https://doi.org/10.1525/luminos.190

Library of Congress Cataloging-in-Publication Data

Names: Jones, Meg Leta, editor. | Levendowski, Amanda Marie, 1990– editor.
Title: Feminist cyberlaw / edited by Meg Leta Jones and Amanda
     Levendowski.
Description: Oakland: University of California Press, 2024. |
     Includes bibliographical references and index.
Identifiers: LCCN 2024002406 (print) | LCCN 2024002407 (ebook) |
     ISBN 9780520388543 (paperback) | ISBN 9780520388550 (ebook)
Subjects: LCSH: Computer networks—Law and legislation. |
     Computer networks—Law and legislation—Criminal provisions. |
     Internet—Law and legislation. | Computer networks—Security measures. |
     Feminist jurisprudence. | BISAC: LAW / Computer & Internet |
     COMPUTERS / Internet / Online Safety & Privacy
Classification: LCC K564.C6 F46 2024 (print) | LCC K564.C6 (ebook) |
     DDC 343.09/944082—dc23/eng/20240129

33 32 31 30 29 28 27 26 25 24
10 9 8 7 6 5 4 3 2 1

For Jinx
For Cameron

CONTENTS

Introduction

Cyberlaw, But Make It Feminist

Meg Leta Jones

When I was a graduate student, a radio show on the Canadian Broadcast Corporation asked to interview me about the right to be forgotten, an idea gaining popularity and the subject of my dissertation. Flattered and excited, I enjoyed my conversation with the talented host and professional staff who asked about feminist themes like non-carceral interventions for content removal and rehabilitation through deletion. After the show aired, I received an email from a man who had taken the time to find my email address and draft a long message explaining that I probably said smart enough things but he couldn't determine one way or another because I sounded so stupid. My voice sounded silly and uneducated. He told me I should take voice lessons. Most of the authors in this volume regularly receive direct messages like this when they engage in public interviews on radio, podcasts, and television to discuss technology policy issues. Most of the messages are far more critical and inappropriate. The cyberspace phenomena of receiving unpleasant and unwelcome direct messages from strange men is a jarring and degrading experience but few of us have changed our tune.

Instead, these voices have grown louder and are collected here to launch a new field called Feminist Cyberlaw.[1] Feminist Cyberlaw represents a radical reimagining of technology law by articulating the way gender, race, sexuality, and disability shape cyberspace and the laws that govern it. Most of the voices, which include a mix of academics, practitioners, and clinicians, trained in a kind of traditional cyberlaw that include a canon of three white men: Barlow, Lessig, and Zittrain. Called the "single most influential essay in the history of Internet law,"[2] John Perry Barlow's 1996 "A Declaration of Independence of Cyberspace" instructed, "Governments of the Industrial World, you weary giants of flesh and steel, I come from

Cyberspace, the new home of the Mind. On behalf of the future, I ask you of the past to leave us alone. You are not welcome among us."[3] A cattle rancher and lyricist for the Grateful Dead, Barlow also cofounded one of cyberlaw's most important organizations: the Electronic Frontier Foundation. Lawrence Lessig's book *Code: And Other Laws Of Cyberspace* came out in 1999 and popularized the idea that "code is law,"[4] meaning code can constrain behavior the way architecture (i.e., a fence) can and as effectively as law can.[5] The idea bolstered an entire line of study in technology law about design and governance that continues to thrive today. In *The Future of the Internet—And How To Stop It*, Jonathan Zittrain argued that the internet's great value lay in its "openness," and that in 2008, when the book was published, the internet operated as an exceptionally generative technology.[6] Zittrain feared that attempts by companies to enclose the internet into proprietary, closed source places and services would end that generativity. All three wrote to ensure a future internet that maintained the aspects they valued and both fought change and called for change.

Voices in Feminist Cyberlaw do the same, but describe different scenes, focusing their lenses on alternative perspectives and values. The authors of this collection build on work that predated, coincided with, and responded to Barlow, Lessig, and Zittrain. In 2000, Jerry Kang asked whether cyberspace could "change the way that race functions in American society" and provided detailed design protocols to answer the question.[7] That same year, Anita Allen revisited her seminal book *Uneasy Access: Privacy For Women in a Free Society*, noting that technology-inspired interest into privacy "had little to do with gender."[8] Intellectual property scholars like Sonia Katyal, Anupam Chander, Madhavi Sunder, and Rebecca Tushnet established critical feminist critique of copyright law through analysis of fair use interpretations.[9] Danielle Citron and Mary Anne Franks centered the experience of marginalized people who endure bullying, threats, and harassment, revealing significant problems that derive from an emphasis on the virtual when seeking justice.[10] And Julie Cohen has consistently demanded attention be paid to power dynamics and institutional structures that make and regulate technology since the 1990s.[11] Feminist Cyberlaw has gained momentum alongside our colleagues working in Information Science, Communications, Science and Technology Studies who established important networks to create change through concrete contributions like the Feminist Data Manifesto-No and Design Justice.[12] These interdisciplinary interventions lead to the same inescapable conclusion. As my coeditor Amanda Levendowski explains, "[Cyberlaw] has always been unified by its reactions to, and governance of, feminist issues—it simply hasn't been understood that way."[13] The authors of this collection also build on the interdisciplinary cohort of scholars, of which they are a part, who have furthered works written over the turn of the millennium that complemented and challenged the cyberlaw canon.[14] In this volume, cyberlaw's focus on universality, virtuality, and novelty gives way to Feminist Cyberlaw's attention to contexts, bodies, and legacies.

Barlow wrote his Declaration in the first person plural *we*. He articulated a universality built from the shared experiences of a particular idea of diversity. He declared, "We are creating a world that all may enter without privilege or prejudice accorded by race, economic power, military force, or station of birth . . . Your legal concepts of property, expression, identity, movement, and context do not apply to us." Barlow's universality fades into the background in Feminist Cyberlaw, which instead highlights *context and locality*. The recognition of unique experiences and relationships to legal concepts in cyberspace is significant to Feminist Cyberlaw. Feminist Cyberlaw makes visible the local contexts in which we can see how cyberspace is part of specific communities, occupations, and relationships. When we hear the stories of those centered in Feminist Cyberlaw, the narratives change the way we see the world. In doing so, Feminist Cyberlaw scholars pursue an ever wider *we*.[15]

Barlow contends cyberspace "is a world that is both everywhere and nowhere, but it is not where bodies live." Lessig further explored that nowhere/everywhere place, *comparing* the design elements of cyberspaces to the layouts of physical environments. Cyberspace is different, according to Lessig, where anonymity is the default. Relieving itself of these virtual versus meatspace analogies and placing anonymity on an ever-present spectrum, Feminist Cyberlaw emphasizes actual *materiality and bodies*. You will find an array of situated, lived bodies undertaking all kinds of activities, and those unique motivations are tied directly to the bodies of many forms, colors, and capabilities. Computers have bodies too and the physical components of the networked infrastructure run under and over different places with different ideas about engaging with the hard drives, servers, and pipes to enforce rules. Feminist Cyberlaw scholars account for the physicality of the network. They know where the bodies are.

Barlow sought to further "the dreams of Jefferson, Washington, Mill, Madison, DeToqueville, and Brandeis," explaining, "These dreams must now be born anew in us." Indeed, the canon utilizes the past in pursuit of the new and novel. Lessig puts novelty in the center of his readers' attention in a way that connects to Zittrain's generativity. They share a distaste for closed systems, those that keep out exciting and innovative new and renewed technologies. For Zittrain, this means that technologies should be built and governed to promote generativity: "a technology's overall capacity to produce unprompted change driven by large, varied, and uncoordinated audiences." The Feminist Cyberlaw authors do not discard novelty but reestablish a legacy of novel uses, hacks, and appropriations from communities overlooked, discarded, or misunderstood by Silicon Valley and its many imitators. Feminist Cyberlaw voices pull us back to note the *legacies of excellence and oppression* found in our most essential social institutions and invisible innovators.

We grouped Feminist Cyberlaw into three broad categories: ownership, access, and governance. Each section includes a set of chapters organized by legal subject and social value, notably not technology. Feminist Cyberlaw is values first, recognizing the power dynamics and possibilities of technology as central to protecting and furthering those values. Values weaved throughout the chapters include accessibility, accountability, advocacy, attribution, autonomy, consent, creativity, dignity, participation, safety, and world building. Together, they are in conversation with those authors noted as canon, as well as the many scholars who, throughout the same period and within their intellectual domains and beyond, increasingly investigated the way oppression played out in cyberspace, its rhetoric, its logics, and its rules.[16] You'll find a unique genealogy built through the feminist citation practices of the authors, acknowledging the "debt to those who came before; those who helped us find our way when the way was obscured because we deviated from the paths we were told to follow."[17]

The first group of Feminist Cyberlaw authors reveal and challenge patriarchal ownership structures in a number of different contexts from various angles. Amanda Levendowski surfaces the "FU" in fair use that degrades and exploits the bodies and labor of women and people of color and develops a new vocabulary for feminist use by delving into the historical context of libraries. Leah Grinvald and Ofer Tur-Sinai highlight the unrealized potential to repair, arguing that copyright furthers the oppressive and exploitative limitations on repair, but seen through a feminist lens, the law can carve out more expansive exemptions to create a bolder right to repair. Nina Srejovic investigates why women, the first computer programmers, don't hold more patents, and finds that it's all about stereotypes of which bodies innovate. Cynthia Conti-Cook uses spillers, fillers, and thrillers to arrange a better procurement process, across its many varieties, that would limit trade secrecy obstruction with the legal precedent of the public's right to know. Alexandra Roberts asks how women and marginalized people can better access and benefit from intellectual property rights instead of being exploited by them and answers by arguing that trademark law can, under the right circumstances, offer disenfranchised groups a means to controlling hashtags. Anjali Vats compares the racial geopolitics of cybercrime using Critical Race Intellectual Property to understand "good" versus "bad" intellectual property actors.

Another set of Feminist Cyberlaw writers investigate the way in which access makes different bodies vulnerable and empowered. Kendra Albert asks whether the law that originally prevented website operators from being held liable for the content posted by users to promote the growth of the web might be accidentally and even inspirationally work against the prison industrial complex. Blake Reid describes how the phenomenon of providing access to those bodies with disabilities consistently brings forth positive effects for those without, but warns that emphasizing this popular policy motive can lead to deprioritizing and erasing disabled users from design and policy processes. Esha Bhandari highlights how those seeking to assess the civil rights legality of algorithms that act on them must do so in an uncertain legal environment due to an outsized corporate influence over antiquated hacking laws. Two chapters describe new threats to bodies after the US Supreme Court overturned its 1973 case *Roe v. Wade*, which established a constitutional right to an abortion, with its 2022 decision *Dobbs v. Jackson Women's Health*. Each tackles a unique facet of the amplified threats facing pregnant people. Michela Meister and Karen Levy describe how a post-*Roe* landscape is incredibly dangerous for a growing number of bodies, highlighting the physical threats of digital invasions and the vast fronts on which those violations may occur. Elizabeth Joh explains that the further limiting of access to safe abortions by *Dobbs* does not take us back to a time before *Roe*, but finds our intimacies brutally exposed in the present, most brutally by those least able to defend themselves, and requires structural changes for the future.

Finally, a collection of Feminist Cyberlaw authors write broadly about governance categories that get at different social values. Using sexual speech as her guide, Hannah Block-Wehba traces early victories for civil society that set the stage for a libertarianism emphasizing government threats to speech and privacy while leaving a conservative, market-minded set of private platforms to shape the moralistic terms of expression and asks whether information about abortions will give rise to an effective wave of civil libertarianism or further marginalize the subject. Gabrielle Rejouis describes the many vulnerabilities experienced by Black women online produced by a lack of intervention from dominant platforms and argues for wielding antitrust law to restructure social media, because these companies use their dominance as both insulation from pressure to protect their Black women users and as an excuse to inconsistently apply their own policies to the detriment of Black women. Jasmine McNealy challenges the viability of consent as a governance tool for data protection by complicating the politics and potential of control surrounding unsolicited dick pics. Iván Chaar López and Victoria Sánchez take an ethnographic dive into the racial politics of AI labor and digital infrastructure maintenance, arguing that current legislative efforts to continually classify and reclassify workers preserve a distinction about which bodies provide exploitable labor. Within the criminal justice context, Ngozi Okidegbe resists the way algorithms lock in existing inequalities by reminding us that algorithmic systems further the interests, attitudes, and values of those that design and employ them; she redirects them toward liberatory ideologies, calling for the meaningful shifts in power to our most oppressed and subjugated people. Kate Darling wraps up this volume by reflecting on how voices from breast pump innovators expressing concerns over historical erasure have shaped her work on the future of robotics policy and invites us all to find those a-ha moments.

These alternative voices provide alternative perspectives, but Feminist Cyberlaw is for everyone.[18] We are overwhelmingly grateful to our authors for giving us so much to introduce, and to you, reader, for joining us in this reunification and reorientation. We organized the collection from a broad, intersectional feminist perspective, utilizing the "prism" to bring to light the dynamics otherwise underappreciated in the analysis of subordination.[19] However, you won't find a unified theory of Feminist Cyberlaw, nor a volume steeped in feminist theory, in the following pages. You also won't find degradations of bro-cyberlaw or attacks on existing cyberlaw scholarship. We hope our volume will supplement the canon and current course materials in cyberlaw, information and communication policy, and computer ethics. Through a tweak to the senses, we hope to expand possibilities. We hope this encouragement leads to further development of Feminist Cyberlaw, for this volume, edited by two white women and largely limited to the United States, is just the beginning. We know there are more perspectives and voices to hear and support. We look forward to doing so.

NOTES

1. We first gathered under this name at the 2020 Privacy Law Scholars Conference.

2. James Grimmelmann, INTERNET LAW: CASES & PROBLEMS (12th ed., 2022).

3. John Perry Barlow, *A Declaration of the Independence of Cyberspace*, EFF (Feb. 8, 1996), https://www.eff.org/cyberspace-independence.

4. Lessig followed Joel Reidenberg's 1998 article *Lex Informatica*, which argued that technology delivers a distinct regulatory force. Joel R. Reidenberg, *Lex Informatica: The Formulation of Information Policy Rules through Technology*, 76 TEX. L. REV. 553 (1998).

5. Lawrence Lessig, CODE: AND OTHER LAWS OF CYBERSPACE (1999).

6. Jonathan Zittrain, THE FUTURE OF THE INTERNET AND HOW TO STOP IT (2008).

7. Jerry Kang, *Cyber-Race*, 113 HARV. L. REV. 1130 (2000).

8. Anita L. Allen, *Gender and Privacy in Cyberspace*, 52 STAN. L. REV. 1175 (2000).

9. Sonia Katyal, *Performance, Property, and the Slashing of Gender in Fan Fiction*, 14 AM. U. J. GENDER SO. POL'Y & L. 463 (2006); Rebecca Tushnet, *My Fair Ladies: Sex, Gender, and Fair Use in Copyright*, 15 AM. U. J. GENDER, SOC. POL'Y & L. 273 (2007); Anupam Chander & Madhavi Sunder, *Everyone's a Superhero: A Cultural Theory of "Mary Sue" Fan Fiction as Fair Use*, 95 CAL. L. REV. 1 (2007).

10. Mary Anne Franks, *Unwilling Avatars: Idealism and Discrimination in Cyberspace*, 20 COLUM. J. GENDER & L. 224 (2011); Danielle Citron, HATE CRIMES IN CYBERSPACE (2014).

11. Julie E. Cohen, *Examined Lives: Informational Privacy and the Subject as Object*, 52 STAN. L. REV. 1373 (2000); Julie E. Cohen, CONFIGURING THE NETWORKED SELF: LAW, CODE, AND THE PLAY OF EVERYDAY PRACTICE (2012); Julie E. Cohen, BETWEEN TRUTH AND POWER: THE LEGAL CONSTRUCTION OF INFORMATIONAL CAPITALISM (2019).

12. Marika Cifor, Patricia Garcia, T.L. Cowan, Jasmine Rault, Tonia Sutherland, Anita Say Chan, Jennifer Rode, Anna Lauren Hoffmann, Niloufar Salehi, and Lisa Nakamura, *Feminist Data Manifest-No* (2019), https://www.manifestno.com/; Design Justice Network, *Design Justice Network Principles* (last updated summer 2018), https://designjustice.org/read-the-principles.

13. Amanda Levendowski, *Defragging Feminist Cyberlaw*, 37 BERKELEY TECH. L.J. 1 (forthcoming 2023).

14. Lilly Irani, *The Cultural Work of Microwork*, 17(5) NEW MEDIA AND SOCIETY, 720 (2013); Andrew Gilden, *Cyberbullying and the Innocence Narrative*, 48 HARV. CIV. RIGHTS-CIV. LIB. L. REV. 357 (2013); danah boyd. IT'S COMPLICATED: THE SOCIAL LIVES OF NETWORKED TEENS (2014); Karen Levy, *Intimate Surveillance*, 51 IDAHO L. REV. 3 (2015); Dan Bouk, HOW OUR DAYS BECAME NUMBERED: RISK AND THE RISE OF THE STATISTICAL INDIVIDUAL (2015); Meg Leta Jones, CTRL+Z: THE RIGHT TO BE FORGOTTEN (2016); Kate Klonick, *Re-Shaming the Debate: Social Norms, Shame, and Regulation in an Internet Age*, 75 MARYLAND L. REV. 1029 (2016); Solon Barocas and Andrew Selbst, *Big Data's Disparate Impact*, 104 CALI. L. REV. 671 (2016); Khiara M. Bridges, THE POVERTY OF PRIVACY (2017);

Mar Hicks, Programmed Inequality: How Britain Discarded Women Technologists and Lost its Edge in Computing (2017); Amanda Levendowski, *How Copyright Law Can Fix Artificial Intelligence's Implicit Bias Problem*, 93 Wash. L. Rev. 579 (2018); Safiya Umoja Noble, Algorithms of Oppression: How Search Engines Reinforce Racism (2018); Ruha Benjamin, Race After Technology: Abolitionist Tools for the New Jim Code (2019); Ari Ezra Waldman, *Law, Privacy, and Online Dating: "Revenge Porn" in Gay Online Communities*, 44 L. & Soc. Inq. 4 (2019); Sarah T. Roberts, Behind the Screen: Content Moderation in the Shadows of Social Media (2019); Scott Skinner-Thompson, Privacy at the Margins (2020); Hannah Bloch-Wehba, *Automation in Moderation*, 53 Cornell Int'l L.J. 41 (2020); Ifeoma Ajunwa, *The Paradox of Automation as Anti-Bias Intervention*, 41 Cardozo. L. Rev. 1671 (2020); Charleton D. McIlwain, Black Software: The Internet & Racial Justice, from the AfroNet to Black Lives Matter (2021); Vincent Southerland, *The Intersection of Race and Algorithmic Tools in the Criminal Legal System*, 80 Md. L. Rev. 487 (2021); Kendra Albert, *Five Reflections from Four Years of FOSTA/SESTA*, Cardozo Arts & Entm't L.J. (forthcoming 2022).

15. Pope Francis, *"Towards an Ever Wider 'We,'"* Message for the 107th World Day of Migrants and Refugees, Summary of Bulletin Vatican Press (June 5, 2021).

16. Some writers at the time went largely overlooked. Two notable examples are Paulina Borsook, Cyberselfish: A Critical Romp through the Terribly Libertarian Culture of High Tech (2001); and Jane Bailey and Adrienne Telford, *What's So Cyber about It: Reflections on Cyberfeminism Contribution to Legal Studies* Can. J. Women & L. 19 (2007): 243.

17. Sarah Ahmed, Living a Feminist Life (2017).

18. Catherine Knight Steele explains that like bell hooks's feminism, digital Black feminism is not about division, but adds that it is "the lived experience, writing, and thought work of Black women that make Black feminism accessible to multiple races and genders." Catherine Knight Steele, Digital Black Feminism (2021); bell hooks, Feminism is for Everybody (2000).

19. Kimberlé Crenshaw, *Demarginalizing the Intersection of Race and Sex: A Black Feminist Critique of Antidiscrimination Doctrine, Feminist Theory, and Antiracist Politics*, 140 Uni. of Chi. Legal Forum, 139 (1989); Katy Steinmetz, *She Coined the Term 'Intersectionality' Over 30 Years Ago. Here's What it Means to Her Today*, Time (May 10, 2018), https://time.com/5786710/kimberle-crenshaw-intersectionality/.

PART I

Ownership × Feminism

Feminist Use

Amanda Levendowski

In 2015, Judge Pierre Leval wrote that copyright isn't about authors, it's about the rest of us. "While authors are undoubtedly important intended beneficiaries of copyright," he explained, "the primary intended beneficiary is the public."[1] He would know—his scholarship has been transformative for how every jurist from the Supreme Court down approaches key copyright questions.[2] But copyright often falls short of this aspiration by benefiting only a sliver of the public.

Copyright law grants exclusive rights to authors of qualifying works, such as books, which protects those works from unauthorized copying.[3] The first copyright legislation, the Statute of Anne of 1710, was drafted and enacted by a British Parliament comprised of privileged white men, largely for the benefit of other privileged white men, to encode men's vision for the intersection of creativity and capitalism.[4] The Copyright Act of 1976, which continues to govern much of copyright law in the United States, was enacted by a Congress comprised of predominantly white men, and it eliminated formalities for copyright registration and extended copyright terms.[5] Those changes make it more challenging for the public to access, read, and remix copyrighted works.[6] Consistently, copyright laws have focused on the creativity of other men, evidenced by their exclusion of arts stereotyped as "women's work."[7]

Scholars like Rebecca Tushnet, Ann Bartow, and Dan Burk have long grappled with how gender shapes copyright,[8] including how feminism frames fair use.[9] The fair use doctrine empowers the public to copy, share, and remake copyrighted works without consent.[10] It transforms would-be infringements into statutorily sanctioned activity under certain conditions, one of which is whether the use is for a preferred purpose that serves the public—such as news reporting, teaching, scholarship or research—which means the use is "not an infringement of copyright."[11] Courts also assess the use under a four-factor test, which analyzes:

1. The purpose and character of the use, including whether such use is of a commercial nature . . .;
2. The nature of the copyrighted work;
3. The amount and substantiality of the portion used in relation to the copyrighted work as a whole; and
4. The effect of the use upon the potential market for or value of the copyrighted work.[12]

Sonia Katyal described how "fair use bears an intimate relationship to the way in which critical legal studies focused its gaze on the role of entitlements for minority groups. Like critical race theory, a critical approach to copyright law tends to ask the question of how entitlements are distributed and their effect on disenfranchised groups, and also to employ tools like fair use to restore some balance between property rights and social justice."[13] As Betsy Rosenblatt has documented, a growing body of critical scholarship seeks to explore the fairness of the fair use doctrine.[14] However, there remains an FU lurking in fair use: fair use doesn't need to be fair, and it often isn't. Qualifying as "fair" legally says nothing about whether the use is "fair" equitably, and many fair uses are oppressive.[15]

When 2 Live Crew parodied Roy Orbison's classic rock hit *Oh, Pretty Woman* with crude lyrics about "big hairy woman," "need to shave that stuff," "bald headed woman," and "two timin' woman," the Supreme Court concluded in its inaugural fair use decision that the band's parody qualified as fair use.[16] The band's misogynistic language was not a one-off. Kimberlé Crenshaw describes lyrics from the band's album *Nasty As They Wanna Be*, the explicit version of the album that *Oh, Pretty Woman* appeared upon, was "virulently misogynist, sometimes violently so," particularly toward Black women.[17] Crenshaw coined the term "intersectionality" to account for "the particular manner in which Black women are subordinated," which is embodied by the band's lyrics.[18] Orbison's original offered one sexist approach to catcalling, but 2 Live Crew's version reinforces another misogynistic stereotype by equating a woman's worth with her appearance and behavior.[19] That decision, *Campbell v. Acuff-Rose*, paved the way for other oppressive fair uses.

In the aughts, Google began displaying thumbnail images of nude models as part of its Google Image Search results without those models', or their photographers', permission.[20] In *Perfect 10 v. Amazon*, the Ninth Circuit concluded that such a use was fair.[21] Even though the models' consent was not relevant legally from a copyright perspective, the court did not address the ethics of broadly publicizing nude photos without consent.[22] More than a decade later, Dr. Safiya Umoja Noble revealed that indiscriminately hoovering up other people's copyrighted works to power an algorithmic Image Search can contribute to a different ethical conundrum: sexist and racist results, like hits for pornography in response to searches for "Black girls."[23]

Gender and race play roles in other fair uses as well. Appropriation artist Richard Prince collaged and painted over portraits of Rastafarians by photographer Patrick Cariou, who spent six years building relationships with Rastafarians in Jamaica for his portraiture.[24] As part of the same series, Prince collaged and painted over photographs of nude women.[25] Both sets of subjects consented to the original photographs but not Prince's alterations—and neither the subjects nor Cariou saw any part of Prince's $10 million in sales.[26] In *Cariou v. Prince*, however, the Second Circuit concluded that Prince's art was mostly fair use.[27] And the secretive company Clearview AI curated a cache of billions of internet users' photographs without their awareness to fuel face surveillance technology for law enforcement.[28] Often, the technology is demographically biased and disproportionately deployed against people of color, activists, immigrants, and other communities who are unjustly targeted.[29] And yet, while a court has not decided the issue, a judge could find some forms of face surveillance to constitute fair use.[30]

"Fair use" can be a misnomer, but the public needs a vocabulary for equitable uses that utilize copyrighted works to challenge oppression or promote liberation. This chapter suggests one: feminist use.

To function effectively, feminist use cannot be limited to abstract theory. It must be a practice. Libraries are already modeling it through the growing library practice of controlled digital lending (CDL).[31] CDL enables libraries to create 1:1 print-to-pixel conversion of their collections, empowering libraries to lend digital versions of print books in lieu of physical ones, which has significant impacts on dismantling oppression and promoting equity.[32] CDL, unsurprisingly, also relies on fair use. Fair use can be flexible, fact dependent, and fraught. But as empirical and qualitative work by Pamela Samuelson, Matthew Sag, and Barton Beebe have shown, it can also be reasonably predictable.[33] That is why a growing number of libraries, librarians, and lawyers have endorsed the idea that CDL is fair use.[34] However, several publishers and some authors vehemently disagree, with the latter charging that CDL makes earning a living as a writer more difficult; the Internet Archive is appealing a recent decision determining that its digital lending program is not fair use.[35] This chapter does not settle that debate. Instead, it uses CDL to illustrate the characteristics of a feminist use.

Feminism is far from the only lens through which to reimagine secondary uses, but it offers one powerful way to discuss how such uses disrupt oppressive power dynamics. In a prior piece, *Defragging Feminist Cyberlaw*, I suggest conceptualizing cyberlaws and policies, including copyright, using three illustrative (but certainly not exhaustive) feminist values: consent, accessibility, and safety.[36] This chapter uses each value to assess CDL in three parts. Section I explains how copyright law is premised on consent—except when it isn't, including rights to create copies that serve the public which predate fair use by a century. In section II, I examine how CDL amplifies the accessibility of copyrighted works, both physically and logistically, to improve access to information. And finally, section III explores how CDL supports the safety of libraries and patrons by protecting resources necessary for a secure, informed public. Rather than reclassify less-than-feminist uses as unfair, this chapter concludes that we should adopt "feminist use" to describe uses that are morally defensible, socially desirable, and politically powerful, regardless of a legal regime that was not built to be feminist.

COMPLICATING CONSENT

Copyright is characterized by its relationship to consent. Without consent, creating copies and making other uses of copyrighted works represents infringement.[37] Members of the public may seek to license a work for appropriation, but a license may generally be denied for almost any reason, including objection to a critical reuse.[38] The alternative, simply using a copyrighted work without consent, carries significant penalties. If someone comes along and infringes a work registered with the Copyright Office,[39] such as by making and distributing copies or preparing derivative works,[40] that person may face up to $150,000 in statutory damages per infringement.[41] Usually.

Fair use is the obvious exception, and the consent-less use of copyrighted works has played a central role in libraries' work for decades.[42] It entitles patrons to copy information for purposes of teaching, scholarship, or research.[43] It empowers libraries to host e-reserves of notable volumes.[44] And it enables libraries to create digital books for patrons with print disabilities, promoting accessibility to information.[45] However, these feminist uses—all of which were also deemed legally fair—would be impossible if libraries were forced to seek consent from copyright owners like publishers, who resisted each of these innovations with litigation, lobbying, or both.[46]

Eschewing copyright owners' consent, however, cuts both ways. It enables fair uses that are sexist, racist, voyeuristic, and colonialist in ways that copyright owners would be unlikely to allow. The fix for oppressive fair uses may seem to be always requiring copyright owners' consent for any secondary use. Some authors might like that to be the case. But it isn't. Requiring consent can prevent oppressive uses, but it has the collateral effect of threatening the good faith fair use arguments underpinning many feminist ones, like CDL.[47] Such a radical policy shift would prevent uses that are both fair and feminist, like many examples of libraries' past and present work.[48]

However, the law has long recognized that consent is not always necessary to create copies. Nearly a century before Judge Joseph Story developed the framework for fair use, eighteenth-century booksellers were frustrated by the newly enacted Statute of Anne's power to extinguish their publishing monopolies, particularly after Parliament declined to extend them.[49] In response, booksellers brought a series of lawsuits arguing that copyright was a common law right of infinite duration.[50] In the landmark case of *Donaldson v. Beckett*, the House of Lords rejected that claim:

> Copies of books have existed in all ages, and they have been multiplied; and yet an exclusive privilege, or the sole right of one man to multiply copies, was never dictated by natural justice in any age or country . . . The common law has ever regarded public utility, as the mother of justice and equity. Public utility requires, that the productions of the mind should be diffused as wide as possible; and therefore the common law could not, upon any principle consistent with itself, abridge the right of multiplying copies.[51]

Donaldson's bold proclamation recognizing that copyright owners' consent to create copies is not and should not always be required is peppered with caveats and exceptions, but the sentiment still animates parts of contemporary copyright policy. Former Register of Copyright Barbara Ringer, who was one of the lead architects of the Copyright Act of 1976, championed authors' rights and also identified one of the three goals comprising the public interest in copyright as "provid[ing] the widest possible access to information of all kinds."[52] The Act encouraged that access by retaining term limitations (albeit extended ones) after which works could be used freely without consent and codified fair use, even while limiting accessibility in other ways.[53] To this day, the Supreme Court, as well as circuit courts, routinely address the "public benefit" of copying even though it is not a formal fair use factor.[54] Whether formulated as public utility, public interest, or public benefit, feminist uses like CDL create copies to serve it.

AMPLIFYING ACCESSIBILITY

As feminist philosopher and disability advocate Anita Silvers recounted, "women with disabilities experience subordination by the dominant culture for being members of the class of women, and again by feminist identity theory when it fails to adopt a disability perspective in recognizing women."[55] Disabled women, as well as other disabled people, often have less access to information.[56] As the American Association of People with Disabilities and its amici explained in *Authors Guild v. HathiTrust*, a prior case recognizing the legality of creating a digital library for disabled people, creating copies to serve disabled patrons "honor[s] the century-long efforts of people with disabilities to seek equal access to copyrighted works," which can be a challenge because there is "strong empirical evidence that people with disabilities are systemically unserved or underserved by copyright holders."[57] CDL continues these efforts by sharing library resources with disabled patrons, who may not be able to use print books or visit physical libraries but can use CDL to access high-quality digital knowledge on their own terms.[58] By making information more easily available than it would be through brick-and-mortar channels, CDL counters epistemic injustices effectively.[59]

Online lending also functionally extends libraries' hours so that anyone who cannot visit a physical library during business hours—including disabled people, as well as working parents or people with eldercare responsibilities, people with limited access to public transit, and a world affected by a global pandemic—still benefit from libraries' resources. Digital materials can also improve literacy for young readers, debunk dangerous misinformation, and make it easier to access resources that promote a candid treatment of sexuality and gender, race and racism, and religion.[60] CDL also makes the histories of marginalized communities more broadly available.[61]

However, materials by and about marginalized people are under threat. In 2021, the American Librarian Association identified more than fifteen hundred books targeted for bans, the highest number since the organization began tracking bans two decades years ago.[62] Not only are more books being banned, but they are being banned broadly. From June 2021 to June 2022, school library book bans occurred in 138 districts across thirty-two states.[63] Students see the problem. "Hiding away things that make us uncomfortable doesn't make them go away," explained Deeya, an Arkansas high school student, "Even if we don't talk about it, racism, sexual assault, genocide, and many other complex issues will still exist. We have to face the discomfort to keep it from happening again."[64] By borrowing books with CDL, all people can access books digitally that explore these and many other urgent issues, even when those books may not be available locally in physical libraries.

SUPPORTING SAFETY

Women flourish when they can safely access information. When books—whether written by women or about gender, sexuality, and reproductive rights—are destroyed or censored, the public suffers. Unfortunately, the safety of libraries, their collections, and their patrons is under siege, both physically and existentially. Physically, library collections are threatened by climate change. That threat inspired the creation of CDL. In 2001, Tropical Storm Allison devastated the University of Houston Law Library.[65] Parts of the library were flooded with at least eight feet of water, submerging many law books; mold destroyed much of the remaining collection.[66] Law librarian Michelle Wu pioneered a new approach to library resilience: CDL.[67] The initial idea driving CDL was, in Wu's words, to "preserve collections while respecting copyright law in a world where natural disasters are a growing threat."[68] Wu published an article outlining her early vision for CDL,[69] and many libraries responded by putting her theory into action.[70] Libraries began scanning physical books and loaning digital versions instead of physical ones, taking steps to mirror physical borrowing by ensuring that only one copy was in circulation at a time, limiting lending terms, and restricting patrons' ability to create copies.[71]

Existentially, libraries' ability to provide patrons with high-quality information is imperiled. Libraries have long been politicized, but that problem is reaching new heights as attacks on library programs and patrons rise.[72] Conservative politicians and school boards ban books about sexuality, race, and gender.[73] Right-wing lawmakers call for book burnings, and several have been held already.[74] And gun-carrying protestors and neo-Nazis threaten drag queen story hours at libraries.[75] But CDL enables libraries to freely, and fairly frictionlessly, lend books that combat oppression without exposing patrons to harassment. While libraries will always be powerful physical presences, CDL provides another way to educate and empower patrons.[76]

REIMAGINING THE FU IN FAIR USE

CDL is promising, but it's not a panacea for knowledge inequality. Digitizing books is not free, posing a hurdle to libraries with increasingly scarce resources.[77] Libraries that *do* engage in CDL may have limited digitized collections or, more dangerously, curate ones that promote oppression and misinformation.[78] Patrons may not have reliable, or any, internet access, putting the benefits of CDL out of their reach.[79] And publishers and authors who oppose CDL raise a challenge: why do libraries have to create their own copies when publishers sell e-books?

Some publishers and authors see every CDL copy as a lost e-book sale; some even see each library lend as a missed potential sale.[80] However, CDL copies and e-books are not interchangeable.[81] Libraries do not own e-books—they're licensed.[82] E-books can cost more than physical books while being subject to contractual restrictions that limit lending, such as requiring libraries to rebuy e-book licenses after lending to a certain number of patrons.[83] Publishers and platforms can also unilaterally remove e-books from libraries' collections, as one publisher did when it pulled more than thirteen hundred titles from academic libraries or another corporation did when it deleted digital versions of *1984* from owners' libraries, both without notice.[84] And publishers do not produce e-books for every title, including for out-of-print books. CDL allows libraries to curate collections that more closely mirror their physical ones than publishers' digital ones. In that sense, CDL magnifies what libraries do best: combatting oppression with access to knowledge.

Regardless of whether an appellate court ultimately finds that CDL is fair use, that term remains a misnomer. Legally, a use need not be equitable to be fair. A use certainly does not need to be feminist, and fair uses often are not. But fair uses can still make way for a new FU: feminist use. Take the sexist, racist, voyeuristic, and colonialist fair uses introduced earlier. Despite their oppressive effects, each one can be invoked to defend the legality of CDL. Losing that legal battle means that the public, the supposed beneficiaries of copyright law, will be robbed of an invaluable tool for combatting oppression—and the feminist goals of consent, accessibility, and safety will be subverted along with it. By embracing the term "feminist use," we gain a vocabulary for describing and distinguishing uses that are legally tolerated from ones are radically transformative. Not in the copyright sense, but in the grand societal one.

NOTES

Thanks to Becky Chambers, Megan Graham, James Grimmelmann, Meg Leta Jones, Chris Morten, Sherry Tseng, Rebecca Wexler, Kit Walsh, Michelle Wu, and Cameron Tepski for generous comments. I am also grateful to former iPIP Clinic students Jay Bober, Dyllan Browne-Bramble, Obi Iloani, Julie Metkus, and Hannah Odenthal, whom I had the pleasure of supervising on controlled digital lending projects for our client, Library Futures, who gave consent for me to write this chapter. The iPIP Clinic has been supported by the Kahle/Austin Foundation. Views are my own and do not necessarily represent the perspectives of iPIP Clinic clients or supporters. Sherry Tseng provided stellar research assistance.

1. Authors Guild v. Google, Inc., 804 F.3d 202, 212 (2d Cir. 2015).

2. *See* Pierre K. Leval, *Toward a Fair Use Standard*, 103 HARV. L. REV. 1105 (1990) (arguing that "transformativeness" ought to be part of the first fair use factor inquiry).

3. 17 U.S.C. §§ 102, 106.

4. Copyright Act of 1710, 8 Ann. c. 21 (encouraging learning by securing limited monopolies to authors and purchasers of copies); *see also* Ann Bartow, *Fair Use and the Fairer Sex: Gender, Feminism, and Copyright Law*, 14 AM. J. GENDER, SOC. POL'Y & LAW 551, 557–58 (2006) (critiquing the patriarchal origins of copyright law). Parts of this paragraph are adapted from Amanda Levendowski, *Defragging Feminist Cyberlaw*, 37 BERKELEY TECH. L.J. 1 (forthcoming 2024) (on file with author).

5. *History of Women in the U.S. Congress*, CTR. FOR AM. WOMEN & POLS., https://cawp.rutgers .edu/facts/levels-office/congress/history-women-us-congress (accessed Apr. 7, 2023). However, it was largely drafted by a woman named Barbara Ringer. For a deeper dive into the remarkable Ringer, whose legislation limited access to copyrighted works but also codified fair use, see Amanda Levendowski, *The Lost and Found Legacy of Barbara Ringer*, THE ATLANTIC (July 11, 2014), https://web.archive.org /web/20210921162304/https://www.theatlantic.com/technology/archive/2014/07/the-lost-and-found -legacy-of-a-copyright-hero/373948/.

6. 17 U.S.C. § 102 (stating that copyright subsists in "original works of authorship fixed in any tangible medium of expression," regardless of notice formalities or registration); 17 U.S.C. § 302 (generally extending term to life of the author plus seventy years).

7. Jessica Litman, DIGITAL COPYRIGHT 105–106 (2017); Bartow, *supra* note 4. *But see* Star Athletica, L.L.C. v. Varsity Brands, Inc., 137 S. Ct. 1002 (2017) (finding copyright protection in conceptually separable aspects of clothing designs).

8. *See, e.g.*, Debora Halbert, *Poaching and Plagiarizing: Property, Plagiarism and Feminist Futures, in* PERSPECTIVES ON PLAGIARISM AND INTELLECTUAL PROPERTY IN A POSTMODERN WORLD (Lisa Buranen & Alice M. Roy eds., 1999); Malla Pollack, *Towards a Feminist Theory of the Public Domain, or Rejecting the Gendered Scope of United States Copyrightable and Patentable Subject Matter*, 12 WM. & MARY J. WOMEN & L. 603 (2006); Madhavi Sunder, *The Romance of the Public Domain*, 92 CALIF. L. REV. 1331 (2004); Bartow, *supra* note 4; Dan L. Burk, *Copyright and Feminism in Digital Media*, 14 AM. U. J. GENDER SOC. POL'Y & L. 519 (2006); Sonia K. Katyal, *Performance, Property, and the Slashing of Gender in Fan Fiction*, 14 AM. U. J. GENDER SOC. POL'Y & L. 463 (2006); Dan L. Burk, *Feminism and Dualism in Intellectual Property*, 15 AM. U. J. GENDER SOC. POL'Y & L. 183 (2007). Beyond the United States, Carys J. Craig has written about gender and copyright. *See, e.g.*, Carys J. Craig, Joseph F. Turcotte & Rosemary J. Coombe, *What's Feminist About Open Access?: A Relational Approach to Copyright in the Academy*, 1 Feminist@law 1 (2011).

9. *See, e.g.*, Rebecca Tushnet, *My Fair Ladies: Sex, Gender, and Fair Use in Copyright*, 15 AM. U. J. GENDER SOC. POL'Y & L. 273 (2007); Bartow, *supra* note 4.

10. 17 U.S.C. § 107.

11. *Id*. Some characterize this as an affirmative defense.

12. *Id*. These factors were inspired by the test created by Justice Story in *Folsom v. Marsh*. 9 F. Cas. 342, 345 (C.C.D. Mass. 1841). Courts commonly ask whether the use is "transformative" under the first factor.

13. Peter Goodrich, Sonia K. Katyal, and Rebecca Tushnet, *Panel 1: Critical Legal Studies in Intellectual Property and Information Law Scholarship*, 31 CARDOZA ARTS & ENT. L.J. 601, 613 (2013) (referencing Molly Shaffer Van Houweling, *Distributive Values in Copyright*, 83 TEX. L. REV. 1535 (2005). Thanks to Betsy Rosenblatt for citing this quote in her work.

14. Betsy Rosenblatt, *Considering the Role of Fairness in Fair Use* (work in progress) (manuscript on file with author) (canvassing relevant scholarship).

15. Examples of sexist, racist, and colonialist fair uses are discussed later in this chapter under Complicating Consent.

16. Campbell v. Acuff-Rose Music, Inc., 510 U.S. 569, 578–94 (1994).

17. Kimberlé W. Crenshaw, *Beyond Racism and Misogyny*, BOSTON REV. (Dec. 1, 1991,), https://www .bostonreview.net/articles/kimberle-w-crenshaw-beyond-racism-and-misogyny/; Kimberlé Williams Crenshaw, *Beyond Racism and Misogyny: Feminism and 2 Live Crew, in* WORDS THAT WOUND: CRITICAL RACE THEORY, ASSAULTIVE SPEECH, AND THE FIRST AMENDMENT (Mari J. Matsuda, et al., eds., 2019).

18. Kimberlé Crenshaw, *Demarginalizing the Intersection of Race and Sex: A Black Feminist Critique of Antidiscrimination Doctrine, Feminist Theory, and Antiracist Politics*, 1 U. CHICAGO L. FORUM 139, 140 (1989).

19. Tushnet, *supra* note 19.

20. Perfect 10 v. Amazon.com, Inc., 508 F.3d 1146, 1155 (9th Cir. 2007).

21. Amazon.com, Inc., 508 F.3d 1146. The models were not the copyright owners, but it remains striking that sharing their nude images broadly, publicly, freely available merited no attention.

22. Levendowski, *supra* note 4.

23. Safiya Umoja Noble, ALGORITHMS OF OPPRESSION: HOW SEARCH ENGINES REINFORCE RACISM (2018); Michelle Ruiz, *Safiya Noble Knew the Algorithm Was Oppressive*, VOGUE (Oct. 21, 2021), https://www.vogue.com/article/safiya-noble.

24. Cariou v. Prince, 714 F. 3d 694, 698–99 (2d. Cir. 2013).

25. Richard Prince, *Djuana Barnes, Natalie Barney, Renee Vivian, and Roman Brooks Take Over the Guanahani* (2008), https://www.ca2.uscourts.gov/docs/opn1197/Prince/A-802,%20Djuna%20Barnes ,%20Natalie%20Barney,%20Richard%20Prince.jpg.

26. *Id*. In another series, Prince appropriated women's images. Jessie Heyman, *SuicideGirls Respond to Richard Prince in the Best Way Possible*, VOGUE (May 28, 2015), https://www.vogue.com /article/suicidegirls-richard-prince.

27. Cariou, 714 F. 3d at 712 (excepting five images and remanding for further proceedings).

28. Kashmir Hill, *The Secretive Company That Might End Privacy as We Know It*, NEW YORK TIMES (Jan. 18, 2020), https://www.nytimes.com/2020/01/18/technology/clearview-privacy-facial-recognition .html.

29. Ethical Use of Facial Recognition Act, S. 3284, 116th Cong. §§ 2(2)–2(3) (2020). Other potential targets include sex workers. Amanda Levendowski, *Resisting Face Surveillance with Copyright Law*, 104 N.C. LAW REV. 4 (2022). Clearview AI settled a lawsuit brought by the American Civil Liberties Union challenging the company's technology under the Illinois Biometric Information Privacy Act, which included a five-year moratorium on selling its face surveillance technology to law enforcement in Illinois. Settlement Agreement & Release at 2, ACLU v. Clearview AI, Inc, No. 2020-CH-04353

(Ill. Cir. Ct. May 4, 2022), https://www.aclu.org/legal-document/exhibit-2-signed-settlement-agreement
?redirect=exhibit-2-signed-settlement-agreement.

30. *Compare* Amanda Levendowski, *How Copyright Law Can Fix Artificial Intelligence's Implicit Bias Problem*, 93 WASH. L. REV. 579 (2018) (detailing why using copyrighted works as machine learning training data is generally fair use) *with* Benjamin L. W. Sobel, *Artificial Intelligence's Fair Use Crisis*, 41 COLUM. J.L. & ARTS 45 (2017) (documenting how AI invocations of fair use may benefit the powerful rather than the public); Levendowski, *supra* note 4 (describing why using profile pictures to train facial recognition algorithms may be an exception).

31. 17 U.S.C. § 107. CDL is also reliant on the common law principle of exhaustion. *Position Statement*, CONTROLLED DIGITAL LENDING BY LIBRARIES (2022), https://controlleddigitallending.org/statement (last visited Apr. 8, 2023).

32. *Position Statement, supra* note 31.

33. *See, e.g.*, Pamela Samuelson, *Unbundling Fair Uses*, 77 FORDHAM L. REV. 2537 (2009) (qualitative analysis of fair use cases); Matthew Sag, *Predicting Fair Use*, 73 OHIO ST. L.J. 47 (2012) (empirical analysis of fair use cases); Barton Beebe, *An Empirical Study of U.S. Copyright Fair Use Opinions Updated, 1978–2019*, 10 N.Y.U. J. INTELL. PROP. & ENT. L. 1 (2020) (empirical review of fair use cases).

34. *Signatories to the Position Statement on Controlled Digital Lending by Libraries*, CONTROLLED DIGITAL LENDING BY LIBRARIES (2022), https://controlleddigitallending.org/signatories (last visited Apr. 8, 2023).

35. Complaint at 3, Hachette Book Group, Inc. v. Internet Archive, 1:20-cv-04160 (S.D.N.Y. June 1, 2020); Hachette Book Group, Inc. v. Internet Archive, 1:20-cv-04160, 2023 WL 2623787 (S.D.N.Y. Mar. 24, 2023) ("Each enumerated fair use factor favors the Publishers, and although these factors are not exclusive, IA has identified no additional relevant considerations. At bottom, IA's fair use defense rests on the notion that lawfully acquiring a copyrighted print book entitles the recipient to make an unauthorized copy and distribute it in place of the print book, so long as it does not simultaneously lend the print book. But no case or legal principle supports that notion."); *Controlled Digital Lending (CDL): An appeal to readers and librarians from the victims of CDL*, AUTHORS GUILD (2019), https://authorsguild.org/app/uploads/2019/02/CDL-Appeal-13FEB2019-v1.pdf. The iPIP Clinic advised the Internet Archive, including while I was on research leave. Client consent was sought and granted. All comments are based on public information and reflect my opinion.

36. Levendowski, *supra* note 4. To be clear, these are not the only feminist values—just a sampling of important ones.

37. 17 U.S.C. § 106.

38. Parodies are a prime example; compulsory licenses are a key exception.

39. Fourth Est. Pub. Benefit Corp. v. Wall-Street.com, LLC, 139 S. Ct. 881 (2019) (requiring registration with the Copyright Office to initiate infringement litigation).

40. 17 U.S.C. § 106 (outlining authors' exclusive rights).

41. 17 U.S.C. § 504(c)(2) (requiring willful infringement).

42. An entire section of the Copyright Act is dedicated to libraries' activities. 17 U.S.C. § 108.

43. Williams & Wilkins Co. v. U.S., 487 F.2d 1345, 1359 (Ct. Cl. 1973). Libraries are also granted an exemption from liability for unsupervised use of reproducing equipment, such as photocopiers, provided the institution posts a notice about copyright laws. 17 U.S.C. § 108.

44. Cambridge Univ. Press v. Patton, 769 F.3d 1232 (11th Cir. 2014).

45. Authors Guild, Inc. v. HathiTrust, 755 F.3d 87, 90–91 (2d Cir. 2014).

46. *Controlled Digital Lending: The Next Chapter in Libraries' Expansion of Access to Knowledge*, LIBRARY FUTURES (on file with author). This policy work was adapted into Kyle Courtney & Juliya Ziskina, *The Publisher Playbook: A Brief History of the Publishing Industry's Obstruction of the Library Mission* (forthcoming 2024), https://dash.harvard.edu/handle/1/37374618.

47. *See, e.g.*, Mattel, Inc. v. Walking Mountain Prod., 353 F.3d 792 (9th Cir. 2003) (observing that Mattel "would be less likely to grant a license to an artist that intends to create art that criticizes and reflects negatively on Barbie's image," which could be described as feminist art).

48. Kyle Courtney & Juliya Ziskina, *The Publisher Playbook: A Brief History of the Publishing Industry's Obstruction of the Library Mission* (forthcoming). Work by the iPIP Clinic inspired this article.

49. Folsom v. Marsh, 9. F. Cas. 342 (C.C.D. Mass. 1841); Donaldson v. Beckett (1774) 1 Eng. Rep. 837; Paul Goldstein, Copyright's Highway: From Gutenberg to the Celestial Jukebox 34–35 (2003).

50. Donaldson, 1 Eng. Rep. 837; *see, e.g.*, Millar v. Taylor (1769) 4 Burr. 2303 (holding that copyrights existed at common law that could not be extinguished by the Statute of Anne's limited terms), *overruled by* Donaldson, 1 Eng. Rep. 837.

51. Donaldson, 1 Eng. Rep. 837. Thanks to Michelle Wu for this citation. For a deeper dive into equitable claims for the right to access information, see Michelle Wu, *Back to Basics: The Balance of Copyright as Natural Law and an Equitable Claim for the Right to Use Knowledge Legitimately Acquired* (on file with author).

52. Barbara Ringer, *Authors' Rights in the Electronic Age: Beyond the Copyright Act of 1976*, 1 Loy. L.A. Ent. L. Rev. 1 (1981). The other two goals were "to induce authors and artists to create and disseminate original works, and to reward them for their contributions to society" and preserve "a fundamental public interest related to . . . freedom of expression, freedom to write and publish whatever one wishes." *Id.*, at 2–4. As discussed earlier, *supra* note 4, the Act codified fair use while limiting access to copyrighted works in other ways. For a deeper dive into Barbara Ringer's legacy, see Levendowski, *supra* note 6.

53. 17 U.S.C. §§ 107, 302.

54. *See, e.g.*, Google LLC v. Oracle Am., Inc., 141 S. Ct. 1183, 1206 (2021) ("[W]e must take into account the public benefits the copying will likely produce . . ."); Perfect 10 v. Google, Inc., 416 F. Supp. 2d 828, 848–49 (C.D. Cal. 2006) ("[S]earch engines such as Google Image Search provide great value to the public."), *aff'd* Amazon.com, Inc., 508 F.3d 1146 (discussing "the significantly transformative nature of Google's search engine, particularly in light of its public benefit"); Authors Guild, 804 F.3d at 212 ("[W]hile authors are undoubtedly important intended beneficiaries of copyright, the primary intended beneficiary is the public."). A use's "public benefit" is usually addressed as part of the first factor.

55. Anita Silvers, *Reprising Women's Disability: Feminist Identity Strategy and Disability Rights*, 13 Berkeley Womens L.J. 81, 82–83 (1998) (citing prominent feminist scholars, including Martha Minow, Susan Sherwin, Rosemarie Tong, and Iris Marion Young, among others, who "made important contributions by commenting on the confluence of disability discrimination with gender oppression").

56. The choice to use identity-first language is a personal one guided by the guidelines of the National Center of Disability and Journalism and my personal preference as a disabled person. *Disability Language Style Guide*, Nat'l Ctr. of Disability & Journalism (Aug. 2021), https://ncdj.org /style-guide/.

57. Amicus Brief of the Am. Ass'n. of People with Disabilities, et al., HathiTrust, 755 F.3d 87.

58. Laura C. Wood, et al., *Libraries: Take AIM! Accessible Instructional Materials and Higher Education*, Repository Serv. Accessible Course Content (Mar. 2017), https://dl.tufts.edu/pdfviewer /d504rx736/fn1079946; Joanne Kaeding, Diane L. Velasquez & Deborah Price, *Public Libraries and Access for Children with Disabilities and Their Families: A Proposed Inclusive Model*, 66 J. Austl. Lib. & Info. Ass'n. 2 (2017), https://www.tandfonline.com/doi/full/10.1080/24750158.2017.1298399.

59. Many of these examples are courtesy of *Controlled Digital Lending: Unlocking the Library's Full Potential*, Library Futures (2021), https://www.libraryfutures.net/policy-document-2021. For deeper dives into how marginalized people use and benefit from libraries, see Mary Case, et al., *Report of the ARL Joint Task Force on Services to Patrons with Disabilities*, Ass'n Rsch. Librs. (Nov. 2, 2012),

https://www.arl.org/wp-content/uploads/2012/11/print-disabilities-tfreport02nov12.pdf; Joanne Kaeding, Diane L. Velasquez & Deborah Price, *Public Libraries and Access for Children with Disabilities and Their Families: A Proposed Inclusive Library Model*, 66:2 J. AUSTL. LIBR. & INFO. ASS'N. 96 (2017); Susan K. Burke, *The Use of Public Libraries by Native Americans*, 77 LIBR. Q. 4 (2007); Debby Warren, *Rural Libraries Take on Growing Role as Agents of Inclusion and Change*, NONPROFIT Q. (Dec. 16, 2019), https://nonprofitquarterly.org/rural-libraries-take-on-growing-role-as-agents-of-inclusion-and -change/; Margaret Barthel, *D.C. Public Library Wants to Build Bigger Neighborhood Branches in Communities Without Easy Access*, DCIST (Nov. 19, 2020), https://dcist.com/story/20/11/19/dc-public -library-bigger-branches-in-communities-without-easy-access/.

60. Irene Pictron, NAT'L LITERACY TRUST, THE IMPACT OF EBOOKS ON THE READING MOTIVATION AND READING SKILLS OF CHILDREN AND YOUNG PEOPLE (2014); Argyri Panezi, *A Public Service Role for Digital Libraries: A Case of Emergency Electronic Access to Library Material and The Unequal Battle Against Misinformation Through Copyright Law Reform*, 31 CORNELL J.L. & PUB. POL'Y 65 (2021); Meghan Gunn, *Recent Surge in Banned Books Targets Titles with Focus on Race, Sexuality*, NEWSWEEK (Apr. 12, 2022), https://www.newsweek.com/2022/04/29/recent-surge-banned-books-targets-titles -focus-race-sexuality-1696575.html (removal of books discussing "critical race theory," as well as books about queerness and gender identities from libraries); Jonathan Friedman & Nadine Farid Johnson, *Banned in the USA: The Growing Movement to Censor Books in Schools*, PEN AMERICA (Sept. 19, 2022), https://pen.org/report/banned-usa-growing-movement-to-censor-books-in-schools/.

61. The Jamestown S'Klallam Tribal Library in Blyn, Washington, for example, was awarded the National Medal for Museum and Library Service for using CDL to share histories of Pacific Northwest tribal nations with patrons. Michael Dashiell, *Jamesdown S'Klallam Library Wins National Medal for Library Service*, DEREK KILMER (May 22, 2019), https://kilmer.house.gov/news/in-the-news/jamestown -sklallam-library-wins-national-medal-for-museum-and-library-service (describing Jamestown S'Klallam Tribal Library efforts to preserve history of Native nations in the Pacific Northwest through a digital collection).

62. Elizabeth A. Harris & Alexandra Alter, *With Rising Book Bans, Librarians Have Come Under Attack*, NEW YORK TIMES (July 18, 2022), https://www.nytimes.com/2022/07/06/books/book-ban -librarians.html.

63. Friedman & Johnson, *supra* note 60.

64. The Learning Network, *What Students Are Saying About Banning Books From School Libraries*, NEW YORK TIMES (Feb. 18, 2022), https://www.nytimes.com/2022/02/18/learning/students-book-bans.html.

65. Lila Bailey, *Protecting Books from Harm with Controlled Digital Lending*, INTERNET ARCHIVE BLOGS (Aug. 28, 2019), https://blog.archive.org/2019/08/28/protecting-books-from-harm-with -controlled-digital-lending/.

66. *Id.*

67. Michelle M. Wu, *Building a Collaborative Digital Collection: A Necessary Evolution in Libraries*, 103 LAW LIBR. J. 527 (2011). Wu's approach, coupled with feminist use, aligns with principles of ecofeminism; *see, e.g.*, Val Plumwood, FEMINISM AND THE MASTERY OF NATURE (1993) (coining the term "critical ecofeminism" to illustrate how feminist critique can integrate theories of gender, race, and class oppression with the domination of nature).

68. Bailey, *supra* note 65.

69. Wu, *supra* note 67.

70. *Controlled Digital Lending: Unlocking the Library's Full Potential*, LIBRARY FUTURES (2021) https://www.libraryfutures.net/policy-document-2021.

71. Michelle M. Wu, *Revisiting Controlled Digital Lending Post-*ReDigi, 24 FIRST MONDAY 5 (2019).

72. Hannah Natanson, *Schools Nationwide Are Quietly Removing Books from Their Libraries*, WASHINGTON POST (Mar. 22, 2022, 9:54 AM), https://www.washingtonpost.com/education/2022/03/22 /school-librarian-book-bans-challenges/.

73. *The Attack on Books in Schools*, Nat'l Coal. Against Censorship (Dec. 2021), https://ncac.org/news/attack-on-books; *Media Factsheet on School Censorship*, GLAAD & Nat'l Coalition Against Censorship (2021), https://ncac.org/wp-content/uploads/2021/12/NCAC-GLAAD-Media-Factsheet-FOR-NCAC-WEB.pdf.

74. Associated Press, *School Library Bill Advances, Sponsor Suggests Book Burning*, U.S. News & World Report (Apr. 27, 2022, 7:54 PM), https://www.usnews.com/news/politics/articles/2022-04-27/school-library-bill-advances-sponsor-suggests-book-burning; Helen Holmes, *Book Banning Is Increasing Across the United States, a Book Burning in Tennessee*, The Observer (Feb. 9, 2022, 4:05 PM), https://observer.com/2022/02/book-banning-is-increasing-across-the-united-states-a-book-burning-in-tennessee/; Bess Levin, *Conservatives Are Just Openly Endorsing Book Burning Now*, Vanity Fair (Nov. 11, 2021), https://www.vanityfair.com/news/2021/11/virginia-school-board-book-burning.

75. Associated Press, *"Drag Queen Story Hour" at Oregon Pub Draws Gun-Carrying Protestors*, The Oregonian (Oct. 25, 2022, 2:58 PM), https://www.oregonlive.com/pacific-northwest-news/2022/10/drag-queen-story-hour-at-oregon-pub-draws-gun-carrying-protesters.html; C. Mandler, *Ohio Drag Queen Storytime Canceled amid Armed Protests by Far-Right Groups*, CBS News (Dec. 4, 2022, 9:17 PM), https://www.cbsnews.com/news/ohio-drag-queen-storytime-event-canceled-amid-armed-protests-proud-boys-patriot-front/; Abby Patkin, *Neo-Nazi Group Interrupts a Drag Queen Story Hour in Taunton*, Boston.com (Jan. 18, 2023), https://www.boston.com/news/local-news/2023/01/18/taunton-drag-queen-story-hour-neo-nazi-protest/.

76. Mia Sato, *Ebook Service Hoopla Brings Anti-vax, Holocaust Denial, and Pro-LGBTQ Conversion Books to Libraries*, The Verge (Apr. 20, 2022), https://www.theverge.com/2022/4/20/23034169/hoopla-ebooks-public-library-conspiracy-theory.

77. However, libraries serving low income or rural communities can partner with other libraries who have CDL programs. As CDL founder and librarian Michelle Wu explained, "[i]t's a way of wealth sharing without much cost to communities." Caralee Adams, Lila Bailey & Chris Freeland, *Transforming Our Libraries: 12 Stories About Controlled Digital Lending*, Controlled Digital Lending (2022), https://archive.org/details/12CDLstories.

78. The risk is not abstract, as a similar problem was posed by ebook lending services in libraries. Claire Woodcock, *Ebook Services Are Bringing Unhinged Conspiracy Books into Public Libraries*, Vice (Apr. 20, 2022), https://www.vice.com/en/article/93b7je/ebook-services-are-bringing-unhinged-conspiracy-books-into-public-libraries. While not CDL, the problem is only a skip away. As Michelle Wu has pointed out, however, CDL collections are not limited to works that a library has digitized itself. Michelle M. Wu, *Piece by Piece Review of Digitize-and-Lend Projects Through the Lens of Copyright Fair Use*, 36 Legal Reference Servs. Q. 51 (2017); Michelle M. Wu, *Shared Collection Development, Digitization, and Owned Digital Collections*, 44 Collection Mgmt. 131 (2019).

79. John Busby, Julia Tanberk & BroadbandNow Team, *FCC Reports Broadband Unavailable to 21.3 Million Americans, BroadbandNow Study Indicates 42 Million Do Not Have Access*, BroadbandNow (Feb. 3, 2020), https://broadbandnow.com/research/fcc-underestimates-unserved-by-50-percent.

80. Dan Cohen, *Libraries Need More Freedom to Distribute Digital Books*, The Atlantic (Mar. 30, 2023), https://www.theatlantic.com/ideas/archive/2023/03/publishers-librarians-ebooks-hachette-v-internet-archive/673560/.

81. *See, e.g.*, 17 U.S.C. § 107.

82. For a deeper dive into the shift away from book and other media ownership and into licensing, see Aaron Perzanowski & Jason Schultz, The End of Ownership: Personal Property in the Digital Age (2018).

83. All Things Considered, *Librarians Worry E-book Pricing Might Affect People's Ability to Borrow Books*, NPR (Nov. 18, 2022), https://www.npr.org/2022/11/18/1137817727/librarians-worry-e-book-pricing-might-affect-people-s-ability-to-borrow-books.

84. *See, e.g.,* Claire Woodcock, *Publishing Company Starts School Year by Removing Over 1,000 E-Textbooks*, VICE (Oct. 5, 2022), https://www.vice.com/en/article/3ad5x8/publishing-company -starts-school-year-by-removing-over-1000-e-textbooks; Brad Stone, *Amazon Erases Orwell Books from Kindle*, NEW YORK TIMES (July 17, 2009), https://www.nytimes.com/2009/07/18/technology /companies/18amazon.html. The publisher announced it would reverse course, at least temporarily. *Statement on Wiley eBooks Featured in ProQuest Academic Complete Library*, WILEY (Oct. 5, 2022), https://newsroom.wiley.com/press-releases/press-release-details/2022/Statement-on-Wiley-eBooks -Featured-in-ProQuest-Academic-Complete-Library/default.aspx.

2

Defending the Right to Repair

Leah Chan Grinvald and Ofer Tur-Sinai

Access to repair information is an essential aspect of an effective right to repair. Yet repair manuals that used to be standard with one's product purchase have gradually disappeared, and intentionally so. Manufacturers argue that products are too complicated to allow self-repair, citing safety concerns.[1] While it is true that products have become more complicated in today's "tethered economy," safety concerns are only part of the reason behind blocking repair. Another reason is that funneling repairs to an authorized repairer can mean big business for some manufacturers—or may mean converting the consumer's desire for repair into an upgrade purchase of the newer version of the product.

There is another hurdle to accessing repair information: copyright law, which provides manufacturers with the ability to claim copyright protection over manuals and block access to repair information. In addition, the Digital Millennium Copyright Act ("DMCA"), gives manufacturers the legal right to block access to their products through software locks (also known as technological protection measures, or TPMs).[2] Under the DMCA, circumventing or "hacking" these software locks can be deemed a criminal offense.[3] While the Copyright Office has recently made hacking for repair purposes exempted from liability,[4] it is still illegal for those who have hacked the lock to share the information under what is known as the anti-trafficking provision, thus limiting the universe of those who can access their products for repair purposes to tech-savvy and entrepreneurial consumers.[5]

There are various convincing justifications for a broad right to repair. While we have previously argued that a right to repair is theoretically compatible with intellectual property protection, this chapter applies feminist legal theory to this issue.

Feminism, as a movement to end all forms of oppression, provides further support for expanded exemptions to the DMCA. Even with limited exemptions currently in place, classism and imperialism are sustained due to an unrealized ability to repair through higher cost and burdensome repair, which also results in e-waste generated by wealthy countries that flows into poor and developing countries.[6] Empowering consumers to utilize third-party repairers and share repair-related information will assist in alleviating these forms of oppression.

REPAIR, COPYRIGHT LAW, AND THE DMCA

The right to repair is having a global moment. Worldwide, the social movement to push governmental change to allow independent repair of products ranging from the everyday (e.g., smartphones) to the extraordinary (e.g., smart cars) is making progress. In the United States, some states have enacted or updated consumer protection laws that provide certain rights to facilitate repair,[7] while the Federal Trade Commission ("FTC") has brought actions against manufacturers who make illegal claims that non-authorized repair voids a product's warranties.[8] In Europe, the European Commission adopted in 2019 a new set of EcoDesign regulations under the framework of the EcoDesign Directive, which included repair-related provisions with respect to ten categories of products.[9] And in Australia, the Productivity Commission issued a "Right to Repair" report, which made several policy recommendations to enable repair in Australia.[10] But despite this progress, challenges to implementing a universal right to repair remain.

A thread that runs throughout the challenges to repairing products outside of a manufacturer's authorized network is the lack of access to information. In the early days of consumer electronic goods, when one purchased a consumer product—for example, a television—a repair manual with the full schematics typically accompanied the purchase.[11] Over time, this repair manual has disappeared and increasingly less information on self-repair has been provided. Some manufacturers made it virtually impossible to obtain any access to repair information, such as Apple in the 2010s.[12]

Unfortunately, manufacturers have a legal ability to bar access to this information through copyright law. Manufacturers routinely claim copyright protection in their manuals, where those manuals have escaped their authorized channels and have appeared online without their consent.[13] Even during the pandemic, a website database dedicated to publishing manuals to repair lifesaving medical devices received a cease-and-desist letter predicated on the manufacturer's copyright protection.[14]

Without access to information regarding how to repair one's product, only those consumers who are tech-savvy and entrepreneurial are able to figure it out on their own—but copyright law makes even this illegal.[15] The Digital Millennium Copyright Act (DMCA) was enacted in 1998 to update and modernize US copyright law in response to the challenges presented by digital technologies and the internet.[16] The DMCA provides protection for TPMs or digital locks (referred to in the DMCA as "a technological measure that effectively controls access to a work protected under [Copyright Law]) used by copyright owners to control access to their copyrighted works."[17] These locks are used by manufacturers of electronic devices to bar access to the product's software that controls how it functions. Access to this software is often needed to repair the product.[18] So even if an enterprising do-it-yourselfer ("DIYer") is able to figure out how to bypass the lock (commonly referred to as "hacking"), the DMCA prohibits this and even may provide for criminal liability in certain situations.[19]

Fortunately, the DMCA authorizes the Copyright Office to promulgate exceptions based on the recommendations of the Library of Congress.[20] These "Section 1201 Promulgations" are issued by the Copyright Office on a three-year cycle and provide exemptions from DMCA liability for various types of activity that would otherwise be considered infringing.[21] As early as 2018, the Copyright Office has included exemptions that recognize that hacking into one's product for purposes of repairing it is not an infringement of the DMCA.[22] But, this exemption is only limited to one part of the DMCA's protection of digital locks—the act of circumventing (or hacking) the digital lock.[23] The exemption does not extend to the anti-trafficking part of the DMCA, which prohibits anyone from distributing the information related to bypassing the digital lock (referred to in the DMCA as "anti-trafficking"). The reason that the Copyright Office has not extended the exemption to anti-trafficking is because it is not authorized to do so.[24]

We have argued in previous work that theories that justify intellectual property law also support a right to repair.[25] Consider, for example, the utilitarian notion of intellectual property rights as a governmental tool to bargain for the development and disclosure of socially valuable information.[26] The DMCA was enacted as an additional form of protection for digital products that were easily copied, in keeping with this incentive rationale.[27] Anti-circumvention measures allow manufacturers to safely release their copyrighted works for consumption because the digital locks protect against the copying of copyrighted works that are embedded in a product.[28] For example, a digital lock placed on a DVD, a music file, or software protects it from being illegally copied.[29] But, with most products these days controlled by software, such software locks are protecting access to the products themselves—and not just the copyrighted software.[30] The Copyright Office exemptions are adopted in recognition of this development. Therefore, while disabling the lock is generally a violation of the DMCA, it is not a violation to so disable it for purposes of repairing the underlying product.[31] The same rationales also seem to support extending the DMCA exemption to cover the dissemination of repair information ("trafficking").

In this contribution, the authors highlight another theoretical frame that provides support for a right to repair: feminism. As conceptualized by scholar Amanda

Levendowski (relying on bell hooks' definition of feminism), "intersectional feminism" extends the feminist movement to all parts of society, seeking to end multiple forms of oppression.[32] Professor Levendowski's conceptualization of "feminist fair uses" of copyrighted works promotes accessibility of information, one of the ways women have long utilized to end their oppression.[33] The authors argue that intersectional feminism, with its goal of ending all forms of oppression, also provides strong support for measures that would end forms of oppression that are furthered through preventing self or independent repair of one's products, including an expansion of the DMCA exemption.[34] Among other things, the inability to repair products has led to pileups of discarded electronic products in developing countries, such as Brazil, Ghana, Mexico, and Nigeria.[35] This has created a form of imperialistic oppression, since North America and Europe are the countries from which this electronic waste (e-waste) originates.[36] Providing greater accessibility to repair would assist in alleviating this oppression. In addition, the inability to repair products leads to the continuation of classism—that is, only the wealthy are able to afford to upgrade their products when they break, whereas the poor must muddle on with products that are semi-functioning.[37] Greater ability to access low cost alternatives to repair would assist in fighting back against this classism. Ultimately, this chapter argues that a "feminist right to repair" would provide further support for expanding the repair exemptions to allow for third party repair and the distribution of repair-related information.

OPPRESSION THROUGH LIMITING ACCESS TO INFORMATION

There are many strands and movements within feminism, but a connecting thread is the fight against the oppression of women in society, albeit white, privileged women.[38] It was in the 1980s with the writings of bell hooks that the scope of feminism was expanded to be defined as "a movement to end sexism, sexist exploitation, and oppression."[39] And, in recognizing that racism, classism, and imperialism were other forms of oppression, includes these within her definition of feminism.[40] Further, "intersectionality feminism" brings these strands together to recognize that oppressed people can experience various forms of inequality and oppression at the same time—and differently—from one another.[41]

hooks defines oppression as "the absence of choices."[42] Given this, one way to end oppression is to be able to provide choices to the oppressed—or access. Access, or "the ability to enter" or the "freedom or ability to obtain or make use of something" can be to resources (like money), information, or knowledge more generally (i.e., education).[43] As Professor Levendowski points out in her chapter, *Feminist Use*, access to free information was recognized early on by feminist movements.[44] Women's associations were the ones to establish close to three-quarters of the early American public lending libraries.[45]

In the modern age, copyright owners are gatekeepers to knowledge and information, such as books, magazines, news articles, documentaries, and on and on, and they want to be paid for such information. This is the "bargain" of copyright that was mentioned earlier, but at the same time, can be seen as the tool of oppression.[46] Where copyright owners believe they have been shortchanged, they can bring a lawsuit (or even just threaten to bring one, which is often just as good).[47] This was seen, for example, in *Kirtsaeng v. John Wiley & Sons, Inc.*, where the copyright owner brought a lawsuit against a graduate student who imported textbooks that had been lawfully sold in his homeland of Thailand.[48] The enterprising graduate student took advantage of the price difference between the cost of the textbooks in Thailand and in the United States, reselling them in the United States to make a profit. The copyright owner believed that it should have been their profit to make and not the student's.[49]

In the digital age, copyright owners continue their gatekeeping function through the use of digital locks (often referred to as technical protection measures or "TPMs") and are aided by Section 1201 of the DMCA in keeping control over access to information.[50] This includes information related to repair, such as repair manuals, schematics, as well as the information to bypass the digital locks that secure access to the underlying products. Manufacturers claim copyright protection in this information and are not shy in enforcing them, even during a pandemic.[51] In allowing copyright owners to maintain control over repair-related information, the DMCA supports the oppression of those who live in poverty (classism) and in developing countries (imperialism).

Classism. The definition of classism, is "the systemic oppression of the lower class and middle class to the advantage of the upper class."[52] A lack of access to repair information sustains classism because only the wealthy can afford to routinely purchase new products when theirs break. Combined with some manufacturers' "planned obsolescence" programs, some products are designed to break down sooner than others.[53] For example, Apple has published the lifecycle expectancies of its iPhones, which is approximately three years.[54]

Even where a consumer (wealthy or not) wishes to have their product repaired instead of purchasing a new one, there are barriers that make it burdensome, even aside from a lack of information needed for self-repair. Some manufacturers require that some repairs be undertaken only by them, which adds additional burdens or makes repairs impossible.[55] Authorized repairers are often more expensive than independent repairers, as well as less conveniently located.[56] And end user license agreements accompanying software embedded in many products can restrict repairs to authorized repairers.[57] During the FTC's workshop held on repair restrictions, Vermont State Senator Christopher Pearson testified that he was told by Apple to mail in his iPhone when the camera broke because, "according to Apple, nobody in Vermont could fix it."[58] This meant that he could not fix his phone because he was using his phone to run his business and a week without his phone was a "nonstarter."[59] In all, making it more difficult to repair products has the effect of sustaining the oppression of those with fewer resources.

Imperialism. The combination of planned obsolescence and lack of repair means that electronic waste (referred to as "e-waste") is being generated at an increasing rate, from an average of 0.6 million tons per year (from 2018 to 2021) to over an estimated average of 2 million tons per year after 2021.[60] While this is a global problem, when one examines the flow of e-waste, it can be seen as a form of modern-day imperialism. The countries that generate the most amount of e-waste are located in North America, Western Europe, and Australia, whereas the countries that receive the most amount of e-waste for disposal are Mexico, Brazil, India, and China.[61] This seems to embody the definition of imperialism, which is the practice "of extending the power and dominion of a nation . . . by gaining indirect control over the political or economic life of other areas."[62]

E-waste is extremely harmful in many aspects. Over 80 percent of e-waste is not collected for recycling.[63] And even where e-waste is recycled, recycling of some types of e-waste is dangerous, with e-waste containing hazardous chemicals.[64] In places where the recycling consists of burning the plastic material around the electronic good in order to obtain the valuable metal inside of them, such processes expose the workers and their community around them to a multitude of toxic substances.[65] More troubling is that in some countries, women and children make up to 30 percent of those employed in these types of recycling facilities, which have long-term consequences.[66] These have included "thyroid function, reproductive health, lung function, growth, and changes to cell functioning."[67] In addition, one systematic review of a number of global studies of e-waste and health outcomes found that "[p]eople living in e-waste recycling towns or working in e-waste recycling had evidence of greater DNA damage than did those living in control towns."[68] This means that the damage done by e-waste will last long beyond the current generation of those living and working in these areas. Developed and wealthy countries are oppressing developing countries through their e-waste, and even if all e-waste shipments were to stop tomorrow, the half-life of these toxic substances would still be felt in generations to come.

TOWARD A FEMINIST RIGHT TO REPAIR

The values underpinning the right to repair movement are feminist values. Repair-related information is power, and access to this information can assist in limiting the classist and imperialistic oppression that the lack of such information sustains.[69] A feminist right to repair provides support for expanding the exemptions provided under Section 1201 of the DMCA to third-party repair and in allowing the distribution of repair information and devices. The question remains, though, as to how these additional exemptions can be obtained, as well as how manufacturers can be compelled to release repair information.

The right to repair movement in the United States has been working to pass state-based legislation that would assist with the latter part.[70] In 2022, the movement saw some success, with New York State being the first to pass a right-to-repair law covering digital consumer products.[71] But the law was narrowed upon the governor's signing. For example, while the law requires manufacturers to make available repair information to independent repairers, it only requires it *if* manufacturers already make such information available to their network of authorized repairers.[72] Also in 2022, Colorado passed a right to repair law focused solely on wheelchairs.[73] Even though these two laws are somewhat more narrow than was advocated, it is still seen as a step in the right direction by some repair advocates.[74] Continued advocacy and lobbying persists in other states to attempt passage of similar, or even broader, legislation.[75]

Additionally, efforts are underway to pass repair legislation at the federal level. During the 2021–2022 session,[76] pro-repair bills were introduced in both the House and Senate, but none of the bills moved beyond being assigned to committees.[77] In addition, the "Freedom to Repair Act of 2022" was introduced in the House and would have amended Section 1201 of the DMCA to permanently exempt from Section 1201 repair-related circumvention and trafficking.[78] This, too, did not make it beyond being assigned to the House Judiciary Committee, despite advocacy to call for a hearing.[79] With the 118th Congressional Session beginning in January 2023, repair bills will need to be reintroduced. To date, H.R. 906 is the first bill introduced related to repair, but focuses on automobiles.[80]

More promising, though, is that self-regulation within the industry appears to be closer for electronic products. If companies would voluntarily allow consumers and independent repairers to have access to repair information and share it freely, it could mean that neither state nor federal legislation is needed in the short term.[81] There are signs that manufacturers themselves are looking into repair options for their products. For example, Google and Samsung have begun to sell some of their phone components on a repair platform, iFixit.[82] Apple began a self-repair service in 2022,[83] although the initial roll out has not gone smoothly.[84] Both the cost and complexity of the tools and parts needed led to some headlines such as "Apple Shipped Me a 79-Pound iPhone Repair Kit to Fix a 1.1 Ounce Battery."[85] The sub-headline to this article was "I'm starting to think Apple doesn't want us to repair them."[86] These articles were released in the early rollout days of the program, and it will likely take time to make self-repair more accessible, but as with the New York State and Colorado legislation, it is a step in the right direction.

Another promising sign is that other technology companies have started studying the issue, with Microsoft bowing to shareholder pressure in 2021 to complete an internal study by 2022 on how to better provide access to repair parts and information.[87] Microsoft released the report in May 2022, which concluded that "all forms of repair offer significant greenhouse gas (GHG) emission and waste reduction benefits."[88] In releasing the report, it was reported that

"Microsoft will continue to use these findings to expand the availability of certain parts and repair documentation beyond Microsoft's Authorized Service Provider (ASP) network, as the company has recently begun, and initiate new mechanisms to enable and facilitate local repair options for consumers. . . ."[89] Like with Google and Samsung, Microsoft has been selling some of its parts for the Surface device on iFixit.[90] However, relying on corporate benevolence to grant consumers the right to repair their own devices means that consumers must trust that the same corporations that prevented access to information previously will not, once again, change their minds.

CONCLUSION

These efforts underscore that consumers, as well as politicians and corporations, are advocating for a right to repair.[91] The momentum appears to be heading in the direction of allowing consumers to have the information to either effectively self-repair or choose to utilize an independent repairer.

The Section 1201 DMCA repair-related exemptions as promulgated by the Copyright Office in 2021 have paved the path for self-repair.[92] But even with these limited exemptions currently in place, anti-feminist oppression, in the forms of classism and imperialism, are sustained due to an unrealized ability to repair through higher cost and burdensome repair, as well as the e-waste generated by wealthy countries that flows into poor and developing countries. A feminist right to repair recognizes how the movement aligns with feminist values and empowers consumers to combat these forms of oppression by being able to utilize third-party retailers and sharing repair information publicly.

NOTES

The authors would like to thank Meg Leta Jones and Amanda Levendowski for the invitation to contribute to this volume.

1. *See* FTC, NIXING THE FIX: AN FTC REPORT TO CONGRESS ON REPAIR RESTRICTIONS 27 (May 2021), https://www.ftc.gov/system/files/documents/reports/nixing-fix-ftc-report-congress-repair-restrictions/nixing_the_fix_report_final_5521_630pm-508_002.pdf.

2. 17 U.S.C. §1201(a)(1)(A), (2) (2022). ("§1201 Circumvention of copyright protection systems (a) Violations Regarding Circumvention of Technological Measures.—(1)(A) No person shall circumvent a technological measure that effectively controls access to a work protected under this title. . . .)

3. 17 U.S.C. §1204.

4. *See* 80 Fed. Reg. 65944, 65954 (Oct. 28, 2015). *See also* USC Gould School of Law, USC Intellectual Property & Technology Law Clinic, Petition for Proposed Exemption Under 17 U.S.C. §1201 (Nov. 3, 2014), https://cdn.loc.gov/copyright/1201/2014/petitions/USC_IP_and_Technology_Law_Clinic_1201_Initial_Submission_2014.pdf (petitioning for a repair exemption for agricultural machinery).

5. *See* Pamela Samuelson, *Right to Tinker*, 17 THEORETICAL INQUIRIES L. 563, 589 (2016) ("Ordinary users rarely have the technical expertise or the inclination to spend time trying to bypass TPMs to tinker with products . . .").

6. *See* WHO, CHILDREN AND DIGITAL DUMPSITES 3–4 (June 15, 2021), https://www.who.int/publications/i/item/9789240023901.

7. *See infra* notes 71–75 and accompanying text.

8. *See* Lesley Fair, FTC Business Blog, *FTC Announces Three Right-to-Repair Cases: Do Your Warranties Comply With the Law?* (July 7, 2022), https://www.ftc.gov/business-guidance/blog/2022/07/ftc-announces-three-right-repair-cases-do-your-warranties-comply-law [https://perma.cc/F2YT-M8G2].

9. European Commission, Commission regulation (EU) 2019/2021. Off. J. Eur. Union 26; Taina Pihlajarinne, *European Steps to the Right to Repair: Towards a Comprehensive Approach to a Sustainable Lifespan of Products and Materials?* (Oct. 9, 2020). University of Oslo Faculty of Law Research Paper No. 2020–32, *available at* SSRN: https://ssrn.com/abstract=3708221. *See also* Anthony D. Rosborough, *Zen and the Art of Repair Manuals: Enabling a Participatory Right to Repair through an Autonomous Concept of EU Copyright Law* (Apr. 21, 2022), *available at* SSRN: https://ssrn.com/abstract=4089949 or http://dx.doi.org/10.2139/ssrn.4089949 (arguing that the EU 2001 Copyright Directive could be interpreted in a manner that provides a repair exception for nonprofit, community repair).

10. *See* Australian Government, Productivity Commission, RIGHT TO REPAIR, FINAL REPORT (Dec. 1, 2021), https://www.pc.gov.au/inquiries/completed/repair#report.

11. *See* Timothy B. Lee, *When Tech Companies Won't Provide Service Manuals, This Guy Writes His Own*, WASHINGTON POST (Jan. 13, 2014), https://www.washingtonpost.com/news/the-switch/wp/2014/01/13/when-tech-companies-wont-provide-service-manuals-this-guy-writes-his-own/ [https://perma.cc/W677-DJF7] (recounting Kyle Wiens's experience).

12. *See id.* In 2022, Apple began offering self-repair to its consumers, arguably in reaction to the progress made by repair activists in getting state legislatures to pass repair-related laws. *See infra* note 83.

13. *See* Kyle Wiens, *The Shady World of Repair Manuals*, WIRED (Nov. 12, 2012, 6:08PM), https://www.wired.com/2012/11/cease-and-desist-manuals-planned-obsolescence/ (recounting the enforcement efforts of Toshiba).

14. *See* Kyle Wiens (@kwiens), Twitter (June 11, 2020, 1:39 PM), https://twitter.com/kwiens/status/1271134890872856577 (posting the cease-and-desist letter that iFixit received from Steris).

15. *See* Samuelson, *supra* note 5, at 589.

16. 17 U.S.C. §§1201 et seq. *See* Jane C. Ginsburg, *Copyright Legislation for the "Digital Millennium,"* 23 COLUM. J. LAW & ARTS 137, 137–8 (1999) [hereinafter, Ginsburg, *Copyright Legislation*].

17. 17 U.S.C. §1201(a).

18. *See* FTC, *supra* note 1, at 23.

19. 17 U.S.C. §1204 ("(a) In General.—Any person who violates section 1201 or 1202 willfully and for purposes of commercial advantage or private financial gain—(1) shall be fined not more than $500,000 or imprisoned for not more than 5 years, or both, for the first offense; and (2) shall be fined not more than $1,000,000 or imprisoned for not more than 10 years, or both, for any subsequent offense.").

20. 17 U.S.C. §1201(a)(1)(C).

21. *See* US Copyright Office, RULEMAKING PROCEEDINGS UNDER SECTION 1201 OF TITLE 17, https://www.copyright.gov/1201/ (accessed June 24, 2023).

22. *See* US Copyright Office, SECTION 1201 RULEMAKING: SEVENTH TRIENNIAL PROCEEDING TO DETERMINE EXEMPTIONS TO THE PROHIBITION ON CIRCUMVENTION 222–25 (2018).

23. *See id.*

24. *See id.*

25. *See* Leah Chan Grinvald & Ofer Tur-Sinai, *Intellectual Property Law and the Right to Repair*, 88 FORD. L. REV. 63, 83–97 (2019) (analyzing various theories of intellectual property law) [hereinafter, Grinvald & Tur-Sinai, *IP and Repair*]. Other theories also support a right to repair, such as antitrust law in the United States or anticompetition law in the EU. *See, e.g.*, Michael A. Carrier, *How the Federal Trade Commission Can Use Section 5 to Strengthen the Right to Repair* 37 BERKELEY TECH. L.J., 1145 (2022), *available at* SSRN: https://ssrn.com/abstract=4200736 (US antitrust law could help repair);

Anthony D. Rosborough, *Unscrewing the Future: The Right to Repair and the Circumvention of Software TPMs in the EU*, 11 (2020) JIPITEC (EU anticompetition law could help repair).

26. *See* Grinvald & Tur-Sinai, *IP and Repair, supra* note 26 at 91–93 (describing the theory in the patent context).

27. *See* Jane C. Ginsburg, *Copyright and Control Over New Technologies of Dissemination*, 101 COLUM. L. REV. 1613, 1618 (2001) ("A goal of the DMCA was to encourage copyright owners to make their works available through digital networks.") [hereinafter, Ginsburg, *Copyright and Control*].

28. *See* Dan L. Burk, *Anticircumvention Misuse*, 50 UCLA L. REV. 1095, 1102–3 (2003).

29. *See* Ginsburg, *Copyright and Control, supra* note 28, at 1618.

30. *See* Ginsburg, *Copyright Legislation, supra* note 17, at 140–43 (arguing that the DMCA has created a new "right of access").

31. *See* Burk, *supra* note 29, at 1106–7 ("Violation of the technological protections on a copyright work is an infringement entirely separate from unauthorized reproduction, distribution, adaptation, public performance, public display, or digital transmission of the controlled material—the technological infringer need engage in none of these exclusive activities to violate the anticircumvention provision.").

32. *See* Amanda Levendowski, *Defragging Feminist Cyberlaw*, 37 BERKELEY TECH. L.J. 1, 7 (forthcoming 2023), *available at* SSRN: https://ssrn.com/abstract=4208296 [hereinafter, Levendowski, *Defragging*].

33. *See* Amanda Levendowski, *Feminist Use, in* FEMINIST CYBERLAW [5] (Meg Leta Jones & Amanda Levendowski, eds., 2024) [hereinafter, Levendowski, *Feminist Use*].

34. *See supra* Grinvald & Tur-Sinai, *IP and Repair*, note 25.

35. *See* Kostyantyn Pivnenko, UN Environment Programme, *Towards a Circular Economy for the Electronics Sector in Africa: Overview, Actions and Recommendations* 20 (2021), https://wedocs.unep.org/handle/20.500.11822/40108; UN Environment Programme, A NEW CIRCULAR VISION FOR ELECTRONICS: TIME FOR A GLOBAL REBOOT 14 (2019), https://wedocs.unep.org/handle/20.500.11822/32762.

36. UN Environment Programme, A NEW CIRCULAR VISION FOR ELECTRONICS: TIME FOR A GLOBAL REBOOT 14 (2019), https://wedocs.unep.org/handle/20.500.11822/32762.

37. The cracked smartphone screen is a paradigmatic example of this. *See* Aaron Perzanowski, THE RIGHT TO REPAIR 2 (2022).

38. *See* Nancy Levit & Robert Verchick, FEMINIST LEGAL THEORY: A PRIMER, x–xi (2nd ed., 2016) ("What makes a theory 'feminist' is itself a subject of considerable scholarly debate, but a pretty good starting point identifies a focus on women, gender relations, power, and inequality"); Hazel Tionloc Biana, *Extending bell hooks' Feminist Theory*, 21 J. INT'L WOMEN'S STUD. 13, 13 (2020).

39. bell hooks, FEMINIST THEORY: FROM MARGIN TO CENTER (Pluto Press, 2nd ed., 2000) (originally published 1984)

40. *See id.*, at 40 ("Individuals who fight for the eradication of sexism without supporting struggles to end racism or classism undermine their own efforts"). *But cf* Biana, *supra* note 38, at 24–27 (critiquing hooks's theory, but offering ways to uplift and extend it).

41. *See* Levendowski, *Defragging, supra* note 32 (quoting Kimberlé Crenshaw).

42. hooks, *supra* note 39, at 5 ("Being oppressed means the *absence of choices*.") (italics in original).

43. Merriam-Webster Dictionary, https://www.merriam-webster.com/dictionary/access.

44. Levendowski, *Feminist Use, supra* note 33, at 5.

45. *Id.* (citing Anne Firor Scott, *Women and Libraries*, 21 J. LIBRARY HISTORY (1974–1987) (1986).

46. *See* Ginsburg, *supra* note 27.

47. *See generally* Leah Chan Grinvald, *Policing the Cease-and-Desist Letter*, 49 U.S.F. L. REV. 409 (2015) (arguing for greater oversight of cease-and-desist letters, since abusive letters often lead to quick capitulation by the recipient of the sender's demands).

48. Kirtsaeng v. John Wiley & Sons, Inc., 568 U.S. 519, 527 (2013).

49. 568 U.S. at 527. Unfortunately for the copyright owner, the Supreme Court held that the first sale doctrine extended internationally, such that the graduate student had the right to import textbooks that had been lawfully first sold in a jurisdiction outside of the United States. *Id.*, at 554.

50. *See supra* notes 2 and 19.

51. Letter from Electronic Frontier Foundation, to Steris, on behalf of iFixit (May 26, 2020), https://www.eff.org/document/letter-eff-steris-behalf-ifixit-5-26-2020.

52. MERRIAM-WEBSTER DICTIONARY, https://www.merriam-webster.com/dictionary/classism [https://perma.cc/6G4F-NZB8].

53. *See* Paul Taylor, ART + Marketing, MEDIUM (June 12, 2016), https://perma.cc/KH28-FB9W.

54. *See* Ryan O'Hare, *How Long Would YOU Wait to Upgrade? Apple Customers Tend to Keep iPhones for Three Years on Average Before Trading In*, DAILY MAIL (Apr. 15, 2016), https://www.dailymail.co.uk/sciencetech/article-3541795/Time-running-iPhone-Macbook-Apple-officially-reveals-products-three-years.html [https://perma.cc/9F7P-A48K].

55. Kaveh Waddell, *People Want to Get Phones and Appliances Fixed—But Often, They Can't*, CONSUMER REPORTS (Feb. 28, 2022), https://www.consumerreports.org/consumer-rights/people-want-to-get-phones-appliances-fixed-but-often-cant-a1117945195/ (citing the cost to repair a broken screen at the Apple store at $279, and at an independent repairer at around $200 [https://perma.cc/ZLJ2-WZ7A].

56. *See* FTC, *supra* note 19, at 38 (citing testimony from Aaron Lowe of the Auto Care Association). *See also* Waddell, *supra* note 55.

57. *See* FTC, *supra* note 1, at 24.

58. FTC, *supra* note 1, at 39.

59. *Id.*

60. *See* UN ENVIRONMENT PROGRAMME, *supra* note 36, at 10 (estimating that from 2021 to 2050, the amount of e-waste is set to rise from 52 million tons to 120 million tons). The average yearly estimate was calculated on dividing the difference in the e-waste generation (68 million tons) by the number of years from 2021 to 2050 (29), which is approximately 2.3 million tons.

61. *See id.*, at 14.

62. MERRIAM-WEBSTER DICTIONARY, https://www.merriam-webster.com/dictionary/imperialism [https://perma.cc/6TZC-97NV].

63. *See* UN ENVIRONMENT PROGRAMME, *supra* note 36, at 12.

64. *Id.* at 13.

65. *Id.*

66. *Id.*

67. *See* Kristen Grant, et al., *Health Consequence of Exposure to E-Waste: A Systematic Review*, LANCET (Dec. 2013), at 353.

68. *Id.*, at 350.

69. The authors are not arguing that a global right to repair would end all poverty, but it could be one indirect way of ending these forms of oppression. However, there is some research that suggests it is not a linear line of causation. *See generally* Chen Jin, Luyi Yang & Cungen Zhu, *Right to Repair: Pricing, Welfare, and Environmental Implications*, 29 MANAGEMENT SCI. 1017 (2023) (arguing that their analytical model shows if repair laws are adopted, there would not necessarily be a reduction in e-waste).

70. *See* Leah Chan Grinvald and Ofer Tur-Sinai, *The Right to Repair: Perspectives from the United States*, 21 AIPJ 98, 102 (2020) (providing overview of state-based legislation).

71. *See* Press Release, *Governor Hochul Signs the Digital Fair Repair Act Into Law* (Dec. 29, 2022), https://www.governor.ny.gov/news/governor-hochul-signs-digital-fair-repair-act-law#:~:text=Governor%20Kathy%20Hochul%20signed%20the,anticompetitive%20efforts%20to%20limit%20repair [https://perma.cc/SH2H-RHM9].

72. *See* NYS The Digital Fair Repair Act (S4104-A/A7006-B), Sec. 3(C) https://www.nysenate.gov/legislation/bills/2021/S4104 (3. Limitations. (C) Nothing in this Section shall be construed to require

an original equipment manufacturer or an authorized repair provider to provide to an owner or independent repair provider access to information other than documentation, that is provided by the original equipment manufacturer to an authorized provider pursuant to the terms of an arrangement described in paragraph (A) of subdivision one of this Section").

73. *See* CO HB22–1031 (2022 Regular Session), https://leg.colorado.gov/bills/hb22-1031; Elaine S. Povich, *Colorado Enacts First 'Right to Repair' Law, But Only for Wheelchairs*, PEW (June 3, 2022), https://www.pewtrusts.org/en/research-and-analysis/blogs/stateline/2022/06/03/colorado-enacts -first-right-to-repair-law-but-only-for-wheelchairs.

74. *See* Cameron Faulkner, *New York Breaks the Right to Repair Bill as It's Signed into Law*, THE VERGE (Dec. 29, 2022, 8:11AM), https://www.theverge.com/2022/12/29/23530733/right-to-repair-law -new-york-tech-hochul-oems-parts (quoting Nathan Proctor, who is the senior right to repair campaign director at the US Public Interest Research Group as saying, "while it's [the NY law] not everything we wanted, it's the first of its kind in the nation, and just the start").

75. *See* REPAIR.ORG, GET INVOLVED, https://www.repair.org/stand-up (providing an interactive map of where bills have been introduced, passed, or where no right to repair bill has been introduced into the state legislature). By February 2023, there were twenty states that had active right to repair bills pending in their state legislature. In Massachusetts, an updated automobile repair law was passed by voters in 2020, but has been under litigation challenges since then. The law would update the 2012 law to include telematics. *See* Maddie Stone, *A Massachusetts Law Protects the Right to Repair Your Own Car. Automakers are Suing.*, GRIST (Jan. 11, 2023), https://grist.org/transportation/a-massachusetts -law-protects-the-right-to-repair-your-own-car-automakers-are-suing/. *See also* Leah Chan Grinvald & Ofer Tur-Sinai, *Smart Cars, Telematics and Repair*, 54 U. MICH. J. L. REF. 283 (2021), 295–98 (detailing the need to update the law to include telematics).

76. S. 3830 and HR 4006, Sec. 2 (117th Congress); H.R. 6566 (117th Congress), Freedom to Repair Act of 2022, https://www.congress.gov/bill/117th-congress/house-bill/6566/text.

77. *See* H.R. 4006, Committees, https://www.congress.gov/bill/117th-congress/house-bill/4006 /committees; S. 3930, Committees, https://www.congress.gov/bill/117th-congress/senate-bill/3830 /committees; H.R. 6566, Committees, https://www.congress.gov/bill/117th-congress/house-bill/6566 /committees; *It's Time for Congress to Hold a Right to Repair Hearing*, Repair.org (Mar. 17, 2022), https:// www.repair.org/blog/2022/3/17/its-time-for-congress-to-hold-a-right-to-repair-hearing.

78. H.R. 6566 (117th Congress), Freedom to Repair Act of 2022, https://www.congress.gov /bill/117th-congress/house-bill/6566/text.

79. H.R. 6566, Committees, https://www.congress.gov/bill/117th-congress/house-bill/6566 /committees (referred to the House Judiciary Committee on Feb. 2, 2022); *see supra* note 77, Repair.org.

80. H.R. 906, To ensure consumers have access to data relating to their motor vehicles, critical repair information, and tools, and to provide them choices for the maintenance, service, and repair of their motor vehicles, and for other purposes (118th Congress), https://www.congress.gov/bill/118th -congress/house-bill/906/text?s=3&r=1&q=%7B%22search%22%3A%5B%22repair%22%5D%7D (accessed June 24, 2023).

81. For example, the automobile industry was successful in 2014 in coming together to agree on a Memorandum of Understanding that provided information and repair parts to independent service providers. Memorandum of Understanding Among Automotive Aftermarket Industry Association, Coalition for Auto Repair Equality, Alliance of Automobile Manufacturers and Association of Global Automakers (Jan. 15, 2014), http://www.njgca.org/wp-content/uploads/Right-to-Repair-national -MOU-01-23-14.pdf [https://perma.cc/5L2F-DF5C]. In addition, there is a separate MOU for commer- cial vehicles. *See* Memorandum of Understanding: National Commercial Vehicle Service Information (Aug. 12, 2015), https://perma.cc/T8YL-FXNM. Unfortunately, the legislation that would update this law to include telematics has been stalled through a lawsuit that has been pending since 2020. *See supra* note 76.

82. *See* Sean Hollister, *The Era of Fixing Your Own Phone Has Nearly Arrived*, VERGE.COM (Apr. 9, 2022, 9:00AM), https://www.theverge.com/23017361/ifixit-right-to-repair-parts-google-samsung -valve-microsoft.

83. *See* Press Release, Apple, Apple's Self Service Repair Now Available (Apr. 27, 2022), https:// www.apple.com/newsroom/2022/04/apples-self-service-repair-now-available/ [https://perma.cc/BG3S -BYEF].

84. *See* Brian Chen, *I Tried Apple's Self-Repair Program with My iPhone. Disaster Ensued*, NEW YORK TIMES, Personal Tech. (May 25, 2022), https://www.nytimes.com/2022/05/25/technology /personaltech/apple-repair-program-iphone.html; Paul Roberts, How Apple's Self-Repair Program Is Engineered to Fail: Repair Roundup, Week of May 23, iFIXIT NEWS (May 28, 2022), https://www.ifixit .com/News/60589/how-apples-self-repair-program-is-engineered-to-fail-repair-roundup-week-of -may-23.

85. Sean Hollister, *Apple Shipped Me a 79-Pound iPhone Repair Kit to Fix a 1.1 Ounce Battery*, Verge.com (May 21, 2022, 3:00AM), https://www.theverge.com/2022/5/21/23079058/apple-self-service -iphone-repair-kit-hands-on?mc_cid=b9cdab4428&mc_eid=3566377881.

86. *Id.*

87. *See* Press Release, *Microsoft Agrees to Expand Consumers' Repair Options, As You Sow* (Oct. 7, 2021), https://www.asyousow.org/press-releases/2021/10/7/microsoft-agrees-expand-consumers-repair -options.

88. Oakdene Hollins, *Executive Summary: An Assessment of the Greenhouse Gas Emissions and Waste Impacts From Improving the Repairability of Microsoft Devices*, at 1 (Apr. 22, 2022), https://www .microsoft.com/en-us/corporate-responsibility/reports-hub#coreui-feature-6w178t7 (link to the report is found under Sustainability Reports, titled "Summary of Sustainability Benefits of Microsoft Device Repair").

89. *See* Press Release, *Microsoft Delivers on Promise to Investors, Releases Study Showing Device Repair Reduces Waste, Climate Emissions, As You Sow* (Apr. 29, 2022), https://www.asyousow.org/press -releases/2022/4/29/microsoft-study-device-repair-reduces-waste-climate-emissions.

90. *See* iFixit.com, *Microsoft Surface Service Tools*, https://www.ifixit.com/Microsoft-Surface -Tools/Microsoft-Surface-Tools (accessed June 24, 2023).

91. *See* Perzanowski, *supra note* 37, at 201 (showing the degree of consumer agreement with right to repair).

92. *Id.*, at 99.

3

Patents and the Gendered View
of Computer Programming
as Drudgery or Innovation

Nina Srejovic

Women were the original computer programmers. Women programmed the ENIAC, the first programmable, electronic, general purpose computer. Women implemented the design to convert that computer into the first stored program computer. And a woman wrote the first compiler program. Despite these many programming firsts, the patent often recognized as the first patent for a computer program, or "software," was granted to a man. While many argue that the waters surrounding the patentability of computer programs are murky even today, the history of computer programming and patents makes clear that judgments about what activity results in patentable subject matter is tied to gendered values society places on different types of work. When women were doing the work, programming was viewed as drudgery, merely the use of a machine, not the innovation or creation of technology that the patent system is designed to reward. As computer programming was professionalized and masculinized, that assessment was reversed, suggesting that at least in the history computer programming, to a large extent gender has determined who gets to invent.

Fundamentally, patents grant an economic right: the right to exclude others from making, using, or selling your invention for the term of the patent. If those rights are violated, patent holders are entitled to monetary damages. But patents are important for other reasons. Patents are used to measure the innovation taking place in society. To many they represent ingenuity, creativity, autonomy. Patent holders list their patents on resumes. In computer programming as in any other industry involving patentable technology, patents influence hiring, determine pay, and impact promotions.[1] Indeed, patent counts have been used as a proxy for "meaningful participation" in the computing field.[2]

On the law's surface, society's reliance on patents to measure and reward innovation should present no problem for women because patent law appears to be gender neutral. The patent statute lays out the requirements for a patent. New and useful processes, machines, manufactures, or compositions of matter, as well as any new and useful improvements are inventions entitled to recognition and exclusive rights.[3] In contrast to these requirements on the subject matter of an invention, patent law has minimal limitations on who can invent. An inventor is simply an "individual" who invents.[4] There are no other qualifications. The Federal Circuit Court of Appeals, the federal court that hears all patent appeals, recently decided that an inventor must be human, but that is an undeniably low bar.[5] So, if the system works according to the text of the law, whether the subject matter of any particular activity is judged to be an "invention" and worthy of a patent should depend on the subject matter that the activity produces not on who performed the activity.

However, the parallel histories of the computer programming profession and patents demonstrate that patent law is far from agnostic with respect to the gender of those who engage in inventive activity. The subject matter of patents both reflects and perpetuates society's judgments about the nature and the relative value of the work that women do. In the early days of computing, women were recruited to program computers because they were considered careful and detail oriented, excelling at repetitive and mundane tasks. Women used technology to make their chores easier. Men, on the other hand, were given the opportunity to develop the hardware of computer systems. Men were considered innovators. Men created technology. Men did the work that patents exist to reward and incentivize. The patent system both perpetuated and reflected those faulty assumptions. This chapter takes advantage of the unique history of computer programming as an activity in which the primary gender of its participants shifted at an identifiable moment from almost exclusively women to largely men. Examining this history in parallel with the history of patenting activity sheds light on how patents reflect and perpetuate society's gendered views of activity as drudgery or innovation. Given the power of patents in the economy and society in general, those working in the patent system should be educated to recognize gendered views of inventive activity, or alternatively patents must be replaced by better measures of innovation in society.

THE HISTORY OF GENDER IDENTITY
IN COMPUTER PROGRAMMING

Unlike the current composition of the programming workforce, the majority of computer programmers in the early days of computers were women. The Electronic Numerical Integrator and Computer (ENIAC), developed during World War II to solve the mathematical equations necessary to determine the ballistics trajectories, is widely recognized as the first programmable, electronic, general purpose computer. The original programmers of the ENIAC were all women—Kay McNulty, Betty Jennings, Betty Snyder, Marlyn Meltzer, Fran Bilas, and Ruth Lichterman. They derived the programs based on block diagrams constructed by another woman, Adele Goldstine.[6] Indeed, according to Herman Goldstine, a senior member of the ENIAC team and Adele's husband, Adele (and, of course, himself) were the "only persons who really had a completely detailed knowledge of how to program the ENIAC."[7]

At the time, women were the obvious choice to program the ENIAC. Before the ENIAC was developed, women manually calculated ballistics trajectories, which was the task the ENIAC was initially designed to perform. These women "computers"[8] already used much simpler machines, such as slide rules and basic calculating machines,[9] to perform what was viewed as their rote, dull, and low status job.[10] They were now just provided a much superior machine in the ENIAC to help them perform the same function.

At the time that women were working to program the ENIAC computer, their government job rating was SP, meaning "subprofessional."[11] They were initially prohibited from entering the ENIAC room because of security concerns, forcing them to learn the machine from wiring diagrams. The account of Herman Goldstine of the history of the ENIAC demonstrates how the contributions of women in the development of the ENIAC were discounted. Goldstine writes, "Holberton [the man in charge of the six women programmers of the ENIAC] and his group had been assigned the responsibility . . . of becoming the programming staff. . . . They were trained largely by my wife, with some help by me."[12] Holberton's "group" was composed of women, here unnamed. During the first public demonstration of the ENIAC, the women programmers were not acknowledged at all.

Other women followed the path of those original ENIAC programmers. Klara von Neumann and Adele Goldstine worked together to convert the ENIAC into the first stored program computer. The first stored programs run on the ENIAC, complex calculations called Monte Carlo simulations tracing the paths of neutrons through an atomic bomb, were written by a woman and run by Klara von Neumann. Klara Dan was the primary programmer of the Mathematical Analyzer, Numerical Integrator, and Computer (MANIAC I), a computer in the 1950s initially designed to perform calculations of the thermonuclear process at Los Alamos National Laboratory. In 1952, Mary Tsingou programmed the first experiment conducted entirely on a computer on the MANIAC.[13]

After the war, Grace Hopper joined the Eckert-Mauchly Computer Corporation and in 1953 wrote the first compiler, written for the COBOL language. Female computer programmers were vital to the computer language development taking place in the 1950s at Bell Labs. Dolores C. Leagus codeveloped the L1 language, and Ruth A. Weiss codeveloped the L2 language. The two languages were used on more the half the IBM computers doing scientific and engineering work in the late 1950s.[14]

Women were not just co-participants with men in developing computer programs. In the days of the ENIAC computer programmers and into the 1950s, there was a clear gender-based line between software developers and hardware developers. As John Knox has observed, when women were doing the programming, the men thought "it was sexier to be around the hardware than software. . . . No one cared about software; it was 'women's work' in a way, even though nothing would have worked without the software."[15] Even some women believed programming was women's work. In Janet Abbate's interviews of early female computer innovators, Elsie Shutt, who was hired by Raytheon in 1953 noted, "it really amazed me that these [men] were programmers, because I thought it was women's work!"[16]

In the postwar years, the demand for computer programmers increased rapidly as computer manufacturers turned their attention to the commercial market. Initially, both women and men were recruited as programmers. Job titles varied from computing engineer to numerical analyst, data processing specialist, computer, or programmer.[17] Recruiters used college degrees, aptitude tests, and experience in other occupations, such as mathematics, engineering, and business as proxy measures for programming skill, each with differing effects on women's opportunities in the field.[18] Some companies and universities affirmatively recruited women by equating the skills necessary for programming to the skills necessary for embroidery or knitting. According to an article in the Guardian, programming required "patience and tenacity, and a common-sense sort of logic. Much of the work is tedious, requiring great attention to detail, and this is where women usually score."[19] But the questions remained, "was computer programming a job for highly skilled scientists, or for clerical workers like secretaries and typists?"[20]

Despite these recruiting efforts, by the late 1960s, discussions about the future of the computing industry were dominated by warnings about the shortage of programmer labor. As more corporate or academically oriented men entered the profession, they "worked to establish professional societies, publish academic journals, develop credentialing programs, and lobby employers and governments for recognition and legitimacy."[21] As late as 1966, computer facilities were funded as tools in other scientific disciplines rather than as research in computing itself.[22] By 1967, the Office for Computing Activities was established at the National Science Foundation, and in 1968, funding for the OCA was increased by 73 percent.[23] The 1969 report proclaimed "the emergence of computer science as an academic discipline."[24]

Nathan Ensmenger has argued that as part of the professionalization of computer programming in the 1960s, computer programming was made masculine as a way to pursue status and autonomy by male programmers.[25] Male academics successfully transformed computer programming, previously viewed as routine and mechanical, into a "highly valued, well-paying, and professionally respectable discipline."[26] Mar Hicks has made a similar case for the masculinization of computer programming work in Britain in the 1960s.[27] "As computer programmers constructed a professional identity for themselves during the crucial decades of the 1950s and 1960s . . . they also constructed a gender identity."[28] The term "software engineering" was adopted in the late 1960s in order to associate programming with a highly masculine occupation. Predictably, the identity of computer programmers became more masculine.[29]

During this time, women were not only replaced by men as programmers. They were also replaceable by computers. Physical computers, which were designed to replace female "computers," were now explicitly marketed as a substitute for women's work and without the distractions that women presented in the workplace. A series of ads by Recognition Equipment Incorporated in the 1960s proclaimed, "Our optical reader can do anything your keypunch operators do. (Well, almost.)"[30] Each ad then recited a presumably annoying skill of female keypunch operators that the optical reader lacked, such as taking maternity leave, suffering from morning sickness, getting mad and making silly mistakes, pouting for days or crying, or being a social butterfly.[31]

WOMEN AS SIDELINED INNOVATORS AND EXCLUDED INVENTORS

In interviews conducted by Janet Abbate for her book *Recoding Gender*[32] and, more recently, by Kathryn Kleiman,[33] the story of early women computer programmers is starting to see the light of day. However, a search of the patent records for the names of these women programming pioneers reveals a puzzling fact: none of them have a patent to her name to recognize her contributions. The patent often recognized as the first patent for a computer program was granted in 1968 to a man.[34] Over the last thirty years, the number of patents granted yearly to inventors working in computer software ranged from thirty thousand to over two hundred thousand.[35] Why were those women innovators not similarly recognized as inventors?

It wasn't because patenting considerations were absent from the programmers' working environment. John Presper Eckert and John W. Mauchly, who have been credited with inventing the ENIAC, applied for a patent for a numerical integrator and computer in 1947.[36] After the patent was finally granted in 1964,[37] Sperry Rand Univac, the assignee of the patent, charged a 1.5 percent royalty on every electronic computer sold in the United States.[38] Several people resigned from the ENIAC project due to disputes over patent rights.[39]

Rather, the inventing was deemed complete once the computer hardware was developed. As John Eckert was quoted claiming, "[John] Mauchly and I achieved a complete workable computer system."[40] No mention was made of the software and the many women who developed it.

In those early days of computing, a clear line divided attitudes about the development of computer hardware versus the development of computer software. The development of hardware was considered inventive enough to warrant a patent, while computer programming, or the development of software, was not. It's possible that this difference in perception was due to the different activities themselves. Perhaps it was easier to conceive of a machine rather than a series of steps as an invention. But the history of computer programming shows that the gender of the people doing the work also influenced that assessment.

When computer programmers were principally women, they were not perceived as inventors. The women who were programming the ENIAC were simply continuing the task of calculating trajectories, now with the technology made possible by the innovation of brilliant men. Photos of the women "programming" the ENIAC depict them standing in front of hundreds of cables resembling an old-time telephone switchboard, programming the computer by plugging and unplugging the cables to alter its functionality.[41] The similarity of the ENIAC's wires and plugs to a telephone switchboard may have made the programmers seem like familiar women telephone operators. Even authors of current feminist retellings of computer history refer to the early programmers of ENIAC as "operators" of the machine.[42] Despite the incredible innovation that was required to develop the logic behind the steps of the calculations and devise ways to program, use, and debug it, the women programmers appeared to be merely operating the "switchboard" of the ENIAC.

Later, as the makeup of computer programmers became more masculine, computer programming took on a different gloss. As described earlier, computer programmers became software engineers tasked with creating rather than merely operating. In addition, the United States Department of Justice began an investigation into whether IBM was committing antitrust violations by selling hardware and software as a "bundled" single product. In 1969, in an attempt to foreclose an antitrust lawsuit against it, IBM announced that it would unbundle software from hardware thus creating a market for computer programs separate from the computer hardware in which they were incorporated. Lawyers and their clients pursued patent protection for computer programs in order to protect their value in the marketplace.

Patent law in the context of computers reflected earlier notions about the primacy of hardware. In the mid-1960s, the Patent Office's guidelines were largely interpreted to exclude computer programs from patentable subject matter because they were either "abstract concepts" or "mental processes." Only when programs were viewed as closely tied to a machine were courts willing to see them as patentable subject matter. In 1969, the US Court of Customs and Patent Appeals, which preceded the Federal Circuit, held that a specialized computer created by programming a general purpose computer was patentable but the computer program itself was not.[43] In response, patents seeking protection for the substance of a computer program were carefully crafted to claim the invention of a machine (in practice, a physical computer together with software) that carried out a particular process. In Gottschalk v. Benson, the first Supreme Court case addressing the patentability of computer programs, the justices focused on whether the program was part of the machine. In oral argument, they repeatedly asked whether the programmed computer was the same or a different machine from the computer before it was programmed.[44] They challenged the assertion that the computer program for which the respondent claimed patent rights should be considered part of the physical computer. Ultimately, the Court sided with the government, which argued that the program was completely separate from the computer, and invalidated the patent. Subsequent Supreme Court cases have been interpreted as either expanding or contracting the patentability of computer programs, but in order to increase the likelihood that their patents will be upheld by a court, patent attorneys today still include some hardware component when writing patents that cover computer programs.

Courts interpreting patent law in the context of computers singled out "technology" as deserving of patent protection. In Application of Musgrave, a case decided in 1970, the US Court of Customs and Patent Appeals considered whether a process is subject matter that can be patented and decided that a sequence of steps was the appropriate subject matter for a patent as long as "it be in the technological arts."[45] Scholars have also argued that patentable inventions should be limited to those that "involve technological contributions" to guard against "render[ing] all human endeavors subject to patenting."[46]

Patent law's requirement that inventive activity must relate to the machine or "technology" made patent lawyers, scholars, and judges party to the agenda of those who sought to professionalize computer programming in the '60s and '70s. Rather than being viewed as simply the use of a machine, programming had to be part of the machine. Only then would it be viewed as creative and innovative (as well as a respected profession). As they argued for the patentability of computer programs, they reinforced the idea that only constructing something that was a part of the machine was inventive. If the machine, or "hardware," is the important contribution, then to be patentable, programming must be a part of that machine. A program, they argued, in its "soft form" was nothing less than instant hardware.[47] Those seeking patents for computer programs also argued that those programs related to "technology," making them more likely to be viewed as the innovation that society values enough to reward with a patent.

Participants in the patent system were quite successful in arguing that computer programming should cross the threshold into machinery, technology, and invention. But when that happened, women were left standing at the door. In asserting that computer programming is part of the machine and related to "technology," participants in the patent system reinforced arguments made by the Association for Computing Machinery (ACM) and other professional organizations and university departments who advocated for treating computer programming as a more technical, and more masculine, occupation. As the perception of computer programming shifted from simply using or operating the machinery of the computer to inventing technology, it was no longer women's work.

COMPENSATING FOR GENDERED ASSESSMENTS OF INNOVATION

Starting in the 1960s, "the problems associated with exploiting fully the potentialities of present and projected computers" were now "difficult and intellectually challenging."[48] The solutions were innovative and creative. They were inventions, and the inventors were male. A 2019 report by the United States Patent and Trademark Office, which provided information inferred from the assumed gender of inventors' names, found that the percentage of patents by either an individual woman inventor or a team of all-women inventors was about 4 percent and has shown little growth since 1976.[49] A 2012 study found that only 1.9 percent of information technology patents listed a woman as sole inventor.[50]

Suggested causes range from the lack of women in senior positions to the particular scientific occupations women pursue to a lack of resources to access the patent system.[51] But the history of computer programming and patents suggests that there is another explanation behind the dearth of patents granted to women in information technology—something an individual inventor can do very little to counteract. Activities performed by women were seen as less innovative and less related to technology and therefore less deserving of patent protection. In addition, patents were only granted to computer programmers once an economic market existed for computer programming. But, as soon as that market was established, women were forced out. Rather than an accurate measure of innovation, patents were part of the system that rewarded the participants, now mostly men, in that market. If the history of computing is representative, these current day patent statistics hide the rich history of women's contributions to innovation, and invoking patents to measure innovation continues to devalue women's innovation.

Computer programming provides a unique case study to examine these attitudes as a single technological field in which patenting once languished when it was predominantly female and later boomed when it became predominantly male. The history of patents and computer programs challenges the notion that the innovative activities of women determine the number of patents they are granted. Efforts to address the gender imbalance in patenting, including the recommendations of the Success Act Report written by the Patent Office focus on resources to assist women in accessing the patent system to increase gender diversity in innovation. Is this the right tactic? Perhaps rather than focusing on levers to increase the likelihood that women will do more to increase patent activity: do more to educate themselves about the patent system, do more to utilize pro bono services to file patent applications, do more innovating; we should be educating men at the Patent Office about women's abilities.

Or should we decouple perceptions of innovation from patenting entirely? If patent protection depends in part on the gender of the person doing the work, are patents even the right tool to measure innovation? Patents are not gender neutral instruments but rather reflect the value that society places—or doesn't place—on women's work. If women do not obtain patents, their contributions are not recognized.[52] While it is important to advocate for space and opportunity for women within the current organizational structure of knowledge production and ownership, a critical evaluation of those structures through a feminist lens shows that rather than measuring innovation, the patent system more accurately measures the value our society places on certain activity—with sexist results.

The view of women's work as less valuable continues today even among different types of computer programming. Women have made some headway in participation in front end programming, but salary in that area tends to be lower than other areas of computer programming.[53] A wage discrimination suit against Google, LLC, alleges that female "Program Managers" are paid less than male "Technical Program Managers" despite performing equal work,[54] and that women are channeled into lower paying roles in the Operations family rather than higher paying roles in the Engineering family.[55] The situation of women of color, particularly non-Asian women, is even worse. Google's recent diversity report acknowledges that gains in women's representation in its workforce have largely been driven by increases in the representation of White and Asian women,[56] and Black women represent only 2.3 percent of Google's workforce in 2022.[57] This recent data makes clear that at least one legacy of the ENIAC programmers lives on. As Miriam Posner, professor of computer science, put it, the industry simply regards anything being done by a woman as easy.[58]

NOTES

1. Rhaina Cohen, *What Programming's Past Reveals about Today's Gender-Pay Gap*, THE ATLANTIC (Sept. 7, 2016), https://www.theatlantic.com/business/archive/2016/09/what-programmings-past-reveals-about-todays-gender-pay-gap/498797/.

2. Catherine Ashcraft & Anthony Breitzman, National Center for Women & Information Technology, WHO INVENTS IT? WOMEN'S PARTICIPATION IN INFORMATION TECHNOLOGY, 2012 UPDATE 3 (2012) [hereinafter WHO INVENTS IT?], https://rdw.rowan.edu/cgi/viewcontent.cgi?article=1005&context=csm_facpub.

3. 35 U.S.C. § 101.

4. 35 U.S.C. § 100(f).

5. The Federal Circuit Court of Appeals has held that "a particular type of connectionist artificial intelligence" computer program known as a "Creativity Machine" cannot be an inventor. Thaler v. Vidal, 43 F.4th 1207, 1209 (Fed. Cir 2022).

6. Adele K. Goldstine, ELECTRONIC NUMERICAL INTEGRATOR AND COMPUTER (ENIAC): ENIAC TECHNICAL MANUAL (1946).

7. Herman Goldstine, THE COMPUTER FROM PASCAL TO VON NEUMANN 330 (1972).

8. W. Barkely Fritz, *The Women of the ENIAC*, 18 IEEE ANNALS HIST. COMPUTING 13, 13 (1996).

9. Sarah McLennan & Mary Gainer, *When the Computer Wore a Skirt: Langley's Computers, 1935–1970*, 29 NASA HIST. PROGRAM OFF. NEWS & NOTES 25 (2012), https://history.nasa.gov/nltr29-1.pdf.

10. Clive Thompson, *The Gendered History of Human Computers*, SMITHSONIAN (June 2019), https://www.smithsonianmag.com/science-nature/history-human-computers-180972202/; *see also* Mar Hicks, PROGRAMMED INEQUALITY (2017).

11. Janet Abbate, RECODING GENDER x (2012) (hereinafter RECODING GENDER).

12. H. Goldstein, see *supra* note 7, 229–30.

13. *A Short History of Women at Los Alamos*, LOS ALAMOS NAT'L LAB'Y (Mar. 22, 2018), https://trace.tennessee.edu/cgi/viewcontent.cgi?article=1163&context=ijns.

14. Bernard D. Holbrook & W. Stanley Brown, BELL LABORATORIES, COMPUTING SCIENCE TECHNICAL REPORT NO. 99: A HISTORY OF COMPUTING RESEARCH AT BELL LABORATORIES (1937–1975) 9 (1982), https://research.swtch.com/cstr99.pdf.

15. Sarah Witman, *The Unheralded Contributions of Klara Dan von Neuwmann*, SMITHSONIAN (June 16, 2017), https://www.smithsonianmag.com/science-nature/meet-computer-scientist-you-should -thank-your-phone-weather-app-180963716/.

16. Abbate, *supra* note 11, at 1.

17. *Id.*, at 43.

18. *Id.*, at 44–64.

19. Maureen Epstein, *Computer Women*, in RECODING GENDER, *supra* note 11, at 67.

20. *Consuming Women, Liberating Women: Women and Advertising in the Mid 20th Century*, DUKE UNIV. (2019), https://sites.duke.edu/womenandadvertising/exhibits/tech-ads-and-women /advertisements-for-technology/.

21. Nathan Ensmenger, *"Beards, Sandals, and Other Signs of Rugged Individualism": Masculine Culture with the Computing Professions*, OSIRIS (2015), at 52.

22. Janet Abbate, *From Handmaiden to "Proper Intellectual Discipline": Creating a Scientific Identity for Computer Science in 1960s America*, in COMMUNITIES OF COMPUTING, COMPUTER SCIENCE AND SOCIETY IN THE ACM 31–32 (Thomas J. Misa, ed., 2017) [hereinafter *Handmaiden*].

23. *Id.*, at 43.

24. *Id.*, at 45.

25. Ensmenger, *supra* note 21. at 65.

26. *Id.*, at 38.

27. Mar Hicks, *Meritocracy and Feminization in Conflict: Computerization in the British Government*, in GENDER CODES: WHY WOMEN ARE LEAVING COMPUTING (Thomas Misa, ed., 2010), 95–114.

28. Nathan Ensmenger, THE COMPUTER BOYS TAKE OVER COMPUTERS, PROGRAMMERS, AND THE POLITICS OF TECHNICAL EXPERTISE 239–40 (2010). A later article extends Ensmenger's work and concludes that "beginning in 1975, new editorial attention to the issues faced by women in the field replaced the open misogyny of a few years before." Although the author notes this interest diminished by the 1980s. William F. Vogel, *The Spitting Image of a Woman Programmer": Changing Portrayals of Women in the American Computing Industry, 1958–1985*, 39 IIEE ANNALS HIST. COMPUTING 49 (2017).

29. Liana Christin Landivar, *American Community Survey Reports, Disparities in STEM Employment by Sex, Race, and Hispanic Origin*, US CENSUS (2013), https://www.census.gov/library/publications /2013/acs/acs-24.html.

30. Nathan Ensmenger, Slides from *Making Programming Masculine: A Gendered History of the Computing Professions Presentation at Stanford University* (Mar. 3, 2011), 64–66, https://homes.luddy .indiana.edu/nensmeng/files/stanford-gender.pdf.

31. *Id.*

32. Abbate, *supra* note 11 at 177–78.

33. *See* Kathryn Kleiman, PROVING GROUND: THE UNTOLD STORY OF THE SIX WOMEN WHO PROGRAMMED THE WORLD'S FIRST MODERN COMPUTER (2022).

34. Gene Quinn, *The History of Software Patents in the United States*, IP WATCHDOG (Nov. 30, 2014), https://ipwatchdog.com/2014/11/30/the-history-of-software-patents-in-the-united-states/id=52256/.

35. Raymond Millien, *Seven Years After Alice, 63.2% of the Patents Granted in 2020 Were Software-Related*, IP WATCHDOG (Mar. 17, 2021), https://ipwatchdog.com/2021/03/17/seven-years-after-alice-63-2-of-the-u-s-patents-issued-in-2020-were-software-related/id=130978/.

36. U.S. Patent App. No. 757158.

37. U.S. Patent No. 3120606.

38. International Business Machines was the only firm exempt from royalty payments due to a cross-licensing agreement between the two companies. The patent was later invalidated by a court because, among other reasons, the invention was derived from work by Dr. John Vincent Atanasoff and the invention was disclosed by John von Neumann too early before the patent application was filed. The decision by the court discussing who among these men invented the electronic computer was over 248 pages long and was preceded by six years of litigation with over thirty thousand exhibits and thousands of pages of deposition testimony. Despite the outcome of the litigation, President Lyndon B. Johnson awarded Eckert and Mauchly the US National Medal of Science for inventing the computer.

39. Nancy Stern, *The Eckert-Mauchly Computers: Conceptual Triumphs, Commercial Tribulations*, 2 TECH. AND CULTURE 569, 571 (1982).

40. J. Presper Eckert, *Co-Inventor of Early Computer, Dies at 76*, NEW YORK TIMES (June 7, 1995); Eckert's obituary is a particularly blatant example of the erasure of both the women "computers" who calculated ballistics trajectories before the ENIAC and the programmers who were critical contributors to the ENIAC's success. According to the obituary, "artillery officers" labored over the calculations, and "ENIAC" was the solution to the problem.

41. *Id.*

42. Abbate, *supra* note 11, at 13 ("Both [Colossus and ENIAC] made important technical advances, both influenced the development of computers after the war, and both employed teams of women to operate the machines").

43. *In re Prater*, 415 F.2d 1393, 1395 (U.S. C.C.P.A. 1969).

44. Gottschalk v. Benson, 409 U.S. 63 (1972), https://www.oyez.org/cases/1972/71-485.

45. Application of Musgrave, 431 F.2d 882 (U.S. C.C.P.A. 1970). As Judge Baldwin points out in his concurrence, this requirement may generate the new problem of "interpreting the meaning of 'technological arts.'"

46. David J. Kappos, John R. Thomas & Randall J Bluestone, *A Technological Contribution Requirement for Patentable Subject Matter: Supreme Court Precedent and Policy*, 6 NW. J. OF TECH. & INTELL. PROP. 152, 153 (2008).

47. Irving Kayton, *Patent Protectability of Software: Background and Current Law*, 9 JURIMETRICS JOURNAL 127, 134 (1969); L. Smilow, *Comments on Computers-in-Law Institute's First Annual Conference*, 50 J. PAT. OFF. SOC'Y 779 (1968).

48. *Handmaiden, supra* note 22, at 38.

49. US Patent & Trademark Off., REPORT TO CONGRESS PURSUANT TO P.L. 115–273, THE SUCCESS ACT (2019), https://www.uspto.gov/sites/default/files/documents/USPTOSuccessAct.pdf.

50. WHO INVENTS IT?, *supra* note 2, at 10.

51. Women are similarly underrepresented as attorneys and agents licensed to practice in the Patent Office. There are more patent practitioners named Michael than racially diverse women. Elaine Spector & LaTia Brand, *Diversity in Patent Law: A Data Analysis of Diversity in the Patent Practice by Technology Background and Region*, 13 LANDSLIDE 1 (2020), https://www.americanbar.org/groups/intellectual_property_law/publications/landslide/2020-21/september-october/diversity-patent-law-data-analysis-diversity-patent-practice-technology-background-region/.

52. Lost Women of Science Podcast put out a request for anyone who knows early computer pioneers. *See* https://lostwomenofscience.org/season-2.

53. The Bureau of Labor Statistics lists the average salary for software developers (designers of computer applications or programs) as $109,020. The average salary for web developers (developers, creators, and testers of website or interface layout, functions, and navigation) is $78,300. US Bureau of Labor Statistics, Occupational Outlook Handbook, https://www.bls.gov/ooh/computer-and-information-technology/web-developers.htm (accessed Sept. 21, 2022).

54. First Amended Complaint at 12, *Ellis v. Google, LLC*, Case No. CGC-17–561299 (Cal. Super. 2017).

55. *Id.*, at 15.

56. Google Diversity Annual Report 2018 11 (2018).

57. Google Diversity Annual Report 2022 34 (2022).

58. Thompson, *supra* note 10.

4

Oppressive and Empowering #Tagmarks

Alexandra J. Roberts

#SayHerName is a hashtag social movement that works to amplify the names and narratives of Black women killed by police and to raise awareness about how state violence intersects with race and gender. Kimberlé Crenshaw, cofounder and executive director of the African American Policy Forum (AAPF), is credited with founding the movement[1] following the police killing of Michelle Cusseaux in 2014.[2] The following year, AAPF hosted "#SayHerName: A Vigil in Memory of Black Women and Girls Killed by the Police" and released a report that outlined the movement's objectives.[3] Since then, and especially following the death of Sandra Bland in police custody, the hashtag has taken off on social media. The AAPF applied to register #SayHerName as a trademark for charitable services and promoting awareness in 2016, but the US Patent and Trademark Office (USPTO) issued an office action refusing registration because it deemed the mark an informational slogan incapable of functioning as a source indicator. Citing copious online evidence, the examining attorney asserted that "because consumers are accustomed to seeing this slogan commonly used in everyday speech by many different sources . . . the public would not perceive the slogan #SAYHERNAME as source-identifying matter that identifies applicant as the source of the services but rather as an expression of support for anti-violence advocates and civil rights groups."

Meanwhile, media consultant Jade Bryan, who says she created the #DeafTalent hashtag used to highlight Deaf and hard of hearing members of the entertainment community and protest the casting of hearing actors in deaf character roles, successfully registered "#DeafTalent" as a trademark for entertainment and education services. She now tries to prohibit others from using the phrase; her website claims that every use of the hashtag requires a license, and she has messaged members of the deaf community to demand they cease use.[4] Bryan also succeeded in getting the UK advocacy group Deaf Talent Collective, which helped many Deaf actors of color earn roles in mainstream film and television productions, suspended from Twitter over a trademark complaint.[5]

The technical trademark analysis arguably does not come down on either AAPF's side or Bryan's. While Crenshaw and AAPF played a key role in making the #SayHerName hashtag go viral, its very virality prevented it from doing what a trademark must do—indicate to consumers that goods or services come from one specific source. And the uses to which Bryan objects are mostly expressive, non-trademark displays of the phrases, making them legally permissible under fair use doctrine. Even commercial uses of marks similar to registered marks can coexist with those registered marks if they don't create confusion, which is more likely when both incorporate descriptive phrases like "Deaf talent." Nonetheless, it's easy to understand AAPF's and Bryan's actions. Bryan secured a registration for a hashtag she adopted, and that registration purports to provide exclusive property rights. AAPF sought to do the same for a hashtag it created and made popular, and in connection with which it provides educational and charitable services. Trademark law is widely acknowledged to be weighted in favor of corporate interests and against individuals and somewhat less widely acknowledged to be more accessible to wealthy white producers than to people of color.

Because of that imbalance, a movement is currently afoot to educate artists, entrepreneurs, activists, and online content creators, particularly those who are members of marginalized groups, about their rights and to help them avail themselves of intellectual property protection. But when members of those groups do apply for trademark registrations or assert common law trademark rights, particularly those based on hashtag social movements and other online uses, they often find their applications refused or their attempts to stop others' uses deemed over-enforcement.[6] Populations that are underrepresented among trademark owners need a clear understanding of what trademark law protects—one that equips them to invest their time and effort building something that they can legally safeguard and effectively enforce. Improving access to information via agency websites and other government resources can help level the playing field. Improving access to competent legal representation, including through law school clinics and opportunities for pro bono advice and representation, is also crucial. And trademark lawyers should work to educate themselves about their clients' artistic, political, or entrepreneurial work and address their own biases or gaps in cultural knowledge to ensure effective advocacy.[7] When resources are free or low-cost, easy to find, and designed for laypeople, members of groups that have traditionally been disenfranchised under intellectual property laws can access the information and protection necessary to formalize and exploit their rights in service of their commercial efforts. And they can enforce those rights in ways that do not use trademark law to silence the speech of other artists, activists, and creators.

A trademark is any device used in connection with goods or services that indicates their source. It can be a word, name, symbol, slogan, or even a scent or shape. It tells consumers who stands behind products or signals that those products come from only one producer. Some categories of marks, such as coined terms or those that don't describe any aspect of the goods or services, can be protected immediately upon use; others, such as marks that describe where the product is made or what it's for or marks that comprise the design of a product, are only protectable upon a showing that they have come to serve as source indicators in the eyes of consumers. In the United States, trademark rights are based on use in commerce and distinctiveness: owners can apply to register matter as a trademark to formalize their federal rights, but registration is not required for rights to accrue, so no single comprehensive list of all enforceable trademarks exists. The goals of trademark law include protecting consumers from deception, promoting economic efficiency and fair competition, and providing trademark owners incentive to invest in producing and marketing high-quality goods and services to generate goodwill. Owners of both registered and unregistered trademarks can sue other entities that create a likelihood of consumer confusion by using a similar mark in commerce; owners of marks that are famous nationwide can also sue for dilution when someone uses a mark that tarnishes the famous mark's reputation or blurs its distinctiveness. Yet most trademark disputes happen outside of the courtroom—cease and desist letters or email demands that someone stop or alter their use are far more common than lawsuits, which means most trademark bargaining and dispute resolution takes place in the shadow of the law.[8]

Intellectual property scholars have decried racial and gender disparities in ownership, prosecution, and examination across all areas of IP, including patent[9] and copyright law.[10] Trademark law is not immune from those inequities. The vast majority of trademark applications are filed by corporate entities, so data on race and gender disparities in trademark registration are somewhat limited compared to other forms of IP.[11] But in a study of over a million trademark applications filed by individuals, researchers found that Black and Hispanic applicants were underrepresented, as were women, while white applicants and male applicants were overrepresented compared to the population.[12]

Individuals and activist groups need opportunities, resources, and support to innovate (patent), create expressive works (copyright), and engage in commerce (trademark).[13] Access to formal IP protection requires access to information, capital, and expertise. What's more, intellectual property laws are structured to privilege and protect some forms of innovation, commerce, and art over others—and those forms of knowing and creating tend to be predominantly white and male.[14] IP is often said to serve the twin goals of incentivizing and rewarding labor and innovation. But the creative and entrepreneurial endeavors of women, people of color, and members of other marginalized groups are less likely to be rewarded with protection and exclusive rights. Unequal numbers in ownership and disparate outcomes at the USPTO and the Copyright Office are not the only reflections of structural inequality. As KJ Greene has written, "A feminist critique recognizes that rights governing cultural production did not arise in a social or cultural vacuum, but in a crucible of gender and racial subordination, the embers of which still burn today."

What happens to ownership of intellectual property in the age of social media? It has become easier than ever to create something that goes viral, but virality rarely begets control—ask Kayla Newman (aka Peaches Monroee), who coined "on fleek"; or Patty Mallette, who created the popular hashtag #LoveWins in the wake of the Supreme Court's recognition of same-sex marriage; or the young, often Black choreographers who create viral TikTok dances[15] only to see white influencers perform them on television.[16] As intellectual property laws intersect with new forms of creativity and creation, the gulf between those who create the content that drives cultural conversations and those who monetize that content becomes increasingly apparent.[17] Several challenges stand in the way of creators profiting from their creativity in this context. One takes the form of barriers to access to intellectual property rights described earlier. Another is the fact that those IP rights are often ill-suited for the particular types of creative works in question.

Take hashtags, which began appearing on social media in 2006. While they were originally designed to sort content and enable people to find posts on particular topics, they have evolved to do much more: social media users employ hashtags to label, link, discuss, criticize, and promote content. They call upon hashtags to build communities and engage in activism.[18] Corporations often use a hashtag as a call to action, encouraging fans to add user-generated content to an advertising campaign or proclaim their affinity for a brand. Some companies use hashtags to celebrate a particular group, as with Equinox's #PoweredByPride, Marriott's #LoveTravels, and American Eagles' #WeAllCan, all designed to broadcast—or, more cynically, perform—the brands' support of their LGBTQ customers.[19] But corporate hashtags are rarely the ones that generate the most engagement. The slogans, catchphrases, and hashtags that catch the public's attention are far more likely to arise organically.

By the end of 2015, over two hundred hashtags were registered with the USPTO as trademarks.[20] In 2023, the number of registered tagmarks is well into the thousands.[21] The Trademark Office added a section on hashtags as trademarks to its Manual of Examining Procedure in 2013,[22] though I have argued that examination of marks in this category is insufficiently stringent.[23] Trademark registration is typically unnecessary for corporations, as owners of plain-text marks like OREO or KFC possess robust rights and receive little or no additional benefit from registering #oreo or #HowDoYouKFC as trademarks.[24] When a hashtag is used like a traditional trademark and affixed to products, trademark protection makes sense.

And hashtag creation may involve labor and creativity. But hashtags as hashtags are unlikely to truly qualify for trademark protection: most fail to function as trademarks for particular goods or services.[25] For those few hashtags that are truly used as marks, many are plagued by functionality, lack of distinctiveness, false association with a celebrity, or likelihood of confusion with another brand.[26] In other words, hashtags frequently fail to meet the requirements for federal protection. They may also be incapable of creating an association with a single source because hashtags are, by their very nature, collectives—the assertion that a hashtag functions as a trademark is often at odds with the way members of the public understand and use hashtags.[27]

But new hashtags are created every day, and when they take off, it is something to behold—consider, for example, the way that survivors of sexual assault and harassment have come together around the #MeToo hashtag; the staying power and emotional resonance of #BlackLivesMatter; the triumph and pride signaled by #LoveWins. #OscarsSoWhite generated dialogue about the awards show that shaped media coverage far beyond the confines of Twitter. It's no coincidence that many of those viral hashtags were created by women or people of color: the hashtag has emerged as a way to center marginalized people and give voice to grassroot movements. Researchers have noted Black Twitter in particular uses hashtags to create a counterpublic within a public space to better communicate about and amplify issues relevant to participants' experiences and concerns.[28] And trademark law, at least in theory, can offer group members a way to assert control over a hashtag and use it to generate revenue and goodwill.

There are trademark applications and registrations for ubiquitous hashtags and phrases including #MeToo, #StopAsianHate,[29] #TransLivesMatter;[30] and #GirlsLikeUs[31]—but the applicants and registrants are not always the hashtag's creators or the movement's leaders. Makeup company Hard Candy applied to register #MeToo as a trademark for cosmetics and fragrances before backlash led it to expressly abandon the endeavor.[32] The expression "Black girls are magic" was coined by CaShawn Thompson in 2013 to celebrate and uplift Black women,[33] but both concept and phrase have been coopted by corporations,[34] as the forty-five trademark applications for variations on the phrase attest: registrations cover everything from wine[35] to curriculum development[36] to charitable fundraising services[37] to apparel.[38] What's more, while hashtag use usually constitutes fair use,[39] some courts have found hashtag uses to infringe existing trademark rights.[40] And for every successful plaintiff, there are many more bullied by mark owners asserting rights broader than those to which their common law or registered rights entitle them. Even Kris Jenner is not immune.[41]

Grassroots organizations seeking to avail themselves of trademark protection have also stumbled, and their stories raise interesting questions for trademark law. The Association for Size Diversity and Health (ASDAH) registered HEALTH AT EVERY SIZE and its acronym HAES, both ubiquitous on social media in hashtag form,[42] as trademarks for educational services in 2012.[43] The phrase originated with the fat acceptance movement and is also the title of a 2010 book, although the movement predates the book and ASDAH has since severed ties with the book's author, Lindo Bacon.[44] In fact, ASDAH leadership warned that Bacon's planned publication of a revised Health At Every Size book would create confusion with ASDAH's registered trademark.[45] Like Jade Bryan, ASDAH lists extensive trademark use guidelines on its website, including requiring that anyone who uses either phrase receive permission in advance, pair the mark with the ® symbol and a generic noun, and prominently display a trademark notice.[46] Those requirements are not mandated by trademark law's supposed "duty to police" and are incompatible with fair use principles. Nominative fair use doctrine provides that anyone can reference a brand by using its trademark, including to describe the user's own goods or services—"we repair TELFAR handbags" or "the Blavity app can be downloaded to Android and Chromebook devices."[47] Members of the public can always use trademarks when they discuss, reference, or criticize a company or brand, and they can also use descriptive terms in their descriptive sense. Enforcing trademark rights against social media posters who talk about how "the #healthateverysize movement changed my relationship with my body" or tag photos "#haes" would chill speech and undermine the organization's very purpose (in addition to constituting trademark bullying). And reporters are certainly not bound to seek permission or approval before discussing the hashtag movement or philosophy by name.

ASDAH articulates its goal in registering the two trademarks as honoring the community-based advocacy work that led to its formation by "protect[ing] th[e] phrase from individuals or large corporations who would seek to co-opt the phrase to hawk their latest diet or weight-loss program."[48] In other words, it frames the registration as a defensive move. Celebrities like Jay-Z and Tom Brady have made similar statements to the press about their efforts to register name-related marks,[49] but trademark law is not designed to enable owners to play defense without also making affirmative use. While some ASDAH community members celebrated the decision, many others have pushed back, noting that the goals of the organization and the strictures of trademark law seem to be in tension.[50] Activists and scholars Drs. Jacqui Gingras and Charlotte Cooper explore that tension in their critique of ASDAH's decision to register the trademarks, arguing that the HAES movement contains multitudes and reflects a rich history of grassroots activism that amplifies different voices, while registering the trademarks relinquishes that history, promotes commodification, and silences those voices and multitudes of meaning by assigning the phrase a singular definition.[51] The decision to register HAES and HEALTH AT EVERY SIZE as trademarks with the goal of prohibiting their exploitation in service of diet culture "fails to interrogate broader misuses of power, particularly under capitalism, or build an intersectional movement that is able or ready to engage with a multiplicity of social justice issues. It is a move that, ironically, concedes powerlessness."[52]

The chilling effects of registration that Gingras and Cooper note are also often seen when private companies seek registration for a phrase or hashtag widely used within a particular community. For example, #a11y is a numeronym that stands for "accessibility." The term is used frequently by digital accessibility practitioners to advocate for accessibility, tag content that discusses it, or identify content that has been made accessible to those using assistive technology.[53] A company called Accessibility Now applied to register A11Y as a trademark for technology that enables users to comply with website accessibility regulations; when the USPTO issued an initial refusal for mere descriptiveness, noting that a11y "appears to be a well-known short-hand for 'accessibility' in the use of computers and related equipment" and that was precisely what applicant's website promised to do, Accessibility Now converted its application from the Principal to the Supplemental Register.[54] While its trademark rights are far less robust based on that registration, the owner can still use the registration to attempt to quash speech it dislikes, as this particular owner has a demonstrated track record of doing.[55] Given the term's widespread use and its utility to a community of users, trademark failure to function doctrine should have barred its registration by deeming it informational matter.[56] Likewise, when the seller of a vibrator labeled "enby" sought to register ENBY as a trademark for sex toys, the USPTO issued two office actions deeming it merely descriptive, given that "enby" is widely-used to mean "nb" or "nonbinary" and the vibrator is for users of any or no gender.[57] The seller then sued a competitor, a Black- and trans-owned online retailer operating at the domain name www .shopenby.com, alleging trademark infringement of its common law rights.[58] The court granted the defendant's motion to dismiss, finding that the plaintiff had not adequately alleged ownership of a valid and protectable trademark, but only after the suit cost the defendant time, money, and energy.[59]

Trademark law is known for its David versus Goliath stories: major corporations regularly use it to silence speech or force much smaller rightsholders to abandon their names. But when it comes to disputes over trademark rights in hashtags and trending terms, there are often no clear villains or victims. The existence of online spaces has helped to amplify diverse voices, broaden access to IP protection, and subvert trademark law's traditional binaries. Members of groups long marginalized by intellectual property law—women, artists, people of color—are finally, at least occasionally, gaining access to trademark and other IP regimes that had long eluded them and perpetuated inequality.[60] But the uses they seek to protect and the uses to which they object don't fit neatly within trademark's core protections and exclusions.

Creators of viral phrases and hashtags need resources and information about which kinds of uses they must make to merit legal protection and which kinds of uses by others they should seek to enjoin. Participants in the content economy equipped with an understanding of trademark law can better resist and bring to light trademark bullying. And trademark law itself must continue to evolve in acknowledgment of both its own systemic biases and new phenomena like memes and viral content.[61] In her book *Branding Black Womanhood: Media Citizenship from Black Power to Black Girl Magic*, Communications professor Timeka Tounsel writes, "In the end, Black Girl Magic matters because it is one process through which a constrained public can access media citizenship. Despite its limitations as a form of enfranchisement . . . this framework offers Black women a pathway to a kind of everyday empowerment."[62] Trademark law can provide voice, access, and economic opportunity. Despite its limitations and potential for abuse, it can enable members of marginalized communities to commercialize and capitalize on their labor and creativity.

NOTES

1. Malika Saada Saar, *#SayHerName: A Q&A with Professor Kimberlé Crenshaw*, YOUTUBE BLOG, https://blog.youtube/news-and-events/sayhername/.

2. Donna M. Owens, *Breonna Taylor, and Hundreds of Black Women Have Died at the Hands of Police. The Movement to Say Their Names Is Growing*, USA TODAY (Mar. 11, 2021) https://www.usatoday.com/in-depth/news/investigations/2021/03/11/sayhername-movement-black-women-police-violence/6921197002/.

3. AAPF, About #SayHerName, https://www.aapf.org/sayhername.

4. Jade Films, https://www.jadefilm.com/deaftalent-trademark.

5. The Limping Chicken, *"Deaf Talent" Trademark Dispute Leads to Fears That Deaf Creatives May No Longer Be Able to Use Hashtag or Term*, https://limpingchicken.com/2021/10/16/deaf-talent-trademark-dispute-leads-to-fears-that-deaf-creatives-may-no-longer-be-able-to-use-hashtag-or-term/ (Oct. 16, 2021).

6. *See* Shontavia Johnson, *Memetic Theory, Trademarks, & the Viral Meme Mark*, 13 J. MARSHALL REV. INTELL. PROP. L. 96, 129 (2013) ("the potential for overenforcement of trademarks is high for viral meme marks").

7. Jordana R. Goodman and Khamal Patterson, *Access to Justice for Black Inventors*, VANDERBILT L. REV. (forthcoming 2024).

8. William T. Gallagher, *Trademark and Copyright Enforcement in the Shadow of IP Law*, 28 SANTA CLARA HIGH TECH. L.J. 453, 456 (2012).

9. Jordana Goodman, *Addressing Patent Gender Disparities*, SCIENCE 376 (694) 706–7 (2022); A. Tulle, et al., *Progress and Potential: 2020 Update on US Women Inventor-Patentees*, US Patent and Trademark Office (2020), https://www.uspto.gov/sites/default/files/documents/OCE-DH-Progress-Potential-2020.pdf; Kyle Jensen, Balàzs Kovács & Olav Sorenson, *Gender Differences in Obtaining and Maintaining Patent Rights*, 36 NATURE BIOTECH. 307–8 (2018); Lisa D. Cook & Chaleampong Kongcharoen, *The Idea Gap in Pink and Black* 1, 28 (Nat'l Bureau Econ. Rsch., Working Paper No. 16331, 2010), https://www.nber.org/system/files/working_papers/w16331/w16331.pdf [https://perma.cc/U6Y9-S2E9]; W. Michael Schuster, R. Evan Davis, Kourtenay Schley & Julie Ravenscraft, *An Empirical Study of Patent Grant Rates as a Function of Race and Gender*, 57 AM. BUS. L.J. 281, 317–18 (2020); Jessica Milli, Barbara Gault, Emma Williams-Baron, Jenny Xia & Meika Berlan, *The Gender Patenting Gap*, INST. FOR WOMEN'S POL'Y RSCH. 7 (2016), https://iwpr.org/iwpr-general/the-gender-patenting-gap/; Jessica Milli, Emma Williams-Baron, Meika Berlan, Jenny Xia & Barbara Gault, *Equity in Innovation: Women Inventors and Patents*, INST. FOR WOMEN'S POL'Y RSCH. 5 (2016), https://iwpr.org/wp-content/uploads/2020/12/C448-Equity-in-Innovation.pdf.

10. Robert Brauneis & Dotan Oliar, *An Empirical Study of the Race, Ethnicity, Gender, and Age of Copyright Registrants*, 86 GEO. WASH. L. REV. 46, 59–60 (2018).

11. A corporate entity may be a large corporation like Nike or Starbucks. But it might also be an individual: for example, each of the Kardashian sisters owns dozens if not hundreds of trademark registrations, but each has created a corporate entity as holder of their intellectual property: Kim's is Kimsaprincess Inc., Kourtney's is 2Die4Kourt, Inc., and Khloe's is Khlomoney, Inc. Meredith Haggerty, *The Kardashians' Corporation Names Are More Embarrassing Than Your First AIM Screen Name*, RACKED (Mar. 22, 2016), https://www.racked.com/2016/3/22/11286814/kardashians-corporation-names-kimsaprincess-khlomoney-2die4kourt.

12. W. Michael Schuster, Miriam Marcowitz-Bitton & Deborah R. Gerhardt, *An Empirical Study of Gender and Race in Trademark Prosecution*, 94 S. CAL. L. REV. 1407, 1439–51 (2021).

13. See generally K. J. Greene, *Intellectual Property at the Intersection of Race and Gender: Lady Sings the Blues*, 16 AM. U. J. GENDER SOC. POL'Y & L. 365 (2008); K. J. Greene, *Copyright, Culture & Black Music: A Legacy of Unequal Protection*, 21 HASTINGS COMMC'NS & ENT. L.J. 339 (1998); Ann Bartow, *Women in the Web of Secondary Copyright Liability and Internet Filtering*, 32 N. KY. L. REV. 449 (2005).

14. Rebecca Tushnet, *My Fair Ladies: Sex, Gender, and Fair Use in Copyright*, 15 AM. U. J. GENDER SOC. POL'Y & L. 273, 303–4 (2007) ("When we compare fields that get intellectual property protection (software, sculpture) with fields that do not (fashion, cooking, sewing), it becomes uncomfortably obvious that our cultural policy has expected women's endeavors to generate surplus creativity but has assumed that men's endeavors require compensation"); *see also* Ann Bartow, *Fair Use and the Fairer Sex: Gender, Feminism, & Copyright Law*, 14 AM. U. J. GENDER SOC. POL'Y & L. 551, 551–52 (2006) ("Copyright laws are written and enforced to help certain groups of people, largely male, assert and retain control over the resources generated by creative productivity. Consequently, the copyright infrastructure plays a role, largely unexamined by legal scholars, in helping to sustain the material and economic inequality between women and men").

15. Morgan Sung, *Black TikTok Creators Are "Striking" to Protest Uncredited Viral Dance Trends*, MASHABLE (June 23, 2021) https://mashable.com/article/black-tiktok-strike-dance-megan-thee-stallion-thot-shit.

16. Ashley Turner, *Social Media Slams "The Tonight Show Starring Jimmy Fallon" TikTok Dance Segment Where Black Creators of the Routines Were Not Credited*, ATLANTA BLACK STAR (Mar. 31, 2021) https://atlantablackstar.com/2021/03/31/social-media-slams-the-tonight-show-starring-jimmy-fallon-tiktok-dance-segment-where-black-creators-of-the-routines-were-not-credited/. The article credits Tiktokkers @noahschnapp, @jazlynebaybee, @yvnggprince, @flyboyfu, @kekejanjah, @macdaddyz, @theemyanicole, and @thegilberttwins as the original choreographers of the dances Addison Rae performed.

17. Jenna Wortham, *The Internet Is Where We Share—and Steal—the Best Ideas*, NEW YORK TIMES (June 6, 2017), https://www.nytimes.com/2017/06/06/magazine/the-internet-is-where-we-share-and-steal-the-best-ideas.html.

18. Alexandra J. Roberts, *Tagmarks*, 105 CAL. L. REV. 599, 605–7 (2017).

19. In fact, Marriott owns a trademark registration for #LoveTravels for entertainment services (Registration No. 5,137,233), Equinox has a pending application to register POWERED BY PRIDE for charitable services and fitness instruction (Serial No. 88,408,050), and American Eagle's parent company applied to register #WeAllCan in sixteen categories (Serial No. 87159504 [abandoned]).

20. Roberts, *supra* note 18, 601.

21. A search on TESS for live registered marks that contain the "#" symbol returned 3,706 hits on June 19, 2023. Most appear to be tagmarks, but some use the hashtag as a number sign or to indicate a censored word—for example, #1 BROTHER'S PIZZA or KINKY MUHF#@KIN HAIR. Without the "registered" and "live" qualifiers, the number of hits is 8,842, indicating far more applications pending than marks registered.

22. TMEP § 1202.18.

23. Roberts, *supra* note 18, 602.

24. #HOWDOYOUKFC was registered for restaurant services but later abandoned. Registration No. 4,523,521.

25. *Tagmarks* at 624–49; Alexandra J. Roberts, *Trademark Failure to Function*, 104 IOWA L. REV. 1977, 2010–2012 (2019).

26. See Dan L. Burk, *Cybermarks*, 94 MINN. L. REV. 1375, 1376 (2010).

27. See Abigail De Kosnik & Keight Feldman, eds., #IDENTITY: HASHTAGGING RACE, GENDER, SEXUALITY, AND NATION 64 ("Despite our ability to trace hashtags such as #YouOkSis to a single origin point [in this case, Twitter user @FeministaJones], hashtags do not follow an unproblematic, hierarchical linearity. . . . Because the hashtag multiplies infinitely—in that it can be taken up and used for almost any purpose that aligns with the hashtag originator's intent or greatly deviates from that intent—a dynamic tension with linearity serves as a fundamental for thinking through the innate nature of the hashtag. Framing hashtags as multiplicitous [technocultural] assemblages provides a way to think through the various strategies users implement to shape engagement with hashtags they have authored or to cultivate certain parameters of use around hashtags on their own timelines").

28. Lyndsay Michalik Gratch & Ariel Gratch, DIGITAL PERFORMANCE IN EVERYDAY LIFE 30 (2021).

29. Serial No. 90,638,513 (abandoned application for apparel). A shooting at three Atlanta spas and growing violence targeting Asians and Asian Americans gave rise to the #StopAsianHate hashtag and movement.

30. TRANS LIVES MATTER was registered for charitable services in 2013 and cancelled in 2018. Registration No. 4,353,324.

31. The hashtag #GirlsLikeUs was created in 2012 by trans writer, director, and activist Janet Mock. Abbie E. Goldberg & Genny Beemyn, eds., *Identity Exploration and Knowledge Sharing*, in THE SAGE ENCYCLOPEDIA OF TRANS STUDIES (2021). An application filed by Kimberly Rose to register GIRLS LIKE US for entertainment featuring LGBTQ people was abandoned before registration. Serial No. 88,288,512.

32. Serial No. 87,653,745.

33. CaShawn Thompson, Bio, https://cashawn.com/ ("Black Girls Are Magic became wildly popular in 2013 after CaShawn began using the phrase online (which was later shortened to the hashtag #BlackGirlMagic) to uplift and praise the accomplishments, beauty and other amazing qualities of Black women"); Tamika N. Tounsel, BRANDING BLACK WOMANHOOD: MEDIA CITIZENSHIP FROM BLACK POWER TO BLACK GIRL MAGIC 14 (2022) ("it was the feeling that Black women were under assault, especially across social media platforms, that prompted CaShawn Thompson to create a hashtag-ready resistance motto in the first place").

34. Tounsel, *supra* note 33, 68–93.

35. BLACK GIRL MAGIC, Registration No. 6,646,502.

36. Registration No. 6,689,956.

37. BLACK GIRL MAGIC BALL, Registration No. 5,874,284.

38. BLACK GIRL MATHGIC, Registration No. 6,608,811; BLK GRL MGC, Registration No. 5,676,917 (Supplemental); "Black girls are . . . magic" logo for drinkware and apparel, Registration No. 5,582,603 (Supplemental) (registered to CaShawn Thompson). *See also* Registration No. 5,372,483 (BLACK GIRL MAGIC for creating and developing concepts for television programs).

39. *Eksouzian v. Albanese*, No. CV 13–00728-PSG-MAN, 2015 WL 4720478, at *10 (C.D. Cal. Aug. 7, 2015) (calling the hashtag "merely a functional tool [and] not an actual trademark" and holding that Plaintiffs did not breach settlement agreement when they used #cloudpen "*as a hashtag*").

40. *Pub. Impact, LLC v. Bos. Consulting Grp., Inc.*, 169 F. Supp. 3d 278, 290 (D. Mass. 2016) (plaintiff had a substantial likelihood of success in proving defendant's use of #PublicImpact hashtag infringed plaintiff's PUBLIC IMAGE trademark); *Chanel v. WGACA, LLC*, No. 18 Civ. 2253 (LLS), 2018 WL 4440507, at *2 (S.D.N.Y. 2018) (plaintiffs plausibly alleged that defendant's use of hashtag

#WGACACHANEL constituted trademark infringement); *Khaled v. Bordenave*, No. 18 CIV. 5187 (PAE), 2019 WL 1894321, at *6 (S.D.N.Y. Apr. 29, 2019) (plaintiffs' allegations as to defendants' use of hashtags including #WeTheBest "clearly state a claim of trademark infringement"); *Fraternity Collection, LLC v. Fargnoli*, No. 3:13-CV-664-CWR-FKB, 2015 WL 1486375, at *5–6 (S.D. Miss. 2015) (use of #fratcollection and #fraternitycollection could plausibly infringe on plaintiff's FRATERNITY COLLECTION trademark); *Align Tech., Inc. v. Strauss Diamond Instruments, Inc.*, No. 18-CV-06663-TSH, 2019 WL 1586776, at *4 (N.D. Cal. Apr. 12, 2019) (preliminarily enjoining defendants' use of plaintiff's marks as hashtags on social media based on likelihood of confusion).

41. The owner of a trademark registration for #ProudMama for jewelry demanded Jenner cease using the hashtag, even though Jenner was only tagging her social media posts and not using #ProudMama in connection with her jewelry sales. Leah Melby Clinton, *Kris Jenner Might Not Be Allowed to Be a #ProudMama on Instagram Anymore*, GLAMOUR (Feb. 1, 2016), https://www.glamour.com/story/kris-jenner-proud-mama.

42. *E.g.* IPS Health, *Health At Every Size, Body-Acceptance and Lizzo: What Does the Dietician Say?* https://www.ipshealth.co.za/health-at-every-size-body/ ("There's a growing social body-positive movement that promotes non-judgement and self-acceptance, particularly of overweight individuals, that has emerged over the past decade. It can be seen under the hashtags #HAES [and others]").

43. Registration Nos. 4,145,545; 3,992,338.

44. ASDAH, *Holding Lindo Bacon Accountable for Repeated Harm in the Fat Liberation & HAES®️ Communities* (Mar. 10, 2022) https://asdah.org/lindo-accountability/.

45. *Id.* ("Your authorship of a revised Health at Every Size®️ book will cause confusion with ASDAH's work promoting Health at Every Size®️. A Health at Every Size®️ book will be reasonably interpreted to be ASDAH's opinions, violating our trademark").

46. ASDAH, *Trademark Guidelines*, https://asdah.org/trademark-guidelines/ (ASDAH does not claim these guidelines are legally binding though; instead it urges "those who espouse HAES®️ to be in right relationship with us by adhering to the following Health at Every Size®️ and HAES®️ trademarks guidelines").

47. To qualify as nominative fair use, courts typically require that (1) the product or service in question is not readily identifiable without use of the trademark; (2) only so much of the mark as is reasonably necessary to identify the product or service is used; and (3) use of the mark does not suggest sponsorship or endorsement by the trademark owner.

48. *ASDAH Announces Health At Every Size ®️ Registered Trademark and Final Schedule for August Conference in San Francisco* (Aug. 1, 2011), http://www.prweb.com/releases/2011/8/prweb8679043.htm.

49. *Jay Z on His Rags-to-Riches Story, Wooing Beyoncé, and How Blue Ivy Is His "Biggest Fan,"* VANITY FAIR (Oct. 1, 2013) https://www.vanityfair.com/culture/2013/10/jay-z-beyonce-blue-ivy-story ("Jay tells Robinson that he and Beyoncé trademarked their daughter's name [BLUE IVY] simply so others couldn't exploit it for profit. . . . "It wasn't for us to do anything; as you see, we haven't done anything"); Mike Reiss, *Not So Terrific: Tom Brady's Trademark Refused*, ESPN (Aug. 23, 2019), https://www.espn.com/nfl/story/_/id/27445881/not-terrific-tom-brady-trademark-refused ("I didn't like the nickname and I [applied to register TOM TERRIFIC because I] wanted to make sure no one used it, because some people wanted to use it. I was trying to keep people from using it").

50. For example, Laurie Toby Edison, *Health at Every Size®️: Now a Registered Trademark*, BODY IMPOLITIC (Aug. 9, 2011), https://laurietobyedison.com/body-impolitic-blog/2011/08/health-at-every-size-now-a-registered-trademark/.

51. Jacqui Gingras and Charlotte Cooper, *Down the Rabbit Hole: A Critique of the ®️ in HAES®️*, J. OF CRITICAL DIETETICS 1 (2012) at 3–4.

52. *Id.*, at 4.

53. The Accessibility Project, https://www.a11yproject.com/about/.

54. US Registration No. 4824150, Office Action (July 24, 2015).

55. *See, e.g.*, Adrian Roselli, *My Cease & Desist from AudioEye* (Apr. 15, 2022) https://adrianroselli .com/2022/04/my-cease-desist-from-audioeye.html (Accessibility Now, Inc., owner of the registration for A11Y, is a subsidiary of AudioEye).

56. TMEP § 1202.04; USPTO, Examination Guide 2–17: Merely Informational Matter (2017), https://www.uspto.gov/trademark/trademark-updates-and-announcements/trademark-user-input.

57. Serial No. 90256449. In fact, some favor the term because it distinguishes nonbinary from non-Black, while sharing the acronym "nb" for both can create confusion. Ana Mardoll, *Storify: Why I Use Enby and Not NB*, ANA MARDOLL'S RAMBLINGS (Feb. 28, 2018), http://www.anamardoll.com/2018/02 /storify-why-i-use-enby-and-not-nb.html. The creation of enby is often credited to Tumblr user @rev-olutionator based on the post captured here: https://cassolotl.tumblr.com/post/620371385484722176.

58. Samira Sadeque, *Sex Toy Company Threatens to Sue Black, Trans-Owned Company over Its Name*, DAILY DOT (Nov. 26, 2020), https://www.dailydot.com/irl/wild-flower-enby-store-trademark -dispute/.

59. *Boyajian Prods. v. ENBY LLC*, 3:20-cv-01991-HZ (D. Or. Nov. 1, 2021).

60. Emma Gray Ellis, *Want to Profit Off Your Meme? Good Luck if You Aren't White*, WIRED (Mar. 1, 2017) https://www.wired.com/2017/03/on-fleek-meme-monetization-gap/ [https://perma.cc/2LQH -K8YU] "[The] problem [for Kayla Newman, who coined the term 'on fleek,'] is part intellectual property law, part access to influence, and all systemic racial inequalities. However egalitarian the internet was supposed to be, creatives' ability to profit off their viral content seems to depend on their race").

61. Johnson, *supra* note 6, at 97 ("Should we revisit current trademark standards as social media, the Internet, and information transmission rapidly change and collide with the historical underpinnings of the law?").

62. Tounsel, *supra* note 33, 125–26.

5

A Bouquet for Battling the Expansion of Trade Secrets in the Public Sector

Cynthia H. Conti-Cook

The best-designed bouquet may appear effortlessly assembled, but bouquets have their own understated architecture—a hearty focal-point flower, fillers for natural aesthetic, and several complimentary supporting flowers.[1] This chapter discusses how trade secrets in the public sector have been imported through new technologies, how they obstruct democracy and cause harm across many communities. It uses the bouquet—a floral arrangement—to illustrate its organization the way pillars or columns typically visualize the blueprint of written organizational structure. The sources gathered here, from the legal history of intellectual property to criminal court decisions to procurement processes to toolkits for organizers, do not always grow near one another or naturally cross-pollinate. Combined, they offer a strategic battle bouquet for organizers to protect the public from corporate control by targeting strategies aimed at the public purse.

This bouquet arrangement features five types of flowers. The focal-point flowers, the big show-stopping wide-open daisies, demand asymmetrical emphasis. Wide-open daisies hide nothing and center the public's right to know as a table-setting motivating principle and magnetized north star. These daisies are surrounded by baby's breath that lend a natural aesthetic—existing legal precedent evincing the historically persuasive logic of prioritizing the public's right to information. Roses are layered and overlapping social harms and bell-shaped wood hyacinths are the social movements already ringing the alarm bells. Finally, peonies are pain-relieving practical tools with which to intervene.

The organizing structure of the bouquet is central to the strategy it offers— to combat trade secrets in the public sector, we must organize ourselves around what we collectively need to know to protect each other and the future survival of all living things. This chapter examines the patriarchal values driving trade secret battles by corporate entities that prioritize property over people, heavily invest in structures of secrecy, and protect dominant yet ahistorical narratives rather than governing through trust and consensus building by informed democratic participation.

By contrast, the healing peonies offered in this chapter prioritize people over property, embody collaborative relational strategies, center addressing harm, learning, and leadership from directly impacted people, and demand inclusive and joyful coalitions. Through the beautiful container of a bouquet, this chapter offers observations of already emerging strategies that address the confluence of state, corporate, and algorithmic secrecy—collaborative advocacy that fertilizes the soil of the public procurement process so that we all may better blossom.

DAISIES—THE PUBLIC'S NATURAL RIGHT TO INFORMATION

Before moving into how trade secrets obstruct access to information about technologies sold to the public sector, we shall set a hearty focal-point—a large wide-open daisy. Indigenous people around the world have long centered collaboration with Earth and all living things based on "a moral covenant of reciprocity [that] calls us to honor our responsibilities for all we have been given, for all that we have taken."[2] Biologist Rachel Carson similarly introduced this enduring reciprocity as a motivating principle in the first chapter of *Silent Spring*, "the classic that launched the environmental movement," with the following: "[the] public must decide whether it wishes to continue on the present road, and it can do so only when in full possession of the facts."[3] The public, *not* corporations, academics, experts, politicians, or billionaires, "*must* decide" how to balance survival with conditions needed to sustain future life. To execute this responsibility effectively, the public requires "full possession of the facts."[4] This principle is not limited to pollutants—it extends to all things potentially harming the public.

Carson grounded her principle not in legal or political history, but in natural rights philosophy.[5] The public's right to decide and be in full possession of the facts grows naturally from "our obligation to endure"—it is an evolutionary-driven natural right protecting our collective ability to sustain existence. Biologist Janine Benyus echoes this emphasis in her book *Biomimicry—Innovation Inspired by Nature*. One of the ten winning strategies she recommends we mimic, based on billions of years of evolution and across complex ecosystems, is to "run on information" and an abundance of feedback. "What makes a mature community run is not one universal message being broadcast from above, but numerous, even redundant, messages coming from the grass roots, dispersed throughout the community structure."[6] This flow of information will determine the sustainability of our collective survival—"the *raison d'être* of mature communities, remember, is to maintain their identity throughout environmental storms and travails, so they can remain, and evolve, in place."[7]

Grounding this chapter in this natural right to information stemming from our "obligation to endure," and not corporate controlled information "broadcast from above," is both relevant to a discussion of trade secrets as well as strategic. Industrial drivers that invented intellectual property (IP) rights like trade secrets—and the courts that have adopted their arguments—have made the source of these rights relevant and central to justifying legal protections for information ownership.[8] Public demand for information is often successfully dismissed based on these dominant invocations of intellectual property, limiting the imaginative solution space to corporate self-audits,[9] protective orders,[10] and nondisclosure agreements.

Invoking natural rights also strategically anchors the conversation about trade secrets around the public's right to information. Hannah Bloch-Wehba called out critical technology scholars for "[neglecting] a critical avenue for promoting public accountability and transparency for automated decision-making: the law of access to government records and proceedings." Her work demonstrates how centering the public's right to know gives advocates a strategic legal advantage in fighting for algorithmic transparency.[11] Fortunately, there is also strong legal precedent for doing so.

BABY'S BREATH—EXISTING LEGAL PRECEDENT

The public's natural right to know is also supported by complimentary existing legal precedent, the baby's breath in this bouquet. Legal scholar Amy Kapczynski resurrected United States Supreme Court precedent "show[ing] that courts even at the height of laissez faire were clear about the *categorical priority of the public*, and rejected trade secret claims when they conflicted with the public's right to know"(emphasis added).[12] While we live in a world where technology companies are claiming everything from diversity policies to how they address gender-pay gaps would cause "competitive harm,"[13] Kapczynski revives a legal history that can shine on "the shadow of trade secret law."[14] We have before and can again subordinate corporate interests to the public good, aligned with the public's natural right to co-create its future through government.

When pressuring procurement systems around the consequences of contract terms, movements can cite this history to emphasize that the public is the primary stakeholder, not the corporate bottom line. Kapczynski asserts this as a "clear principle . . . [legislatures] and agencies have the right to disclose anything—even core trade secrets like product formulas—anytime they seek to reveal something relevant to consumers about the marketed product or service."[15] This is especially true in the context of new technologies. Advocates' attempts to reveal the extent of preventable harms by public access requests simply seek information that the government using the technology has, the corporation has, but the person subjected to the technology often does not have access to. Optimistically, Kapczynski asserts that "together, these points indicate that Congress can condition [vendors'] market access on the turning over of trade secret data, and make that data public without working a takings, *at least if there is no express governmental promise before the submission of the data that [government] will refrain from doing this.*"[16] The caveat, as mentioned earlier, is one we must pay attention to: when procurement officers and courts concede to corporate claims of confidentiality, it may unintentionally feed a factual corporate narrative that seeks to expand secrecy.

This trend is simply counterintuitive for a democracy, as David S. Levine presciently warned, "[if] we do nothing, [trade secrets] will be the infrastructure itself—owned and operated by private interests with commercial values like business advantage and secrecy of corporate information—that will direct the law involving public activity, rather than the law creating the conditions under which public infrastructure operates."[17] And as Bloch-Wehba said so well, the real obstacles to understanding technologies "are attributable, not to the sophistication of decision-making methodologies but to a more basic shift toward privatization and automation in government."[18] Increased secrecy is simply a feature, not a bug, of expanded neoliberalism.

ROSES—OVERLAPPING AND LAYERED HARMS

Intentionally documenting and articulating the overlapping and layered harms corporate secrecy introduces into the public sector must be done strategically and be led by people most deeply impacted. New technology researched and developed by private companies is bought by government agencies every day, from systems used for police investigation through electronic incarceration on parole supervision. It includes predictive policing, cell-site simulators, biometric tools, risk assessment tools, communications systems for detained people, and many more tools state actors use to surveil.[19]

Each of these technologies have context and technology-specific issues that contribute to its harms. Former public defender Vincent Southerland observed that "technology in the hands of law enforcement is a force multiplier"[20] and, therefore, also a harm multiplier.[21] Many tools in the hands of law enforcement cause various iterations of harm at varied degrees of severity—from potentially lethal and routinely abusive police interactions, to detention, family separation, deportation, and many more.[22] These layered harms and their solutions are best understood by those in immediate proximity to them. Those people tend to be disproportionately feminine, pregnant, Black, poor, disabled, migrating, or part of another historically oppressed community. Like layers of rose petals, these harms are occasionally obscured and overlapping, compounding suffering on those at the intersections. Southerland describes how "[the] technologies erect digital borders around communities of color, fortifying the colony-in-a-nation status that defines those communities."[23] These conditions require arduous effort to organize against. Through legal constructs that promote secrecy, these efforts are often suppressed.

I have seen these efforts to organize thwarted firsthand. Around 2017, I represented a man incarcerated in New York who, along with two others, noticed discrepancies across the "COMPAS" scores relied on by the prison to evaluate eligibility for release.[24] This assessment is done by prison staff at a computer. My client introduced me to the two men, Glenn Rodriguez and Jose Piñeda, with whom he compared "risk" scores.[25] Mr. Rodriguez surveyed others and analyzed their risk scores to how staff used vast discretion to interpret a single subjective question.[26] Question 19 asked, "Does this person appear to have notable disciplinary issues?" How that specific question was answered, despite how vaguely it was written and how differently prison staff were interpreting it, determined whether it gave you a score of high ("yes"), medium ("unsure"), or low risk ("no").

Mr. Piñeda, whose counselor answered "unsure" for Question 19, made another observation—when the counselors were scrolling through the assessment, a bubble popped up above the question with additional instructions. He filed a Freedom of Information Law (FOIL) request with the prison for that language and for the training manual issued by COMPAS to train the state prison's counselors to try and understand what his counselor was "unsure" about—he only had two infractions in the last decade. The government responded that the information sought "are trade secrets or are submitted to an agency by a commercial enterprise or derived from information obtained from a commercial enterprise and which if disclosed would cause substantial injury to the competitive position of the subject enterprise."[27]

We sued to demand disclosure. The State argued that disclosure of the training manual "would cause substantial injury to the competitive position of this enterprise" despite failing to point to any evidence "or even a suggestion as to how the material requested" could be considered a trade secret.[28] The Court ruled in favor of a limited disclosure after a year of litigation. An officer brought the training manual to Mr. Piñeda's cell where he read what the bubble said: "Using all the information available to you and in your professional judgment did this person have significant disciplinary problems."[29] For Mr. Piñeda, the harms introduced by this risk assessment were layered. Forcing his mostly decades-old disciplinary history into a "yes, no, unsure" box and reducing his years of accomplishments into an estimated score dehumanized him in front of the parole board. After denied parole, his inability to access information that would help him correct the mischaracterization of his disciplinary history hampered his ability to appeal his denial and prevent the same thing from happening again.

More broadly, the obstruction meant that other people in prison could take only limited proactive action to protect their scores and push back on the use of risk assessment's all together. The prison's deference to protecting the property interests of a company above the liberty interests of a person in prison fighting for parole release against an algorithm crystalizes how corporate secrecy creep manifests in the public sector.

This perversion of public sector values was even more explicit when a DNA software company appeared in an appellate criminal case out of California to fight against the accused's access to its calculations.[30] To support its claim for trade secrecy, the company offered what is likely a routine comparison in trade secret battles—its hours invested in the business.[31] Yet instead of competing against another business's number of hours, its adversary was a man facing fifty years in prison. Nevertheless, the company essentially argued "its property interests of 27,600 hours (or a little over three years) should weigh more than the hundreds of thousands of hours [the accused] potentially faces in prison, deprived of his liberty, freedom and family."[32] For a business to invest so much in a tool meant for criminal prosecutions without also expecting constitutional confrontation rights, like adversarial testing, to require disclosures demonstrates how problematically corporate claims to secrecy have eclipsed public protections in the procurement process.[33]

Some governments even agree explicitly to confidentiality terms in their contract.[34] As these trade secret cases emerged, they inspired a nascent research effort, joined by Jeanna Matthews and the NYU Technology Law and Policy clinic, to request law enforcement technology contracts across the country. We found contracts explicitly protecting the public's interest in accessing information—for example, in Allegheny County's Purchase Agreement with Cybergenetic—but we also found multiple contracts, like the Harris Corporation's contract in Chicago, that attempted to bind the state to confidentiality.[35] These confidentiality agreements do not, however, only hinder people seeking release after conviction from accessing information, like Mr. Piñeda. As Rebecca Wexler wrote, they also obstruct people accused of crimes from accessing and confronting evidence presented against them at trial. Public defenders are additionally generally under-resourced to combat both prosecutors and corporate legal teams in trade secret battles, and when they do win access and find errors, faulty programs are rarely replaced.[36] When the systems are replaced,[37] the underlying government failures to filter for similar system errors in new programs still go unaddressed—simply put, litigation is not a viable strategy for preventing harm.[38]

In addition to the obstructions trade secrets introduce to a person's literal ability to fight for their freedom from incarceration, they also smuggle a more subtle danger into the public sector. Corporations in the future may try to point to government adoption of confidentiality terms and trade secret claims as factual precedent in attempts to limit public or even government access to aspects of their technologies.[39] While some court decisions allowing defense counsel more expansive access to materials under protective orders are celebrated for achieving balance between competing interests, by consistently conceding the existence of trade secrets, courts feed corporate secrecy campaigns.[40] These fights will not be won in courts—we must follow movements now pointing at procurement.

WOOD HYACINTHS—MOVEMENTS RINGING ALARM BELLS

Social justice movements are responding to these harms by targeting local budgets and corporations, as well as organizing campaigns around aligning public funds with the public's interest. Wood-hyacinths are tiny flowers shaped like bells, and this section shines on a handful of movements already ringing alarm bells over corporate secrecy. Organizations like Worth Rises are creating tools to educate the public about corporate influence on government.[41] Advocates like Mijente, Surveillance Resistance Lab, and Just Futures Law are evolving their pressure campaigns to target shareholders and workers at specific corporations, like Equifax, that are sharing utility data with immigration enforcement.[42] Organizers are targeting contract cycles like election cycles[43] and mapping corporate capture like electoral maps.[44] Accessing information about these companies' contractual relationships to government is a crucial part of this work.

Media Justice, for example, hosts an interactive map about e-carceration, or electronic monitoring ("EM") companies. E-carceration companies in the United States alone operate app and ankle strap monitoring businesses worth hundreds of millions of dollars in government contracts for people before and after conviction.[45] "The average daily caseload of monitored individuals in . . . North America . . . amounted to about 282,000 . . . during 2020" and that number is projected to double by 2025, with additional "strong focus" projected for embedded software and analytics.[46]

Media Justice's Roadmap, "How to Build an Unshackling Freedom Campaign," targeting EM emphasizes "your starting point is information." It recommends that organizers, in addition to gathering stories from people subjected to e-carceration, understand the importance of "[accessing] as much official data on EM as you can" . . . "to effectively mobilize people to your campaign or challenge the talking points offered by proponents of EM."[47] Media Justice's own website marshals information about contracts, fees lobbed on those subjected to EM, taxpayers, and in some states, like Louisiana, they connect dots between judges ordering EM and company kickbacks.[48]

As EM companies incorporate more software and analytics into their devices, accessing information through public records requests may be increasingly obstructed by trade secret exemptions, as the prison attempted to do in Mr. Piñeda's case. Indeed, it is exactly this corporate entanglement that Media Justice's founder, Malkia Cyril, highlights as dangerous to the public's influence on the state: "e-carceration helps states become indebted to corporations and corporate power."[49] Trade secrets, as currently tolerated by the public sector, serve to obscure the extent of this debt and power—they shroud corporate stakeholders invested in maintaining an expansion of carceral technology in secrecy.

PEONIES—PAIN-RELIEVING PRACTICAL TOOLS FOR PROCUREMENT INTERVENTIONS

The public procurement process is how government contracts for goods or services are established with private corporations and it can look different depending on whether it is federal, state, or local. The introduction of new technologies like risk assessment tools, surveillance systems, or any of the many other technologies and bundled services currently sold to governments requires a new procurement process—one that first interrogates the assumption that a data-driven tool will solve the problem presented and opens opportunities for public participation.

Procurement officers generally have the power to issue directives to its staff about what standards any new vendor or contract must meet. For example, for some specialized contracts, specific rules dictate how agencies can contract IT consulting services.[50] Similarly, procurement processes for technology vendors must introduce some threshold questions about what problem they are solving for—and invite public participation in that problem definition process early and often. Engaged public participation throughout the process of identifying a problem, understanding the scope of that problem, the potential for that problem to be addressed by a data-driven solution (or not) as well as the potential harms it introduces could better protect the public from harmful technologies. If public participation confirms that a technology solution would address the problem defined, additional opportunities for public input must arise to inform impact assessments, identify potential harms and mitigation strategies, consider a company's history, and identify metrics by which to measure the technology intervention's success. For now, these procurement processes are often opaque and difficult to pierce.

Fortunately, there are a handful of peonies—known for pain-relief—we can add to our bouquet. Rashida Richardson's *Guidance for Key Stages of Government Technology Procurement* can be used by advocates to support engagement with their local procurement officer. "This guidance offers high level considerations and recommendations that can improve transparency, accountability, oversight, and public trust in government technology procurement without legislative or regulatory reform."[51] Richardson identifies methods such as documenting presolicitation technology assessments, assessing solicitation approaches, proposal evaluation and contract negotiation, which procurement officers can use to better understand a technology—and the problem it seeks to solve. Similarly, Stephen Raher created a useful set of "Best Practices for Prison and Jail Tablet Procurement" through the Prison Policy Initiative applicable to many other digital contexts.[52] He identifies ways procurement of prison telecommunications services can be "reinvented" by "[opening] up aspects of the procurement process to oversight" and "simply by modifying contracts or the terms of requests for proposals."[53] Catherine Crump also offers procurement "remedies to democratize local surveillance policy making" at federal, state, and local levels. Her suggestions include requiring involvement of elected representatives in technology procurement processes, requiring that technologies be governed by use policies, and additional state and local remedies.[54]

Elizabeth Joh also highlights public access laws as an important oversight mechanism.[55] An online resource, *Breaking the Lock: Accessing Public Records to Map Systems, Algorithms, and Data* specifically supports this strategy to help "activists, lawyers or anyone interested in filing an open records request to determine what to look and ask for in order to assess and potentially challenge government use of algorithmic systems."[56] For organizers working on corporate accountability campaigns, "Tech Inquiry" is a tool that can help uncover layers of intermediaries, subcontractors, and subsidiaries that make tracing a company's contracts challenging.[57] The website's creator, Jack Poulson, explains its importance: "[even] when investigating a single form of influence . . . the official government data sources (e.g., USASpending.gov) at best partially expose corporate hierarchies."[58] These are all tools that organizers can use to brainstorm research strategies, develop actionable toolkits, and build strategies targeting procurement of technology.

Too often, "[in] criminal justice software and in many other examples of black box decision-making software in areas like hiring or credit, the interests of those purchasing the software to make decisions can be very different than the interests of those being decided about."[59] Opening up the procurement process to more democratic engagement introduces the interests of "those being decided about" in both defining the problem, evaluating whether the technology solution is responsive or potentially introducing new harm that weighs against its use, or requires impact assessments or other harm mitigation efforts.

Through multiple strategies including research, pressure campaigns on procurement officers, corporate accountability campaigns, public record litigation, communications strategies, and more, advocates can begin to push for more public interest values by pulling at purse strings.[60]

A BOW TO TIE IT ALL TOGETHER—IN CONCLUSION

Silent Spring's last chapter was "The Other Road."[61] Carson writes "[the] other fork of the road—the one "less traveled by"—offers "our last, our only chance to reach a destination that assures the preservation of our earth."[62] For the same reasons that Carson argued the insecticide industry cannot shape climate policy, we must also not allow states and corporations to govern us through a triple threat of police, corporate, and algorithmic secrecy that prioritizes corporate wealth above the public's right to co-create its future.

Protecting our right to information through interventions with the procurement process will become increasingly important harm management given future battles over data ownership, the inextricable connection between bodily and digital autonomy,[63] and the increased production of data-extraction tools set in communal infrastructures (i.e., "smart" cities). As Kapczynski explained, "trade secret law, because it protects only commercially valuable information that has been kept secret, neatly excludes ordinary people as 'owners' of data produced by or about them—even as it has expanded to incorporate an almost limitless amount of business data."[64] The expansion of technologies and trade secrets into the public sector combined with the toxic appetite companies have for claiming all data is their trade secret leaves little room left for democracy.

To imagine beyond harm mitigation strategies, if we were to let ourselves be led by Indigenous people's governance and agricultural practices, take Carson's "other road" or perhaps be the bouquet thrown by Banksy's *Rage, the Flower Thrower* into futures we define, how would the world look?[65] If the public's right to know dominated as a motivating principle over corporate financial interests and power, as the Supreme Court previously said it should, how might organizers, wise to the dangers of corporate capture of the state, recreate public procurement policies to ensure vendors capitulate to the public's demand for "full possession of the facts"? Perhaps we would prohibit privatized public sector technology contractors in the first place and return such services to more accountable government agencies and entirely rethink the privatization of punishment, or state-sanctioned punishment itself.

Rooting ourselves back into our collective right to be in full possession of the facts—stemming naturally from "our obligation to endure"—perhaps also leads to a place without prisons, private vendors, or bow-tied bouquets. Flowers remain rooted in the ground, growing wild; they are never overplanted with pesticides, picked by underpaid people, separated, or sold. A place where public procurement prioritizes principles of permaculture in government services—care for Earth, care for people—and protect the public's right to know what it needs to know in order to collectively endure.[66]

NOTES

Cynthia Conti-Cook extends many blue hydrangeas of gratitude for thoughtful feedback and encouragement to her former Legal Aid Society colleagues Terri Rosenblatt, Rebecca Wexler, Jessica Goldthwaite, Jerome Greco, as well as Glenn Rodriguez, Jose Piñeda, Vincent Southerland, Jeanna Matthews, Dana Delger, Michelle Shevin, and Paromita Shah. My gratitude also goes to the many inspiring people and organizations whose lived experiences, organizing, writing, and research is described within—flowers to all of you for striving to make this world more beautiful by being here. And to the late Chris Kuhlman, my hometown florist who taught me that flowers have their own language, a bushel of forget-me-nots for consulting with me on this bouquet last year. Rest well under the shade of big, beautiful petals.

1. *How to Make a Floral Bouquet in 6 Simple Steps*, MASTERCLASS (June 7, 2021), https://www.masterclass.com/articles/how-to-make-a-bouquet#3-tips-for-picking-flowers-for-a-bouquet.

2. Robin Wall Kimmerer, BRAIDING SWEETGRASS—INDIGENOUS WISDOM, SCIENTIFIC KNOWLEDGE, AND THE TEACHINGS OF PLANTS, 384 (2013).

3. Rachel Carson, SILENT SPRING, 13 (1962).

4. Not all facts are helpful to this end—overwhelming data dumps that drown out important information, for example, are not helpful.

5. Carson, *supra* note 3 (quoting natural philosopher Jean Rostrand).

6. Janine Benyus, BIOMIMICRY: INNOVATION INSPIRED BY NATURE, 274 (1997).

7. *Id.*

8. Letter from A. R. Wallace to Charles Darwin, n.5 (July 2, 1866), *in* DARWIN CORRESPONDENCE PROJECT, https://www.darwinproject.ac.uk/letter/DCP-LETT-5140.xml#back-mark-5140.f5 (industrialist Herbert Spencer, pointing to Charles Darwin's research, coined the phrase "survival of the fittest").

9. Central Digital & Data Office, *Data Ethics Framework*, GOV.UK (Sept. 16, 2020), https://www.gov.uk/government/publications/data-ethics-framework/data-ethics-framework-2020#specific-actions.

10. Rebecca Wexler, *Life, Liberty, and Trade Secrets: Intellectual Property in the Criminal Justice System*, 70 STAN. L. REV. 1343, 1418 (2018).

11. Hannah Bloch-Wehba, *Access to Algorithms*, 88 FORDHAM L. REV. 1265 (2020).

12. Amy Kapczynski, *The Public History of Trade Secrets*, 55 U.C. DAVIS L. REV. 1367, 1367 (2022).

13. Julienne Pepitone, *Black, Female, and a Silicon Valley "Trade Secret,"* CNN (Mar. 17, 2013, 8:00 AM), https://www.cnn.com/2013/03/17/us/black-female-and-a-silicon-valley-trade-secret/index.html.

14. Kapczynski, *supra* note 12, at 1428.

15. *Id.,* at 1440.

16. *Id.,* at 1418.

17. David S. Levine, *Secrecy and Unaccountability: Trade Secrets in Our Public Infrastructure*, 59 FLA. L. REV. 136, 140 (2007).

18. Bloch-Wehba, *supra* note 11, at 1270–71.

19. *See id.,* at 1273–86 (a more exhaustive list).

20. Vincent Southerland, *The Master's Tools and a Mission: Using Community Control and Oversight Laws to Resist and Abolish Police Surveillance Technologies*, 70 UCLA L. REV. (June 16, 2023).

21. *Id.,* at 15–18.

22. Aaron Sankin, Dhruv Mehrotra, Surya Mattu & Annie Gilbertson, *Crime Prediction Software Promised to Be Free of Biases. New Data Shows It Perpetuates Them*, THE MARKUP (Dec. 2, 2021, 8:00 ET), https://themarkup.org/prediction-bias/2021/12/02/crime-prediction-software-promised-to-be-free-of-biases-new-data-shows-it-perpetuates-them.

23. Southerland, *supra* note 20, at 19.

24. N.Y. State Dep't of Corrs. and Cmty. Supervision, COMPAS ASSESSMENTS/CASE PLAN (Aug. 14, 2019), https://doccs.ny.gov/system/files/documents/2020/11/8500.pdf ("COMPAS" stands for "Correctional Offender Management Profiling for Alternative Sanctions"); *see also* Julia Angwin, Jeff Larson, Surya Mattu & Lauren Kirchner, *Machine Bias*, PROPUBLICA (May 23, 2016), https://www.propublica.org/article/machine-bias-risk-assessments-in-criminal-sentencing.

25. Both Mr. Rodriguez and Mr. Piñeda consented to their stories being shared in this chapter.

26. Rebecca Wexler, *Code of Silence*, WASHINGTON MONTHLY (June 11, 2017), https://washingtonmonthly.com/2017/06/11/code-of-silence/; *see also* Wexler, *supra* note 10, at 1370. Mr. Rodriguez presented his research in multiple venues. Brookings Institution, *Forensic Algorithms: The Future of Technology in the US Legal System* at 22:29, YOUTUBE (May 12, 2022), https://www.youtube.com/watch?v=YNFEdElUT-4. Mr. Rodriguez and myself also presented his research and its implications. Ass'n for Computing Mach., *2019 Implications Tutorial: Parole Denied: One Man's Fight against a COMPAS Risk Assessment*, YOUTUBE (Feb. 22, 2019), https://www.youtube.com/watch?v=UySPgihj70E.

27. N.Y. PUB. OFF. LAW § 87 (McKinney 2022).

28. Jose Piñeda, N.Y. State Dept. of Corrs. and Cmty Supervision, No. 903104–19, 10 (Oct. 11, 2019).

29. As documented in correspondence from Mr. Piñeda, in possession of author.

30. The type of software system in question was a probabilistic genotyping system (or PG system). Marc Canellas describes PG systems in Defending IEEE Software Standards in Federal Criminal Court as "heuristically developed forensic science driven by law enforcement goals, not science. It uses Markov chain, Monte Carlo methods that purportedly enable the identification of individuals from tiny samples of DNA that contain a mix of people's genetic material." Marc Canellas, *Defending IEEE Software Standards in Federal Criminal Court*, COMPUTER (June 7, 2021), at 15.

31. People v. Superior Court (Dominguez), 28 Cal. App. 5th 223 (ESR brief filed 05/10/2018 at 3) (2018). People v. Superior Court (Dominguez), 28 Cal. App. 5th 223, at 227 (2018). The procedural history was summarized by the court—"Dominguez was initially tried in 2011; that jury hung. Upon his subsequent retrial, he was convicted of first-degree murder (Pen. Code, § 187, subd. [a]) and conspiracy to commit murder (id. §§ 182, subd. [a][1], 187). We upheld that conviction in People v. Dominguez (July 5, 2013, D060019) [nonpub. Opn.]). In 2017, the superior court granted Dominguez's petition for writ of habeas corpus, reversing his conviction." *Id.*, at 227 n.1. He had previously been serving a fifty-year sentence on the same charge. Greg Moran, *Murder Case That Highlighted DNA-Analysis Controversy Ends with Plea to Reduced Charge, Release*, SAN DIEGO UNION-TRIBUNE (Dec. 6, 2019), https:// www.sandiegouniontribune.com/news/courts/story/2019-12-06/murder-case-that-highlighted-dna -analysis-controversy-ends-with-plea-to-reduced-charge-release.

32. Brief for the Legal Aid Society as amicus curie at 28, People v. Superior Court, 28 Cal. App. 5th 223 (2018)(filed 07/05/18) (I co-authored this brief with Legal Aid colleagues).

33. See Wexler, *supra* note 10.

34. Stingray Equipment Under GSA Contract *(# GS-35F0283J, § 4.5); See also* Tim Cushing, *Harris Stingray Nondisclosure Agreement Forbids Cops from Telling Legislators*, TECHDIRT (Jan. 25, 2018), https://www.techdirt.com/2018/01/25/harris-stingray-nondisclosure-agreement-forbids-cops-telling -legislators-about-surveillance-tech/.

35. *Allegheny County's Purchase Agreement with Cybergenetics (Purchase Agreement #73948, § 10.2)* (Feb. 19, 2009).

36. Rachel B. Warren & Niloufar Salehi, *Trial by File Formats: Exploring Public Defenders' Challenges Working with Novel Surveillance Data*, PROS. OF THE ASS'N FOR COMPUTING MACH. ON HUMAN-COMPUTER INTERACTION (Apr. 2022), https://dl.acm.org/doi/pdf/10.1145/3512914.

37. By the time ProPublica won access to a tool developed by the Office of Medical Examiners in New York City, the agency already procured a vendor to replace it. Lauren Kirchner, *Federal Judge Unseals New York Crime Lab's Software for Analyzing DNA Evidence*, PROPUBLICA (Oct. 20, 2017), https:// www.propublica.org/article/federal-judge-unseals-new-york-crime-labs-software-for-analyzing -dna-evidence.

38. "If, in 5–10 years, defense attorneys are alone and still fighting over access to source code . . . we will have failed." Marc Canellas, Att'y, Off. of the Pub. Def., Cnty. of Arlington & the City of Falls Church, Engineers v. PGS: A Strategy for the War against Carceral Technology at the Legal Aid Society's DNA Unit's Foundation of DNA Defense: Unpacking the 2021 NIST Report (Apr. 1, 2022).

39. Kapczynski, *supra* note 12, at 1418.

40. *See State v. Pickett*, 466 N.J. Super. 270 (N.J. Super. Ct. App. 2021).

41. *The Prison Industry: Mapping Private Sector Players.* WORTH RISES (Apr. 2020), https:// worthrises.org/theprisonindustry2020.

42. Drew Harwell, *Utility Giants Agree to No Longer Allow Sensitive Records to Be Shared with ICE*, WASHINGTON POST (Dec. 8, 2021), https://www.washingtonpost.com/technology/2021/12/08 /utility-data-government-tracking/.

43. Fran Spielman, *ShotSpotter Contract Comes Under Heavy Fire.* CHICAGO SUN-TIMES (Nov. 12, 2021), https://chicago.suntimes.com/city-hall/2021/11/12/22778971/shotspotter-contract-police-districts-city -council-gunfire-violence-crime.

44. *Electronic Monitoring Hotspot Map*, MEDIA JUSTICE (2022), https://mediajustice.org/electronic-monitoring-hotspots/; Nat'l Immigration Project, Immigrant Def. Project & Mijente, *Who's Behind ICE: the Tech Companies Fueling Deportations*, MIJENTE (Oct. 23, 2018), https://mijente.net/wp-content/uploads/2018/10/WHO%E2%80%99S-BEHIND-ICE_-The-Tech-and-Data-Companies-Fueling-Deportations-_v1.pdf.

45. *Electronic Offender Monitoring Solutions Market Trends and Drivers 2021: Stronger Focus on Software and Analytics within Offender Monitoring—ResearchAndMarkets.com*, BUSINESS WIRE (Dec. 14, 2021), https://www.businesswire.com/news/home/20211214005999/en/Electronic-Offender-Monitoring-Solutions-Market-Trends-and-Drivers-2021-Stronger-Focus-On-Software-and-Analytics-Within-Offender-Monitoring.

46. *Electronic Offender Monitoring Solutions—2nd Edition*, RESEARCHANDMARKETS (Dec. 14, 2021), https://www.researchandmarkets.com/reports/5509412/electronic-offender-monitoring-solutions-2nd#src-pos-1.

47. *Unshackling Freedom Toolkit*, MEDIAJUSTICE, https://mediajustice.org/unshackling-freedom/what-you-can-do/ (accessed Apr. 3, 2023).

48. *Electronic Monitoring Hotspot Map: Louisiana*, MEDIAJUSTICE, https://mediajustice.org/electronic-monitoring-hotspots/louisiana/ (accessed Apr. 3, 2023).

49. MediaJustice, *Understanding E-Carceration: A Community Event on the Future of Surveillance & Mass Incarceration* at 10:19, YOUTUBE (Mar. 23, 2022), https://www.youtube.com/watch?v=nwZIUqTmao4.

50. The City of New York Office of the Comptroller, *Internal Control and Accountability Directives: Directive #31: Special Audit Procedures for Information Technology Consulting and Other Information Technology Professional Services Payment Requests under Contracts Specifying Payment to a Vendor Based on Time* (July 1, 2014), https://comptroller.nyc.gov/wp-content/uploads/documents/Directive-31-Special-Audit-Procedures-for-IT-Consulting-etc.-Reformatted.pdf.

51. Rashida Richardson, *Best Practices for Government Procurement of Data Driven Technologies: A Short Guidance for Key Stages of Government Technology Procurement*, CTR. FOR L., INFO., AND CREATIVITY (May 2021), https://riipl.rutgers.edu/files/2021/05/Best-Practices-for-Government-Technology-Procurement-May-2021.pdf. Richardson adds parenthetically "(though modernization of procurement laws and policies is highly encouraged)".

52. Stephen Raher, *Best Practices for Prison and Jail Tablet Procurement*, PRISON POLICY INITIATIVE (July 14, 2022), https://www.prisonpolicy.org/messaging/rfp_guidance.html.

53. Stephen Raher, *The Company Store and the Literally Captive Market: Consumer Law in Prisons and Jails*, 17 HASTINGS RACE & POVERTY L.J. 3, 77 (2020).

54. Catherine Crump, *Surveillance Policy Making by Procurement*, 91 WASH. L. REV. 1595, 1655–60 (2016).

55. Elizabeth E. Joh, *The Undue Influence of Surveillance Technology Companies on Policing*, 91 N.Y.U. L. REV. ONLINE 101, 125 (2017).

56. Rashida Richardson, Amba Bak & Ian Head. *Breaking the Lock: Accessing Public Records to Map Systems, Algorithms and Data*, FOIA BASICS FOR ACTIVISTS (Mar. 2022). https://www.foiabasics.org/breaking-the-lock.

57. TECH INQUIRY, https://techinquiry.org/ (accessed Apr. 3, 2023).

58. Jack Poulson, *Easy as PAI (Publicly Available Information)*, TECH INQUIRY 1–2 (Sept. 10, 2021), https://techinquiry.org/EasyAsPAI/resources/EasyAsPAI.pdf.

59. Jeanna Matthews, et al., *When Trusted Black Boxes Don't Agree: Incentivizing Iterative Improvement and Accountability in Critical Software Systems*, in AIES' 20: PROCEEDINGS OF THE AAAI/ACM CONFERENCE ON AI, ETHICS, AND SOCIETY, 13 (2020).

60. For example, Boston, MA, centered its constituents in technology procurement in this playbook. Mayor's Office of New Urban Mechanics, BOSTON SMART CITY PLAYBOOK, https://monum.github.io/playbook/#play6 (accessed Apr. 3, 2023).

61. Carson, *supra* note 3, at 277.

62. *Id.*

63. Rebecca Chowdhury, *America's High-Tech Surveillance Could Track Abortion-Seekers, Too, Activists Warn*, TIME (June 6, 2022), https://time.com/6184111/abortion-surveillance-tech-tracking/.

64. Kapczynski, *supra* note 12, at 1442.

65. "Rage, the Flower Thrower" by Banksy was the subject of a famous trademark battle. Anny Shaw, *Banksy Loses Trademark Battle over His Famous Flower Thrower*, THE ART NEWSPAPER (Sept. 17, 2020), https://www.theartnewspaper.com/2020/09/17/banksy-loses-trademark-battle-over-his-famous-flower-thrower-image.

66. *How to Start a Permaculture Garden*, MASTERCLASS (June 7, 2021), https://www.masterclass.com/articles/how-to-start-a-permaculture-garden#what-is-permaculture.

6

Chinese and Russian Cybercrime in Global Racial Orders of Intellectual Property

Anjali Vats

When President Joseph Biden retired the China Initiative,[1] an economic espionage program created in 2018 by the US Department of Justice to combat an alleged epidemic of trade secret theft carried out by those of Chinese descent, many rejoiced.[2] The government policy was derided then and now by racial justice advocates as a McCarthy style witch hunt,[3] that involved cases reminiscent of the attack on nuclear scientist Wen Ho Lee.[4] Though civil rights advocates have made clear that retiring the China Initiative is insufficient to completely upend the racist narratives routinely imposed upon people of East Asian descent,[5] some maintain that forcing prosecutors to drop cases against academics such as Anaming Hu and Gang Chen will encourage them to confront and even address their Sinophobic bias.[6]

The Trump Administration's rationale for the China Initiative, which Biden has openly criticized, stereotyped Chinese people as inherently disloyal.[7] This is the same troubling theme that prosecutors leveraged in Lee's case, now widely regarded as a Clinton Era political prosecution used to provide an alibi for trade policy that Republicans critiqued as Sinophilic.[8] As political scientist Stephen del Visco shows, the contemporary recurrence of the trope of East Asians as turncoats is not a historical accident but an intentional rhetorical strategy crafted by conservative commentators to unite the party around whiteness and capitalism.[9] Perhaps the most compelling evidence of the China Initiative's systemic bias is the case-by-case deconstruction of the indictments in the *MIT Technology Review* that revealed a prosecutorial pattern of targeting those who were #Researching-WhileAsian.[10] US officials have not yet outlined how they will restructure the China Initiative.[11] But comments by Matthew Olsen, Assistant Attorney General for National Security, that "the department's work will not be hampered" suggests that future policy will continue to be racially problematic.[12]

The China Initiative's Sinophobia reflects American use of *intellectual property rights talk*, a term I introduce as a play on Mary Ann Glendon's notion of "rights talk," as a means of explicitly and implicitly deploying racist and sexist dog whistles to justify inequitable knowledge production, ownership, and circulation policies grounded in white and masculine theories of rights.[13] The desire to protect American intellectual property rights is so intense that it spills over into nearby areas of law—here theft of trade secrets via cyberespionage[14]—and encourages aggressive and imprecise prosecutions in the name of national security.[15] The concept of intellectual property rights talk is a useful entrée into understanding how "relational racialization," racial bias that operates *across* racial groups, operates to produce durable forms of gendered racism.[16] In this case, the China Initiative, a reflection of the white nationalist ideologies that became tools of Sinophobic populist incitement during the Trump Administration, invoked and reproduced anti-Asianness.[17] This is partly because it privileged intellectual property *rights* over intellectual property *responsibilities*, specifically about whether US demands were fair and just and what obligations might come with the US legal conceptions of trade secret infringement, especially with respect to legal issues such as cybercrime, around which there is little international consensus.[18] A wealth of literature already compellingly makes the case that imposing intellectual property standards on other nations reenacts (neo)colonial power relations, especially when done without regard for the histories and economies of those places.[19]

This chapter compares the laws imposed and punishments enforced against China with those laws imposed and punishments enforced against Russia, another nation engaged in the theft of trade secrets via cyberespionage, in order to show how (neo)colonialism emerges in international arenas, vis-à-vis disparate raced and gendered treatment in geopolitical dealings. While Chinese nationals have been historically and contemporarily singled out for acting as what I have previously described as "bad intellectual property citizens,"[20] Russian nationals have been treated with near impunity despite creating similarly alarming threats to political and economic stability.[21] Reading US engagements with these nations in relation to one another reveals a lack of racial evenhandedness in economic espionage policy that reinforces global racial and gender hierarchies of intellectual property. Greater focus on intellectual property rights responsibilities and the ethical obligations that flow from them with respect to race, gender, and nation can help to create more equitable forms of policymaking.

This chapter also complicates the binary of good intellectual property citizenship/bad intellectual property citizenship that I have previously proposed by showing that groups do not merely comply with or violate intellectual property laws. Rather, intellectual property rights talk constantly defines and redefines "intellectual property" and "infringement" in response to real and perceived threats, frequently by employing rhetorics of race, gender, and nation to justify expansive and inequitable definitions of both. For instance, China *becomes* a worse intellectual property citizen and Russia *becomes* a better bad intellectual property citizen when Former Attorney General Jeff Sessions declares: "Perhaps this threat [from China] has been overshadowed in the press by threats from Russia or radical Islamic terrorism. But while it has been in the shadows, the threat has only grown more dangerous."[22] By positioning the two nations in relation to one another, in a hierarchy anchored by terrorism, he amplifies the Chinese threat. Here, I consider three recurring racist and sexist representations of China as populated by individuals (1) who are devious and suspect, loyal only to their nation of origin; (2) whose way of being is effeminate and weak; and (3) who engage in economic espionage via cybercrime that threatens the United States. I maintain that the United States is comparatively soft on comparable or worse Russian violations partly due to their shared commitments to white supremacy. Geopolitically speaking, this casts Russia not as Edward Said's Orientalized Other but as Richard Dyer's "bad white."[23] The bad white is without a doubt a villain—but one that is familiar and sympathetic enough to allow "good whites" to position themselves as morally superior heroes among their own kind. Russia exemplifies a racial and moral gray area that breaks with ideal (colonial) foreign policy but facilitates the maintenance of white supremacy and aggressive masculinity. I show this by detailing how multiple stakeholders describe Russian saboteurs with (1) more generous attribution of motive, (2) more respect for raced and gendered strongman and mafioso behavior, and (3) more technological awe at infringing behaviors as compared to their Chinese counterparts. Chinese infringement is presented as uniquely threatening to global legal orders.

My argument proceeds in three parts. Part I outlines two theoretical frameworks for examining how racialization unfolds in the context of economic espionage specifically and intellectual property law generally: Critical Race Intellectual Property (CRTIP) and Third World Studies (TWS). CRTIP applies the intersectional insights of Critical Race Theory (CRT) to intellectual property to understand how race operates in the laws of copyright, patent, trademark, trade secret, unfair competition, and rights of publicity. TWS decenters the United States by considering how global liberation theories might approach the problems of racial and gender hierarchy in knowledge governance regimes. Intellectual property scholars relatedly speak of Third World Approaches to International Law (TWAIL) as a lens for thinking about the international inequities produced by Euroamerican knowledge ownership regimes.[24] Part II examines how China is racially represented and geopolitically managed in conversations about cybercrime and espionage in the larger context of histories and formations of Asianness. Part III considers how Russia is racially represented and geopolitically managed in conversations about hacking and disinformation in the larger context of the histories and formations of whiteness. The conclusion posits that drawing upon feminist cyberlaw's articulations of ethics and fairness can help build equitable global racial orders of intellectual property that divest from whiteness.

RACE AND GLOBAL GEOPOLITICS

CRTIP is a term that Deidré Keller and I use to organize and describe a body of race and gender progressive intellectual property scholarship and activism from the past three decades that is largely authored by people of color.[25] We maintain that bringing CRT, the current racial boogeyman of the fascist right, together with intellectual property encourages intentional consideration of race as an organizing concept in a wide range of legal contexts. As we understand it, CRTIP functions as a set of questions that aid in drawing nuanced intersectional conclusions about the cultural and political superstructures of intellectual property regimes.[26] Like CRT, a set of principles and praxes for understanding how race remains entrenched in facially race neutral laws and addressing that embedded inequity, CRTIP focuses on where and how intellectual property law fails to produce racially just and racially equitable outcomes. As a theoretical lens, CRTIP is not confined to analyses of the United States or race. Asking questions about transnational intellectual property regimes and how they are deployed in the service of larger systems of colonialism can illuminate when and how punishment for violation of intellectual property norms is actually punishment for deviation from Euroamerican norms— for example, an implicit form of "intellectual property imperialism."[27] By making these interventions intersectionally, CRTIP can invoke and complement feminist cyberlaw's theorizations of fairness and equity.

Gary Y. Okihiro explains TWS as an interdisciplinary movement centered on finding commonality in the struggle for liberation.[28] Unlike Ethnic Studies and its progeny, which he maintains can produce divisive forms of identity politics, TWS is grounded in global solidarities.[29] I am interested in how TWS offers a path to reimagining knowledge governance regimes, around a wide range of transformative cultural values. I embrace the phrase "Third World" alongside "Global South" in this chapter as a means of calling upon histories of radical racial activism rooted in 1960s era frameworks of alliance in liberation,[30] as well as invoking the ideological and methodological imperatives of TWAIL.[31] James Gathii, who is interested in transformative justice approaches to international law, proposes that "there is an opportunity for learning, sharing, and collaboration between CRT and TWAIL scholars" that emphasizes both colonial extraction and white supremacy as meaningful analytics.[32] J. Janewa Osei-Tutu has compellingly applied TWAIL to intellectual property law by highlighting the need to decenter American epistemologies while focusing on equitable ownership and egalitarian access to knowledge across the globe.[33] This chapter draws upon the often intersecting approaches of CRTIP, TWS, and TWAIL scholars in intersectionally examining intellectual property's racial orders, the logics of which implicitly and explicitly structure rhetorics around Russian and Chinese theft of trade secrets via cyberespionage.

THE FEMINIZED ASIANNESS
OF CHINESE CYBERCRIME

In a recent article for the *South China Morning Post*, Leo Yu observed that ongoing Congressional investigations into Tik Tok as spying technology are rooted not in fact but in the "original sin" of Chinese ownership.[34] During the hearings, Republican Jay Obernolte asked accusatorily: "How could looking at the algorithm confirm that [Tik Tok is] free from foreign influence?"[35] while confrontationally informing CEO Shou Zi Chew "you are not trusted here."[36] Reasonable people may disagree about the nature and scope of the privacy issues associated with Tik Tok but the evidence that Chinese-owned companies are held to higher and racialized standards than white-owned ones is difficult to deny. A bipartisan majority of US policymakers appear committed to the narrative of China as a nation of disloyal spies, who mobilize new technologies in the service of global political and economic domination. Their prejudices are evident in the long history of actions intended to rein in Chinese trade secret theft that the National Counterintelligence and Security Center (NCSC), among other US government agencies, has characterized as "active and persistent."[37] While the NCSC's conclusion has its kernel of truth, the assumptions upon which it is based are troubling and hypocritical.

Multiple independent analyses of the China Initiative characterize it as a racist policy that targeted Chinese researchers for "relatively minor errors and omissions in grant applications, rather than spies stealing national security secrets or proprietary technology at the direction of the Chinese government."[38] A recent Brennan Center report historicizes the program, observing that "the FBI and Justice Department tendency to stretch facts and jump to conclusions in Chinese espionage cases pre-dated the China Initiative."[39] For instance, FBI counterintelligence training materials otherize those of Asian descent.[40] And earlier policies and actions, including the Economic Espionage Act of 1996 (EEA), reflect similar racial animus. The EEA, which turned theft of trade secrets into a federal crime,[41] marked an uptick in criminalizing previously accepted forms of competitive behavior, with an eye to Asia.[42] In 2022, the Stanford Center on China's Economy and Institutions noted that "[a] significant increase in the number of cases charging EEA-related offenses against suspects of Chinese heritage began in 2009 under the Obama administration."[43] The report goes on to propose that this is a symptom of disproportionate and racist targeting of Chinese people.[44] In a detailed review of the EEA, Andrew Chongseh Kim finds "significant disparities in the rates at which people of Asian descent are prosecuted for espionage and the outcomes of those prosecutions."[45] He concludes that "Chinese and other Asian defendants are twice as likely to be innocent as those of other races."[46]

This, of course, reinforces Del Visco's argument, that Sinophobic logics are reflexive in American political culture, including among Democrats.[47] CRT scholars and activists have long argued that "yellow peril" and "model minority" stereotypes organize American thinking about Asianness.[48] Within this binary, East Asians are presented as dangerous and disloyal "forever foreigners," who threaten to overrun the nation.[49] All too often, Asianness is also feminized, for instance through the association of spying with gossip and the association of disloyalty with weakness.[50] Such gendered tropes are evident in representations of the Chinese government as an all-powerful regime and Chinese citizens as eternally committed ideologues. Consider, for instance, the FBI's semi-fictional propaganda film, *The Company Man* (2015), which promotes yellow perilism by telling a story that contrasts a loyal American businessman with two disloyal Chinese cybercriminals in search of trade secrets. Circulated as a both an agency training video and public awareness campaign, *The Company Man* encourages multiple audiences to embrace American exceptionalism and Sinophobic paranoia.[51] The film tells a gendered, as well as raced, tale in which the dishonorable Chinese men, who shamelessly sneak around industrial spaces and offer exorbitant bribes, fail to live up to the honorable white masculinity of their American target.[52] As evident in the short film, representations of yellow perils and forever foreigners often feminize and emasculate East Asians,[53] representing them as obedient and cowardly automatons, dishonestly and submissively slinking through the shadows while sabotaging others and destroying relationships.[54]

Techno-Orientalism, Betsy Huang argues, emerged in the 1880s with descriptions of Asians as mechanistic alien bots without emotions.[55] In a longer history of the Asian as "model machine," a feminized robotic model of race, Long Bui highlights the many ways that US public culture consistently expresses ambivalence, specifically hate and reverence, about Asian technological prowess.[56] Though most often applied in science fiction studies, the term techno-Orientalism is useful in theorizing political rhetoric as well, specifically in highlighting how US trade, innovation, internet, and technology policy has collided with racial and gender anxieties. As Lok Sui and Claire Chun put it, "techno-orientalism . . . is the expressive vehicle . . . by which Western and Eastern nations articulate their fears, desires, and anxieties that are produced in their competitive struggle to gain technological hegemony through economic trade and scientific innovation."[57] They trace the concept of techno-Orientalism, through the work of David Morely and Kevin Robin, back to fears of Japanese technological superiority in the 1980s.[58] These fears played out in the VCR Wars, a series of conflicts over Asian production of video recording technologies that became lightning rods for national security and economic downturn rhetoric.[59] With respect to the former, the Supreme Court, in a decision that largely sidestepped the race and gender anxieties of the moment, held that the production and use of Betamax recorders did not constitute copyright infringement, only "time shifting" of programming that viewers could watch at the originally scheduled time.[60] Still techno-Orientalism continued to rear its head, first in disputes over semiconductors and automobiles and later in disputes over cybercrime and platforms.

Despite the Supreme Court's decision, Motion Picture Association of America president Jack Valenti doubled down on the Japanophobic sentiments of the time. In 1982, he testified before Congress, at a hearing on home recording:

> "The single one American-made product that the Japanese, skilled beyond all comparison in their conquest of world trade, are unable to duplicate or displace or to compete with or to clone . . . this asset, [the US film and television production industry], which is unlike steel or silicon chips or motor cars or electronics of all kinds—a piece of sardonic irony that while the Japanese are unable to duplicate the American films by flank assault, they can destroy it by this video cassette recorder."[61]

This eerily familiar language expresses ambivalence about Japan, a nation "skilled beyond all comparison in the conquest of world trade," but nonetheless incapable of competing with America's creative moviemaking spirit. Technology operates as a tool of conquest in Valenti's analogy, as well as an anchor for racist and sexist intellectual property rights talk. War metaphors such as "flank assault" add a militant and patriotic urgency to the fight, with Japan engaging in feminized treachery and pathologized virality. Perhaps more importantly, they transform intellectual property rights talk into a raced and gendered conversation that disparages Japanese peoples' ability to produce artistic works and engage in war. The backhanded compliment that implicitly broadens copyright to include economic espionage, is discrimination deployed in the service of ownership rights.

The Japanophobia of the 1980s is intertwined with contemporary Sinophobia because, as Stanford Lyman puts it, anti-Asian racisms are overlapping and interchangeable, despite cultural and geopolitical differences: "The yellow peril appeared first as China, then as Japan, then as China and North Korea, then as China and Vietnam, then briefly as a temporarily prosperous Japan again, and, at the moment—once again as China."[62] Moreover, both are orientalist in their demonization of the so-called Orient as a means of validating Euroamerican white supremacy and legal regimes. Over time, the yellow peril narrative of the "Chinese copy" came to be treated as bipartisan fact, with the Bush Administration and the Clinton Administration cracking down on infringement, while bashing China's intellectual property policies. Under the Obama Administration, Biden declared: "Why have they not become [one of] the most innovative countries in the world? Why is there a need to steal our intellectual property? Why is there a need to have a business hand over its trade secrets to have access to a market of a billion, three hundred million people? Because they're not innovating."[63] This racist and gendered intellectual property rights talk is perpetually justified through moving goalposts: when China agrees to international norms, the US demands greater compliance with its visions of knowledge ownership and economic norms.[64] Copying is treated as weakness not as resilience or choice.

America consistently shores up support for white supremacist intellectual property policies, including around trade secrets, through the mobilization of public emotions of fear and anger. These feelings are frequently rooted in national and geopolitical anxieties about the sustainability of the economy and whiteness.[65] But, as Sara Ahmed might contend, these "racial feelings" about employment, resources, and more are dishonest projections, defensive postures that ignore how the United States built its own economy on infringement and imposes double standards on other nations.[66] Indeed, good faith international intellectual property engagements require acknowledging the unique knowledge production trajectories and economic flows of nations in the Global South.[67] Yet according to US racial epistemes, Chinese people are quintessential bad intellectual property citizens who constitutionally refuse to comply with global norms, and Euroamerican nations are quintessentially good intellectual property citizens who intuitively steward international norms. These heroic myths of whiteness and masculinity are further normalized through relational racialization.

THE MASCULINE WHITENESS OF RUSSIAN HACKING

In 2020, CNN published an article with the headline "37 Times Trump Was Soft on Russia."[68] According to the article, Trump not only urged Russia to hack more, stating: "Russia, if you're listening, I hope you're able to find the 30,000 emails that are missing," he also proposed cybercrime cooperation with Putin.[69] The NCSC, in contrast to its assessments of China's economic espionage, describes Russia as a "sophisticated adversary," focused on military and economic domination.[70] While the Chinese threat originates in "persistence," a trope of mechanistic overrun, the Russian threat originates in "[sophistication]," a trope of elegant wrongdoing. If US policy toward China with respect to intellectual property and economic espionage can be characterized as condescending managerialism, its Russia policy can be described as begrudging acceptance. This hands-off approach has persisted for many years in the face of egregious violations of geopolitical norms, such as invasions of sovereign nations and interference in national elections, as well as a litany of intellectual property and economic espionage transgressions. This is curious given that cybersecurity experts consistently rank Russia in the top cybercrime threats to the US, alongside China. Russian hackers are described as "sowing chaos."[71] China's mechanistic precision is contrasted with Russia's thuggish cold-bloodedness.[72] Yet the consequences for the two nations are very different.

Barron's reports that there are two primary reasons for US nonintervention in the latter issues: that Russia is careful to stay within applicable legal boundaries, here of infringement and cybercrime, and that the United States lacks the political will to enforce its policies. Vladimir Putin himself is aware that "there is little Western countries have been willing to do to stop them . . . If there was little incentive in Russia to stop cybercrime before Ukraine, there is no incentive now.[73] Indeed, even when Putin declared, in March 2022, that Russian nationals would no longer be required to pay patent owners in "unfriendly countries," the US barely responded.[74] One of the few comparative studies of US treatment of Chinese and Russian infringement, a decades old essay, states what is now obvious: "In general, the United States has appeared to pursue different political, economic, and military goals in its relationships with Russia and China."[75] In practice, this means that the US has punished China for even those infractions that may fall under the gray areas of international law while permitting Russia to engage in similar acts with little more than a slap on the wrist.[76] The carte blanche that the United States has offered to Russia is entangled with white supremacy.

While the end of the Cold War produced détente with the US in the 1990s and 2000s, Putin's rise to power shifted the dynamic of the bilateral relationship.[77] The latter has been described as a "strongman," a term "historically deployed to describe autocrats who rule by violence and see themselves, or want to be seen, as worthy of fear."[78] Over the past twenty years, Putin has led an increasingly aggressive Russia, invested in transnational white supremacy. Indeed, multiple white nationalist leaders, including David Duke and Richard Spencer, have identified Putin's Russia as central to maintaining the global authority of whiteness.[79] Yet despite warnings about the destabilizing effects of Russia's white nationalism, the United States has declined to consistently condemn it.[80] I posit that this is largely because Russia, a "contingently white" country, has strategically exploited its whiteness in its geopolitical dealings.[81] The concept of contingent whiteness presupposes that race is produced through racialization, a process of constant change that explains "why certain groups become accepted as 'white,' how and why they adopt white identity claims, and what consequences those identity claims have for social relations."[82] Russia has endeavored to become whiter over time and Euroamerican nations have largely accepted this. Ian Law writes that "there have been striking changes in racial ideas, practices, exclusions and violence in Russia since the 1990s . . . the notion of a 'civilised country' has become a synonym for racial whiteness and Russianness a form of privileged whiteness."[83] Marina Levina observes that Russian investments in whiteness are used to reinforce what Jasbir Puar calls a "politics of debilitation"[84] on racially othered peoples such as Syrians and Ukrainians.[85] Russians choose whiteness because they benefit from its privileges, including relative impunity. The United States allows this because it benefits from Russia's whiteness, including regional counterbalancing.

Despite its chosen and bestowed whiteness, Russia has retained its long-standing identity as a political foil and imperial actor that requires containment. This is evident in multiple areas of friction with the United States, including discussions over NATO expansion. Conflict over intellectual property and economic espionage extends at least as far back to the Soviet Era when, as Debora Halbert observes, national intellectual, political, and economic investments functioned as tools for proving cultural and artistic superiority.[86] Yet the contemporary American refusal to hold Russia accountable for its misdeeds suggests that the ideological dispute is embedded within a larger context. I propose that, while Russians continue to operate as "bad whites"[87] against whom Americans can demonstrate their global moral authority via soft power, it is also beneficial for the United States to engage in performative admonishments instead of meaningful consequences. Three racial outcomes flow from the toothless US response to Russia: (1) it normalizes the US position as the heroic "good white"[88] who appears to seek justice in the global arena; (2) it allows the United States to chastise Russia while also simultaneously colluding with Putin; and (3) it positions China below Russia in a divide-and-conquer style intellectual property and economic espionage racial order. US intellectual property rights talk with Russia thus supports larger architectures of white supremacy by letting the former off the hook while simultaneously deriding China for its illegal and illicit acts. It also exemplifies how realpolitik itself is constituted relationally, through categories of race and gender.

Returning to EEA data with this context around Russia illustrates how the United States uses intellectual property rights talk to reinforce Sinophobic racial hierarchies through relational racialization. The Stanford Center on China's Economy and Institutions notes that "Chinese-named defendants were 13.2% more likely to have their [EEA] cases dismissed or acquitted compared to other defendants, and 13.5% less likely to be found guilty of EEA-related charges than defendants with non-Chinese names."[89] In terms of sentencing, "Chinese-named defendants on average received 12.5 months longer jail terms compared to all other defendants and 12.4 months longer jail terms compared to defendants with Western names.[90] The targeting of Chinese defendants relative to other defendants is even more stark when considered over time. The number of Western defendants has declined from 59 percent of the total of all defendants in 1996–2008 to 28 percent of the total defendants in 2016–2020.[91] In comparison, approximately 50 percent of the total defendants prosecuted since 2009 have been Chinese.[92] These numbers are particularly notable given that Russian actors are growing increasingly bold. "US intelligence officials do not . . . rate China as the biggest threat to the US in cyberspace. The Russians are definitely better, almost as good as we are,' said one," Richard Clarke and Robert Knake reported in 2010.[93]

The Obama Administration and Biden Administration both imposed sanctions against Russia for engaging in economic espionage via cybercrime.[94] However, those sanctions were narrow and limited, especially compared to those imposed upon China.[95] The racialized rhetorics that American policymakers use to talk about Russia provide some insight about why the US shows this geopolitical rival such deference. A 2009 report released by the Rand Corporation describes Russia as a literal host and harbor for cybercrime, emphasizing that infringers use Russian websites to sell pirated and counterfeited goods because they operate as "protected spaces for crime to arise."[96] Instead of being intertwined with narratives of threatening criminality like Black mafia rhetorics,[97] or narratives of devious yellow perils like Asian mafia rhetorics,[98] Russian mafia rhetorics suggest a worthy, masculine, strongman foe. Russian hackers are managers of the infringement world, whose ingenuity and infrastructure helps exceptional fakes to circulate. In 2008, Former Attorney General Michael Mukasey declared: "A Russian mobster selling fake handbags through a middleman in New York may also be selling pirated DVDs in London, counterfeit AIDS medication in Africa, and child pornography over the internet."[99] The "Russian mobster" is the protagonist of the story, here because he manages the sale of multiple goods. In 2006, the *Los Angeles Times* proclaimed, in an article entitled "Russians Able to Fake It Like No One Else," that "if there is a world capital of audacious fabrication, it must be Moscow, where fake is never a four-letter word."[100] It went on to describe Russian copies through "the French notion of *faire montrer* [sic]," noting "it's better to look like something than to be something. It's a very Eastern way of thinking."[101] Fakes may be Eastern, but Russian fakes are exceptional, certainly better than those Made in China. This racialized rhetoric of expertise positions Russia as strong and China as weak. Invoking France moves Russia closer to Europe—and whiteness.[102]

DECONSTRUCTING INTELLECTUAL PROPERTY'S RACE AND GENDER HIERARCHIES

This chapter has focused on how US intellectual property rights talk around economic espionage, trade secrets, and cybercrime prosecution uses comparative racialization, with gendered elements, as a means of justifying and enforcing inequitable knowledge governance policies. When speaking about China, the United States employs intellectual property rights talk that plays on fears of feminized yellow perils associated with racial deficiencies, viral replication, and overwhelming numbers. When speaking about Russia, the United States employs intellectual property rights talk that plays on respect for strongman mafiosos operating cybercrime rings to build and sell counterfeit goods. Russian hackers are imagined as deft and capable emblems of white masculinity even though, as Ruth Ben-Ghiat observes, they "are actually weak and insecure individuals but they appear [to supporters in] their countries as saviors, defenders, sex symbols at times, and other male archetypes."[103] Asian cybercriminals, unlike their white counterparts, are presented as femininely devious, thus undeserving of an empathetic counternarrative, despite their nations facing centuries of extractive colonialism.

US policies toward China and Russia are anything but independent. Their race and gender contrasts amplify one another while also reinforcing whiteness, a "relatively uncharted territory that has remained invisible as it continues to influence the identity of those both within and without its domain."[104] CRTIP, TWS, and TWAIL are useful intersectional tools for deconstructing intellectual property rights talk because they make racial and gender hierarchies visible. Those using these methods would benefit from applying and deepening feminist cyberlaw's insights about ethics and fairness in the area of theft of trade secrets via cyberespionage as part of their theoretical inquiries. Doing so will not only highlight the intersectional race issues that arise with respect to the theft of trade secrets but also aid in building more equitable knowledge governance regimes with evenhanded application of laws and policies across racial groups.

NOTES

My gratitude to Amanda Levendowski and Meg Leta Jones for the opportunity to contribute to this groundbreaking collection and Hayley Behal for her adept research assistance on this project. Thank you as well to Jeremy Wu, Sharon Sandeen, and Peter Yu for their thoughtful input on this piece. I had the privilege of presenting an early version of this work at the Symposium on Trade Secrets for Scholars and Practitioners, organized by Nicola Searle.

1. Jeff Sessions, "Attorney General Jeff Sessions Announces New Initiative to Combat Chinese Economic Espionage," *The United States Department of Justice* (Nov. 1, 2018), https://www.justice.gov /opa/speech/attorney-general-jeff-sessions-announces-new-initiative-combat-chinese-economic -espionage. The US has passed no equivalent law to target Russia.

2. Katie Benner, *Justice Department Is Set to Modify Trump-Era Program Aimed at Fighting Chinese Threats*, NY TIMES (Feb. 20, 2022), https://www.nytimes.com/2022/02/20/us/politics/justice -department-china-trump.html.

3. Bethany Allen-Ebrahimian, *DOJ's China Initiative Under Scrutiny as Cases Fall Apart*, AXIOS (Jan. 25, 2022), https://www.axios.com/justice-department-china-initiative-scrutiny-41113cf0-14a8-42b9 -9ba3-074446239bbf.html.

4. Spencer K. Turnbull, *Wen Ho Lee and the Consequences of Enduring Asian American Stereotypes*, 7 UCLA ASIAN PAC. AM. L.J. 72 (2001).

5. Ellen Barry & Katie Benner, *U.S. Drops Its Case Against M.I.T. Scientist Accused of Hiding China Links*, NY TIMES (Jan. 20, 2022) https://www.nytimes.com/2022/01/20/science/gang-chen-mit -china-initiative.html; Matt Schiavenza, *How the China Initiative Went Wrong*, FOREIGN POLICY (2022), https://foreignpolicy.com/2022/02/13/china-fbi-initiative-spying-racism/.

6. Allen-Ebrahimian, *supra* note 3.

7. Benner, *supra* note 2.

8. Turnbull, *supra* note 4.

9. Stephen Del Visco, *Yellow Peril, Red Scare: Race and Communism in National Review*, 42 ETHNIC & RACIAL STUDS. 626 (2019) (illustrating how the *National Review* trafficked in fearmongering about those of Asian descent as a way of producing political unity among conservatives).

10. Eileen Guo, Jess Aloe & Karen Hao, *The US Crackdown on Chinese Economic Espionage Is a Mess. We Have the Data to Show It.*, MIT TECH. REV. (2021), https://www.technologyreview .com/2021/12/02/1040656/china-initative-us-justice-department/.

11. Benner, *supra* note 2.

12. George Pence, *While China Initiative May Have Ended, Foreign Influence Remains DOJ Enforcement Priority*, REUTERS (Mar. 28, 2022), https://www.reuters.com/legal/legalindustry/while-china -initiative-may-have-ended-foreign-influence-remains-doj-enforcement-2022-03-28/.

13. MARY ANN GLENDON, RIGHTS TALK: THE IMPOVERISHMENT OF POLITICAL DISCOURSE (2008).

14. For a detailed discussion of how these laws are unfairly leveraged against China, *see* Peter Yu, *Trade Secret Hacking, Online Data Breaches, and China's Cyberthreats*, 2015 CARDOZO L. REV. DE-NOVO 130 (2015).

15. Former Cybersecurity and Infrastructure Security Agency Director Chris Krebs linked Chinese hacking, patent theft, and public health in justifying the need for harsher legal penalties for cybercrime. Amanda Macias, "Former Cybersecurity Chief says Russia, China, Iran, and North Korea Are Trying to Steal Coronavirus Vaccine IP," *CNBC* (Dec. 6, 2020), https://www.cnbc.com/2020/12/06 /former-top-cybersecurity-chief-says-russia-china-iran-and-north-korea-are-trying-to-steal-coronoavir .html; *see also* Nicole Sganga, "Chinese Hackers Took Trillions in Intellectual Property from About 30 Multinational Companies," *CBS News* (May 4, 2022), https://www.cbsnews.com/news/chinese -hackers-took-trillions-in-intellectual-property-from-about-30-multinational-companies/ (citing FBI Director Christopher Wray in linking Chinese cybercrime and industrial espionage with intellectual property theft).

16. Natalia Molina, *Understanding Race as a Relational Concept*, 1 MOD. AM. HIST. 101 (2018).

17. *See generally* Ian Haney López, DOG WHISTLE POLITICS: STRATEGIC RACISM, FAKE POPULISM, AND THE DIVIDING OF AMERICA (2022).

18. Glendon, *supra* note 13.

19. *See e.g.*, Madhavi Sunder, *IP3*, 59 STAN. L. REV. 257 (2006).

20. ANJALI VATS, THE COLOR OF CREATORSHIP: INTELLECTUAL PROPERTY, RACE, AND THE MAKING OF AMERICANS (2020).

21. *See e.g.*, Sessions, *supra* note 1.

22. *Id.*

23. RICHARD DYER, WHITE: ESSAYS ON RACE AND CULTURE, 35 (1997).

24. Athena D. Mutua, *The Rise, Development and Future Directions of Critical Race Theory and Related Scholarship*, DENV. U. L. REV. 339 (2006).

25. Anjali Vats & Deidré A. Keller, *Critical Race IP*, 36 CARDOZO ARTS & ENT. L.J. 735 (2018).

26. *Id.*

27. Alpana Roy, *Copyright: A Colonial Doctrine in a Postcolonial Age*, 26 COPYRIGHT REP. 112 (2008); *see also* Lateef Mtima, *What's Mine Is Mine but What's Yours Is Ours: IP Imperialism, the Right of Publicity, and Intellectual Property Social Justice in the Digital Information Age*, 15 SMU SCI. & TECH. L. REV. 323 (2012).

28. GARY Y. OKIHIRO, THIRD WORLD STUDIES: THEORIZING LIBERATION, 2 (2016).

29. *Id.*

30. *Id.*

31. Mutua, *supra* note 24.

32. James T. Gathii, *Writing Race and Identity in a Global Context: What CRT and TWAIL Can Learn From Each Other*, 65 UCLA LAW REVIEW 1610, 1612 (2021).

33. J. Janewa Osei-Tutu, *Denying Cultural Intellectual Property: An International Perspective on Anjali Vats's The Color of Creatorship*, 55 NEW ENG. L. REV. 79 (2020).

34. Leo Yu, *TikTok Is Targeted in the US for Being Chinese, Not For What It Has or Has Not Done*, SOUTH CHINA MORNING POST (Mar. 26, 2023), https://www.msn.com/en-xl/news/other/tiktok-is -targeted-in-the-us-for-being-chinese-not-for-what-it-has-or-has-not-done/ar-AA194p7j (accessed Mar. 29, 2023); *see also* Leo Yu, *From Criminalizing China to Criminalizing the Chinese*, 55 COLUM. HUM. RTS L. REV. (forthcoming 2024).

35. Gopal Ratnam, *Obernolte, Johnson Use Tech Backgrounds to Question Tik Tok CEO*, ROLLCALL (Mar. 8, 2023), https://rollcall.com/2023/03/28/obernolte-johnson-use-tech-backgrounds-to-question -tiktok-ceo/.

36. Yu, *supra* note 34.

37. *Foreign Economic Espionage in Cyberspace*, NATIONAL COUNTERINTELLIGENCE AND SECURITY CENTER, 2018, https://irp.fas.org/ops/ci/feec-2018.pdf.

38. Michael German & Alex Liang, *End of Justice Department's "China Initiative" Brings Little Relief to U.S. Academics*, BRENNAN CTR. FOR JUST. (2022), https://www.brennancenter.org/our-work/analysis-opinion/end-justice-departments-china-initiative-brings-little-relief-us.

39. *Id.*

40. *Id.*

41. Hanming Fang & Ming Li, *Racial Profiling Under the Economic Espionage Act*, STAN. CTR. ON CHINA'S ECON. & INSTS. (2022), https://sccei.fsi.stanford.edu/china-briefs/racial-profiling-under-economic-espionage-act.

42. Julia Jayne and Ashley Riser, *Theft of Trade Secrets: The Economic Espionage Act, China Initiative, and Silicon Valley*, THE CHAMPION (Sept./Oct. 2019), https://www.nacdl.org/Article/SeptOct2019-TheftofTradeSecretsTheEconomicEspionag.

43. Fang and Li, *supra* note 41.

44. *Id.*

45. Andrew Chongseh Kim, *Prosecuting Chinese Spies: An Empirical Analysis of the Economic Espionage Act*, 40 CARDOZO L. REV. 749 (2018).

46. *Id.*

47. Dexter Roberts, *Biden Makes a Habit of Dissing Chinese Innovation*, BLOOMBERG BUSINESSWEEK (2014), https://www.bloomberg.com/news/articles/2014-05-29/biden-makes-a-habit-of-dissing-chinese-innovation.

48. Yuko Kawai, *Stereotyping Asian Americans: The Dialectic of the Model Minority and the Yellow Peril*, 16 HOW. J. COMMC'NS 109 (2005).

49. MIA TUAN, FOREVER FOREIGNERS OR HONORARY WHITES?: THE ASIAN ETHNIC EXPERIENCE TODAY (1999).

50. *See e.g.*, Marika Cifor, *Acting up, Talking Back: TITA, TIARA, and the Value of Gossip*, 12 INTER-ACTIONS: UCLA J. OF EDUC. AND INFO. STUD. 1 (2016); JOSEPH CHEAH AND GRACE JI-SUN KIM, THEOLOGICAL REFLECTIONS ON "GANGNAM STYLE": A RACIAL, SEXUAL, AND CULTURAL CRITIQUE (2014).

51. Federal Bureau of Investigation, *The Company Man: Protecting America's Secrets* (2015), https://www.fbi.gov/video-repository/newss-the-company-man-protecting-americas-secrets/view.

52. Cifor, *supra* note 50.

53. *See e.g.*, Michael Park, *Asian American Masculinity Eclipsed: A Legal and Historical Perspective of Emasculation Through US Immigration Practices*, 8 MOD. AM. 5 (2012–2013).

54. LONG T. BUI, MODEL MACHINES: A HISTORY OF THE ASIAN AS AUTOMATON, 2 (2022).

55. Betsy Huang, *Premodern Orientalist Science Fictions*, 33 MELUS (2008).

56. BUI, *supra* note 54.

57. Lok Siu & Claire Chun, *Yellow Peril and Techno-Orientalism in the Time of Covid-19: Racialized Contagion, Scientific Espionage, and Techno-Economic Warfare*, 23 J. ASIAN AM. STUD. 421 (2020).

58. *Id.*

59. JAMES LARDNER, FAST FORWARD: HOLLYWOOD, THE JAPANESE, AND THE ONSLAUGHT OF THE VCR (1987).

60. Sony Corp. of America v. Universal City Studios, Inc., 464 U.S. 417 (1984).

61. *Home Recording of Copyrighted Works: Hearings Before the Subcommittee on Courts, Civil Liberties, and the Administration of Justice of the Committee on the Judiciary*, 97th Cong. (1981) (testimony of Jack Valenti), https://cryptome.org/hrcw-hear.htm.

62. Stanford M. Lyman, *The "Yellow Peril" Mystique: Origins and Vicissitudes of a Racist Discourse*, 13 INT'L J. POLS., CULTURE, & SOC'Y 683 (2000).

63. Roberts, *supra* note 47.

64. Yu, *supra* note 14.

65. *See e.g.*, Michelle Murray Yang, *At War with the Chinese Economic Yellow Peril: Mitt Romney's 2012 Presidential Campaign Rhetoric*, 45 J. INTERCULTURAL COMMC'N RSCH 45 (2016).

66. Sara Ahmed, *Affective Economies*, 22 SOCIAL TEXT 117 (2004).

67. *See e.g.*, ROSANA PINHEIRO-MACHADO, COUNTERFEIT ITINERARIES IN THE GLOBAL SOUTH: THE HUMAN CONSEQUENCES OF PIRACY IN CHINA AND BRAZIL (2017).

68. Marshall Cohen, *37 Times Trump Was Soft On Russia*, CNN (Nov. 11, 2019), https://www.cnn.com/2019/11/17/politics/trump-soft-on-russia/index.html.

69. *Id.*

70. *Foreign Economic Espionage in Cyberspace, supra* note 37.

71. Joseph Marks, *Analysis | Is Russia or China the Biggest Cyber Threat? Experts Are Split*, WASHINGTON POST (Jan. 20, 2022), https://www.washingtonpost.com/politics/2022/01/20/is-russia-or-china-biggest-cyber-threat-experts-are-split/.

72. *Id.*

73. *Id.*

74. Helen Holmes, *Putin's War on Intellectual Property Has Only Just Begun*, OBSERVER (Mar. 17, 2022), https://observer.com/2022/03/putins-war-on-intellectual-property-has-only-just-begun/.

75. Connie Neigel, *Piracy in Russia and China: A Different US Reaction*, 63 L. & CONTEMP. PROBS. 179 (2000).

76. *Id.*

77. Stephen Handelman, *The Russian "Mafiya,"* FOREIGN AFFAIRS, March 1, 1994, https://www.foreignaffairs.com/articles/russia-fsu/1994-03-01/russian-mafiya.

78. Daniel King, *There Are Many Words for Vladimir Putin. Is He Still Your "Strongman"?*, MOTHER JONES (Feb. 27, 2022), https://www.motherjones.com/politics/2022/02/there-are-many-words-for-vladimir-putin-is-strongman-one/.

79. Elizabeth Grimm Arsenault & Joseph Stabile, *Confronting Russia's Role in Transnational White Supremacist Extremism*, JUST SEC'Y (Feb. 6, 2020), https://www.justsecurity.org/68420/confronting-russias-role-in-transnational-white-supremacist-extremism/.

80. *See e.g.*, Cohen, *supra* note 68.

81. Vic Satzewich, *Whiteness Limited: Racialization and the Social Construction of "Peripheral Europeans,"* 33 SOCIAL HIST. 271 (2000).

82. *Id.* at 273.

83. Ian Law, *Review of Attaining Whiteness. A Sociological Study of Race and Racialisation in Russia*, 51 SOCIOLOGISK FORSKNING 87 (2014).

84. JASBIR PUAR, THE RIGHT TO MAIM: DEBILITY, CAPACITY, DISABILITY (2017).

85. Marina Levina, *Epidemiology as Methodology: COVID-19, Ukraine, and the Problem of Whiteness*, 19 COMMC'N & CRITICAL/CULTURAL STUDS. 112, 114–17 (2022).

86. DEBORA J. HALBERT, THE STATE OF COPYRIGHT: THE COMPLEX RELATIONSHIPS OF CULTURAL CREATION IN A GLOBALIZED WORLD (2014).

87. DYER, *supra* note 23.

88. *Id.*

89. Fang and Li, *supra* note 41.

90. *Id.*

91. *Id.* The remaining categories—Other Asian, Hispanic, Middle Eastern, Unknown, and Firm—are inapplicable to Russia.

92. *Id.*

93. RICHARD A. CLARKE AND ROBERT KNAKE, CYBER WAR: THE NEXT THREAT TO NATIONAL SECURITY AND WHAT TO DO ABOUT IT, 34 (2010). For instance, 74 percent of revenue from ransomware attacks goes to hackers linked to Russia. Joe Tidy, *74% of Ransomware Revenue Goes to Russia-Linked Hackers*, BBC (Feb. 14, 2022), https://www.bbc.com/news/technology-60378009.

94. Marcus Lu & Christina Kostandi, *A Recent History of U.S. Sanctions on Russia*, Visual Capitalist (2022), https://www.visualcapitalist.com/history-us-sanctions-on-russia/.

95. Steve Ranger, *Can Russian Hackers Be Stopped? Here's Why It Might Take 20 Years*, TechRepublic (2018), https://www.techrepublic.com/resource-library/downloads/can-russian-hackers-be-stopped-here-s-why-it-might-take-20-years-cover-story-pdf/.

96. Gregory F. Treverton et al., Film Piracy, Organized Crime, and Terrorism, Rand Corporation (2009).

97. Vats, *supra* note 20.

98. *See e.g.*, Mike Dillon, *The Immigrant and the Yakuza: Gangscapes in Miike Takashi's DOA*, Studies in the Humanities (June 1, 2012), https://www.proquest.com/docview/1539524714?pq-origsite=primo.

99. Michael Mukasey, *Remarks Prepared for Delivery by Attorney General Michael B. Mukasey at the Tech Museum of Innovation*, US Department of Justice (Mar. 28, 2008), https://www.justice.gov/archive/ag/speeches/2008/ag_speech_080328.html.

100. Kim Murphy, *Russians Able to Fake It Like No One Else*, Seattle Times (July 15, 2006), http://seattletimes.com/html/nationworld/2003128478_fakerussia15.html.

101. *Id.*

102. Vats, *supra* note 20.

103. King, *supra* note 77.

104. Thomas Nakayama and Robert Krizek, *Whiteness: A Strategic Rhetoric*, 81 Q. J. of Speech 291–301 (1995).

PART II

Access × Feminism

7

Accidental Abolition?

Exploring Section 230 as Non-Reformist Reform

Kendra Albert

Depending on who you listen to, Section 230 of the Communications Act is "the closest thing there is to a perfect law"; the "twenty six words that created the Internet"; a "subsidy" to tech platforms; or "a law [from] the 90's that lets tech companies get away [with catastrophic injuries]."[1] But most scholars do not cite Section 230 as an example of abolition of the police state or prison industrial complex, despite the fact that Section 230 may represent the largest single carve-out of people and entities from state criminal liability in US history.

This makes sense facially, because the original proponents of Section 230, Christopher Cox and Ron Wyden, do not have voting or public statement records that suggest that they were trying to get rid of policing. Nor, in 1996, when Section 230 was passed as part of the broader Communications Decency Act, was "abolition feminism" named in the way it is now, although certainly its organizing lineages reach back that far and further. But abolition feminism, a critique that comes out of both work against the prison industrial complex and feminist communities of color advocating against using the criminal legal system to address interpersonal violence, has much to teach us about how to think about Section 230.[2]

With a small number of exceptions created by the Fight Online Sex Trafficking Act of 2018, owners or operators of computer services cannot be held liable under state criminal law for the acts of their users, even when their behavior might otherwise rise to the legal standard of aiding and abetting.[3] This fact is usually framed as negative: "the Internet is lawless!"; "bad people will not be held accountable!" In this chapter, I approach Section 230 differently. I name the possibilities that Section 230 creates and use the tools of abolitionist feminism to explore the failure of many platforms and people to fully perform the imagining work necessary to make use of those possibilities.

Before I dive in, a caveat: I am not saying that Section 230 *is* abolitionist. Section 230 and most of the advocates who support it do not center the experiences of the formerly incarcerated and those most likely to be targets of the systems of violence of American policing (disabled/queer/trans Black people and people of color). This makes Section 230 a strange fit for the abolitionist framework or an analysis of non-reformist reforms. But yet, my own experience working on Section 230 has taught me that the same arguments that caution against criminal liability for online platforms apply more so to individuals. Thus, I position 230 similarly to how some advocates invoke the suburbs, with a full awareness that such an invocation is contested and appealing primarily to White readers and reinforcing the idea of abolition as absence.[4]

The work of abolition is not solely the elimination of the criminal legal system, policing, jails, or the policing of families. Rather, it requires imagining and creating the things that take the place of those systems. Section 230 has cleared space for such imaginings, and that the failure by major platforms to meaningfully make use of this space reinforces the call to be doing both forms of work at once.

Toward that imagining, this chapter proceeds as follows: I provide a brief background sketch on abolition feminism, and then I use the questions produced by Critical Resistance, an abolitionist organization, to explore whether Section 230 is an example of a non-reformist reform. Through that process, I also explain what it does. I close by reflecting on how tech platforms have generally failed to build meaningful non-carceral solutions in the absence of criminal liability.

WHAT IS ABOLITION FEMINISM?

Abolitionist or abolition feminism takes its name from those who fought against slavery. It is dedicated to rendering obsolete and eliminating the prison industrial complex and policing. As Mariame Kaba argues in her essay published during the George Floyd uprising, "We can't reform the police. The only way to diminish police violence is to reduce contact between the public and the police."[5] In short, abolition names that the problems that prisons attempt to solve are solvable by other means and attempts to build a world such that prisons are no longer necessary, at the same time as mobilizing and organizing for reduction in the power of carceral institutions.[6]

Abolition feminist work does not solely focus on policing. Its analysis has been extended to the child welfare system,[7] institutionalization of people with intellectual and developmental disabilities,[8] and borders.[9]

Although there are many lines to trace abolitionist feminism to, modern organizing that most directly relates to the work being done now started in the early 2000s, with conferences thrown by the anti-prison industrial complex group

Critical Resistance, as well as earlier work by INCITE! Women of Color Against Violence.[10] INCITE!, in particular, was a group of women of color organizing against domestic and intimate partner violence who rejected the move by the mainstream White feminist movements to use policing and carceral apparatus. Abolitionist organizing often focuses on local campaigns, to resist the construction of prisons, for example, or participatory defense, rather than broader legal or regulatory reform strategies.[11] By 2019, the *Harvard Law Review* dedicated an entire issue to prison abolition, after formative work by Amna Akbar, Dean Spade, and Allegra M. McLeod.[12]

Abolitionist feminist thinkers are engaged with technology. Stop LAPD Spying, a group based in Los Angeles, builds community power to abolish surveillance and policing, both methods that use technology and those that don't.[13] Sarah Hamid, an organizer with #8toAbolition and the Carceral Tech Resistance Network, has argued that technological reformers and critics have played a similar role to prison reformers.[14] Likewise, formerly incarcerated activists like James Kilgore have brought abolitionist advocacy to areas like ankle monitors and other forms of digital incarceration.[15]

Of course, it is not just those that explicitly name technology in their work that have something to say about technological developments in policing and surveillance. The idea that abolition feminism that does not explicitly discuss technology is not concerned with it has been rejected by many scholars. Abolition feminists often resist the move to segregate technology from other areas of policing. As an example, the consensus "why" document produced by carceral tech resistance network explains that "the history of carceral tech does not begin with computational policing or risk assessment algorithms. This kind of periodization only services police-adjacent academics, media, and system reformists."[16]

230 AS NON-REFORMIST REFORM?

A fundamental premise of abolition feminism is that reforming prisons is not possible—the system is not broken, it is working as intended.[17] Thus, all efforts at reforming the existing system must be evaluated in terms of their chances of retrenching those systems, ultimately making it harder to dislodge them or to imagine alternatives. The primary frame through which this evaluation is done is the idea of "non-reformist reforms," building on the work of Andre Gorz.[18]

Non-reformist reforms aim to reduce harm without entrenching existing systems. They are "determined not by terms of what can be, but what should be," and are reliant on and in relation to a fundamental modification of the relations of power.[19] But because abolition feminism is not just a theoretical framework but a living way of organizing, Gorz's more abstract idea only serves as a starting point. Organizers have developed tools to determine which steps serve to reinforce the criminal legal system, policing, and prisons, and which might serve to lessen its impact. In particular, a chart produced by Critical Resistance aims to help a reader evaluate if a particular step is an abolitionist step to end imprisonment.[20]

"Does a particular reform . . .

- reduce the number of people imprisoned, under surveillance, or under other forms of state control?
- reduce the reach of jails, prisons, and surveillance in our everyday lives?
- create resources and infrastructures that are steady, preventative, and accessible without police and prison guard contact?
- strengthen capacities to prevent or address harm and create processes for community accountability?"[21]

Section 230, as mentioned earlier, provides blanket immunity to the provider of an interactive computer service for claims under state criminal law where they would be held liable as the publisher or speaker of information from another content provider.[22] Generally, in order to claim immunity under Section 230, a person must show that (1) they are a provider or user of an interactive computer service, (2) the information for which the state seeks to hold the defendant liable was information provided by another information content provider, and (3) the claim seeks to hold the defendant liable as the publisher or speaker of that information.

This can be quite abstract, so let's take an example. If, for example, North Carolina passed a law making it a crime to aid and abet the sharing of information about self-managed abortion, online service providers whose facilities are used for this information could face criminal liability.[23] An online service provider (say a small forum) who had not banned their users from discussing abortion could be prosecuted under the law after a user self manages an abortion based on information shared by another user. But Section 230 would prevent the online forum from being held criminally liable for the speech of their users, even if it were found to rise to the level of aiding and abetting under state criminal law.[24]

Section 230 may eliminate state criminal liability for the online forum in that case. But is it a non-reformist reform under the Critical Resistance questions?

(1) Does Section 230 reduce the number of people imprisoned, under surveillance, or under other forms of state control, or (2) reduce the reach of jails, prisons, and surveillance in our everyday lives?.   Of course, the type of liability involved in our example or in most Section 230 cases is quite different than ordinary arrests based on street level surveillance. But nonetheless, Section 230 greatly reduces the reach of state criminal law online.

In these circumstances, Section 230 may at least partially serve as a non-reformist reform. It does reduce the number of people imprisoned/under surveillance/under other forms of state control by eliminating criminal liability for a particular population.

This risk reduction allows for online platforms to make more nuanced choices about how to handle speech without necessarily focusing on state criminal law as the primary arbiter. There have been instances in which platforms, because of the limits on their legal liability for online materials, have allowed for behavior that would have otherwise potentially been criminalized.[25] This created spaces that focused on harm reduction rather than overenforcement.

(3) Does Section 230 create resources and infrastructures that are steady, preventative, and accessible without police and prison guard contact?.   For the third question, the answer is more complicated. It is specious to suggest that the absence of criminal liability for the online speech of others has made internet infrastructure a cop-free zone. Online services are rich in information that leads to criminal prosecutions.

But it is true that many technology companies have built infrastructure for dealing with what would otherwise be criminal behavior that exists separate from that of traditional policing. For example, if Facebook removes a post for discussion of illegal drugs, it does not automatically report such a post to law enforcement.[26] Not so for child sexual abuse material, which earns an automatic referral to the National Center for Missing and Exploited Children (NCMEC), as required by federal law. Although it may not fit within the original imaginings of abolitionists who formulated the question, online platforms can create infrastructure for eliminating or reducing some forms of harm without police.[27]

(4) Does Section 230 strengthen capacities to prevent or address harm and create processes for community accountability?.   It is the fourth question posed about non-reformist reforms where Section 230 fails entirely. Although Section 230 may reduce the scope of potential criminal proceedings and thus the risk of state surveillance, those who make use of its benefits often have not meaningfully created alternative structures that allow for thinking beyond the law. It is true that online platforms are often infrastructures that do not depend upon the police. Section 230 fits well into the false imaginary of abolition as absence, like the suburbs.

But even in the absence of criminal law, online platforms engage with the harms they cause through a fundamental conservative and carceral frame. Rarely do we see online service providers devote time and energy to building in processes of meaningful community accountability, or resourcing those harmed by the side effects of the decisions they have made.[28] Section 230 may provide space to do things differently, but as Kate Klonick has articulated, when it comes to speech, platforms have ended up building on the American speech tradition,[29] and then basically speedrunning First Amendment law.[30]

In previous work, I called the role of laws in this space "talismanic," noting that they are evoked not for their actual legal requirements but to hold space for a set of arguments occurring elsewhere.[31] Experts such as Sarah Hamid, Rachel Kuo, and others have called this "carceral content moderation," noting that the binary "keep up or take down" model often exhibits the same lack of imagination as more carceral apparatuses, to say nothing of the way in which digital surveillance tools feed directly into real world policing.[32] In short, there is an utter failure of imagination to figure out what we could do differently, perhaps partially because of the sheer scale of major platforms content moderation efforts (which, of course, is no one's fault but the platforms and perhaps their investors).[33]

Despite that failure of imagination, or perhaps because of it, a number of scholars have begun to suggest abolitionist approaches to online spaces based on alternative, non-carceral models. In her essay in Logic Magazine, Niloufar Salehi lays out a restorative justice frame to approaching online harassment, centering on the needs of those who have been harmed.[34] Similarly, Sarita Schonenbeck and Lindsey Blackwall conceptualize a move toward accountability and repair, proposing governing principles that align social media platforms with frameworks separate from criminal punishment.[35] And as with abolition more generally, these efforts are not limited to the academy. Tyler Musgrave's work on Black women and Femmes' experiences with harassment show how users, whether platforms facilitate it or not, can transform the harm they experience.[36] These practical efforts and theoretical frames demonstrate Gorz's points that non-reformist reforms both imagine a different world at the same time that they build popular support.

REIMAGINING SECTION 230 AS ABOLITIONIST
ARGUMENT GATEWAY

Did Christopher Cox and Ron Wyden accidentally imagine something consistent with the work of Critical Resistance? No. And Section 230 might not even be a non-reformist reform. As it currently stands, its proponents and its primary beneficiaries have done the first part of abolition—the elimination of policing and criminal law; but not the second—the building of alternatives that transform violence and harm.[37]

But perhaps Section 230 can nonetheless serve as a gateway to abolition. Section 230 does have many advocates who would not identify themselves as abolitionists admitting that the imposition of criminal liability creates bad incentives and leads to unworkable solutions. In the context of Section 230, we often see widespread agreement that state criminal law is arbitrary, uneven, holds the wrong people to account, is fundamentally regressive, and does not successfully deal with real problems. Although not all of these are abolitionist arguments, it is fascinating to see critiques that could be crafted to describe the felony murder rule or conspiracy liability used to suggest avoiding online liability for online platforms. What does it mean that in the context of the internet, state criminal law has been accepted as an arbitrary, negative force, that prevents the operators of platforms from dealing with content in ways that genuinely promote harm reduction? How could that analysis be expanded to so many other spaces where criminal liability eliminates pro-social options? And how can this analysis be re-centered to focus not on platforms, but on those who bear the primary harms of policing?

If we can answer these questions, perhaps Section 230 could be abolitionist. It says, quite clearly, that there are places where criminal liability does harm, not good. It clears space for an imagined alternative. Perhaps, building on the work of feminists, we can imagine online communities that take seriously the responsibility to build non-carceral, community-based solutions to transform harm. Some of them may already exist. And if they do not, Section 230 might help us, if only we moved beyond absence to a politics of care.

NOTES

Thank you to Amanda Levendowski and Meg Leta Jones for their encouragement, flexibility, and always perceptive comments, to the group chats for everything, as usual, to Sarah Hamid for her clarity of vision, and to Rachel Kuo for both her writing and her labor in creating space for thoughts that aren't yet fully formulated. Finally, I owe a debt of gratitude to the many abolitionist organizers and experts outside of the academy. Their work, though not always citable in a traditional sense, is the ground upon which this piece is built. To them, and all the people who imagine different and better worlds, thank you.

1. Preston Byrne, *Section 230 is the Closest Thing There is to a Perfect Law*, @prestonjbyrne (July 26, 2022), https://twitter.com/prestonjbyrne/status/1551891254186745858; David Chavern, *Section 230 Is a Government License to Build Rage Machines*, WIRED, https://www.wired.com/story/opinion-section-230-is-a-government-license-to-build-rage-machines (calling Section 230 a subsidy for big tech); Jeff Kosseff, THE TWENTY-SIX WORDS THAT CREATED THE INTERNET (2019), Congressional Testimony from Carrie Goldberg, *Holding Big Tech Accountable: Targeted Reforms to Tech's Legal Immunity: Hearings Before the Subcommittee on Communications and Technology, of the House Committee on Energy and Climate*, 117th Cong. (2021).

2. *See, e.g.*, Angela Y. Davis, ARE PRISONS OBSOLETE? (2003); Ruth Wilson Gilmore, GOLDEN GULAG: PRISONS, SURPLUS, CRISIS, AND OPPOSITION IN GLOBALIZING CALIFORNIA (2007); Angela Y. Davis, et al., ABOLITION. FEMINISM. NOW (2022); Mariame Kaba & Andrea J. Richie, NO MORE POLICE: A CASE FOR ABOLITION (2022).

3. Section 230 does not immunize providers or users of online services against federal criminal law, but as well documented elsewhere, most criminal enforcement happens at a state, not a federal level. An additional caveat is that it is also unclear how much user behavior providers or other users would be liable for without 230, but given the fact that criminal law primarily results in plea bargaining rather than trial, 230's impact at eliminating the possibility of liability is profound.

4. josie duffy rice, *Many People in America Already Exist in a World Where Police and Prisons Do Not Exist. Go to Any Middle to Upper Class Suburb in America. Cops Arent Wandering the Streets. People Aren't Being Arrested. Neighbors Aren't Being Sent to Prison. and Generally Everyone is. . . . Fine.*, @jduffyrice (May 28, 2020), https://twitter.com/jduffyrice/status/1265957718260690944. *But see* Tamara K. Nopper, *Abolition Is Not a Suburb*, THE NEW INQUIRY (July 16, 2020), https://thenewinquiry.com/abolition-is-not-a-suburb/.

5. Mariame Kaba, *Opinion | Yes, We Mean Literally Abolish the Police*, NEW YORK TIMES (June 12, 2020), https://www.nytimes.com/2020/06/12/opinion/sunday/floyd-abolish-defund-police.html.

6. See Mariame Kaba, WE DO THIS 'TIL WE FREE US: ABOLITIONIST ORGANIZING AND TRANSFORMING JUSTICE, 20–22 (2021); Dylan Rodríguez, *Abolition as Praxis of Human Being: A Foreword*, 132 HARV. L. REV. 1575, 1577 (2019).

7. *See, e.g.*, Dorothy E. Roberts, *I Have Studied Child Protective Services for Decades. It Needs to Be Abolished*, MOTHER JONES (Apr. 5, 2022), https://www.motherjones.com/crime-justice/2022/04/abolish-child-protective-services-torn-apart-dorothy-roberts-book-excerpt/.

8. *See, e.g.*, Liat Ben-Moshe, DECARCERATING DISABILITY: DEINSTITUTIONALIZATION AND PRISON ABOLITION (2020).

9. *See, e.g.*, Anita Yandle, *Open Borders, Then Abolish Them*, ABOLITION AND DEMOCRACY 13/13 (Mar. 31, 2021), https://blogs.law.columbia.edu/abolition1313/anita-yandle-open-borders-then-abolish-them/.

10. *See History*, CRITICAL RESISTANCE, http://criticalresistance.org/about/history/. For a more general history, *see* Davis, et al., *supra* note 2.

11. *See Local Chapters*, CRITICAL RESISTANCE, https://criticalresistance.org/local-chapters/; Emily L. Thuma, ALL OUR TRIALS: PRISONS, POLICING, AND THE FEMINIST FIGHT TO END VIOLENCE (2019); see Kaba, *supra* note 6.

12. *Introduction*, 132 HARV. L. REV. 1568 (2019); Amna A. Akbar, *Toward a Radical Imagination of Law*, 93 N.Y.U. L. REV. 405, 410 (2018); Dean Spade, *The Only Way to End Racialized Gender Violence in Prisons Is to End Prisons: A Response to Russell Robinson's "Masculinity as Prison,"* 3 CALIF. L. REV. CIR. 184, 186 (2012); Allegra M. McLeod, *Prison Abolition and Grounded Justice*, 62 UCLA L. REV. 1156, 1161 (2015).

13. Stop LAPD Spying Coalition, STOP LAPD SPYING COALITION, https://stoplapdspying.org/ (accessed Sep 23, 2022); *see also* Stop LAPD Spying, *Co-optation and Counterinsurgency in Surveillance Reform*, LPE PROJECT (Mar. 15, 2022), https://lpeproject.org/blog/co-optation-and-counterinsurgency-in-surveillance-reform.

14. Sarah T. Hamid, *Community Defense: Sarah T. Hamid on Abolishing Carceral Technologies*, LOGIC MAGAZINE (Aug. 31, 2020), https://logicmag.io/care/community-defense-sarah-t-hamid-on-abolishing-carceral-technologies/.

15. James Kilgore, *Electronic Monitoring Is Not the Answer: Critical Reflections on a Flawed Alternative* (2015), https://mediajustice.org/wp-content/uploads/2015/10/EM-Report-Kilgore-final-draft-10-4-15.pdf.

16. *why //*, CARCERAL TECH RESISTANCE NETWORK (2020), http://carceral.tech/why.

17. Mariame Kaba, WE DO THIS 'TIL WE FREE US: ABOLITIONIST ORGANIZING AND TRANSFORMING JUSTICE (2021), at 13.

18. André Gorz, STRATEGY FOR LABOR: A RADICAL PROPOSAL (1967).

19. *Id.*, at 7–8.

20. *Reformist Reforms vs. Abolitionist Steps to End IMPRISONMENT*, CRITICAL RESISTANCE, https://criticalresistance.org/wp-content/uploads/2021/08/CR_abolitioniststeps_antiexpansion_2021_eng.pdf. *See also* Mariame Kaba, *Police "Reforms" You Should Always Oppose*, TRUTHOUT (Dec. 7, 2014), https://truthout.org/articles/police-reforms-you-should-always-oppose/.

21. *Reformist Reforms vs. Abolitionist Steps*, see *supra* note 20.

22. 47 U.S.C. § 230.

23. There would likely also be First Amendment challenges to such a law, but as Eric Goldman has argued, Section 230 may provide more procedural protection than the First Amendment. Eric Goldman, *Why Section 230 Is Better Than the First Amendment*, 95 NOTRE DAME L. REV. REFLECTION 33 (2019).

24. Reporting by Melissa Gira Grant has noted that as part of the passage of the Communications Decency Act, the bill that contained Section 230, the Comstock Act (a federal law that prohibits the distribution of information related to abortion) was broadened to cover online platforms. *See* Melissa Gira Grant, *A Forgotten 1990s Law Could Make It Illegal to Discuss Abortion Online*, NEW REPUBLIC (Aug. 1, 2022), https://newrepublic.com/article/167178/1990s-law-abortion-online-illegal-cda. Although this unfortunate addition is unlikely to be relevant to Section 230's state law preemptions, it does make the example choice more evocative.

25. *See, e.g.*, Melissa Gira Grant, *7 Sex Workers on What It Means to Lose Backpage*, THE CUT (Apr. 10, 2018), https://www.thecut.com/2018/04/7-sex-workers-on-what-it-means-to-lose-backpage.html.

26. Of course, this may be in part because it would be time-consuming or difficult to figure out who the appropriate law enforcement body is.

27. *But see* Rachel Kuo and Sarah T. Hamid, *Towards Collective Safety: Transformative Methodologies, in* FIRST MONDAY, SPECIAL ISSUE ON ONLINE HARM AND ABUSE, at 12 (forthcoming), noting that many forms of online violence have been turned into policing problems.

28. Facebook's funding of journalists notwithstanding.

29. Kate Klonick, *The New Governors: The People, Rules, and Processes Governing Online Speech*, 131 HARVARD LAW REVIEW 1598, 1618 (2018).

30. The idea of referring to this process as speedrunning is one I owe to Mike Masnick. *See, e.g.*, Mike Masnick, *Parler Speedruns The Content Moderation Learning Curve; Goes From "We Allow Everything" To "We're The Good Censors" In Days*, TECHDIRT (July 1, 2020), https://www.techdirt .com/2020/07/01/parler-speedruns-content-moderation-learning-curve-goes-we-allow-everything -to-were-good-censors-days/.

31. Kendra Albert, *Beyond Legal Talismans*, BERKMAN KLEIN CENTER FOR INTERNET AND SOCIETY LUNCH TALK SERIES (2016), https://cyber.harvard.edu/events/luncheons/2016/10/Albert.

32. See Rachel Kuo and Sarah T. Hamid, *supra* note 27, *citing* CTRN Organizers' Working Session: Police Surveillance and Platform Policies Workshop (Feb. 8, 2020), Camarillo, CA.

33. *See* Kuo and Hamid, *supra* note 27, at 17, explaining how the failure to "scale" is used as critique of transformative justice methodologies; *see also* Amy A. Hasinoff & Nathan Schneider, *From Scalability to Subsidiarity in Addressing Online Harm*, 8 SOCIAL MEDIA + SOCIETY, no. 3 (2022); Tarleton Gillespie, *The Fact of Content Moderation; Or, Let's Not Solve the Platforms' Problems for Them*, 11 MEDIA AND COMMUNICATION (June 28, 2023), https://www.cogitatiopress.com/mediaandcommunication /article/view/6610.

34. Niloufar Salehi, *Do No Harm*, LOGIC MAGAZINE (Aug. 31, 2020), https://logicmag.io/care/do -no-harm/.

35. Sarita Schoenebeck and Lindsey Blackwell, *Reimagining Social Media Governance: Harm, Accountability and Repair*, 23 YALE J. OF L. & TECH. 113 (2021).

36. Tyler Musgrave, Alia Cummings & Sarita Schoenebeck, *Experiences of Harm, Healing, and Joy among Black Women and Femmes on Social Media, in* PROCEEDINGS OF THE 2022 CHI CONFERENCE ON HUMAN FACTORS IN COMPUTING SYSTEMS 1 (Apr. 2022), https://doi.org/10.1145/3491102.3517608.

37. *Id.* ("Transformative justice is the work of building new models of justice and safety through accountability and harm repair practices that attend to the *root conditions* of violence and harm").

8

The Curb-Cut Effect and the Perils of Accessibility without Disability

Blake E. Reid

The *curb-cut effect* is an oft-observed phenomenon that occurs when technology designed to dismantle barriers to the accessibility of society for disabled people affords positive benefits—positive externalities or spillovers in economic terms[1]—for nondisabled people.[2] However, this chapter argues that unduly focusing on those benefits risks subordinating the needs and interests of disabled people in the development and application of disability and communications law aimed at technology accessibility in cyberlaw contexts.

Given the long-running discourse on the spatiality of cyberspace and its relationship to physical space,[3] it should come as no surprise that a critical phenomenon at the intersection of cyberlaw and disability law—the curb-cut effect—has its roots in the built world's rhetoric and technology. Indeed, the titular curb-cut effect is observed with the built-world technology of literal "curb cuts"—ramps "cut" into (or built up to) curbs on sidewalks and other walkways[4] that grew to prominence in part after a group of UC-Berkeley student wheelchair users who called themselves the "Rolling Quads" snuck out at night with attendants and literally mixed their own concrete to build ramps.[5] Physical curb cuts are nominally intended to ensure that disabled people who use wheelchairs, scooters, walkers, or other mobility devices can safely navigate to and from a walkway, avoid the danger of traveling in the street, where they risk being struck by cars, and access homes, public accommodations, and other buildings that must be accessed from the walkway. Yet physical curb cuts can be used to beneficial effect by nondisabled people pushing strollers, hand trucks, or grocery carts, or pulling luggage, runners, cyclists, skateboarders, roller-bladers, people who do not identify as disabled but have temporary injuries that require the use of mobility devices, and people using other wheeled tools and conveyances to easily transit to and from walkways that might otherwise be difficult or impossible to navigate.

More generally, then, the curb-cut effect has come to be known as the positive spillover that occurs for society (or some members thereof) when accessibility-oriented technology designed for disabled people benefits nondisabled people for purposes other than accessibility. Examples from the built world abound—for example, replacing or supplementing steps with ramps, adding elevators, widening entrances and doorways, clearing floor paths, and so forth, all confer similarly pluralistic navigational benefits to nondisabled people.

In cyberspatial discourse, the built-world rhetoric of curb cuts has transitioned to a shorthand for accessible affordances of virtual spaces, such as the inclusion of closed captions and image descriptions, the construction of web architecture to be compatible with screen readers, and software configuration settings to provide legible contrast for color-blind users. More generally, it includes the deployment of a wide range of technologies and techniques in and adjacent to virtual spaces to ensure their accessibility and usability by disabled users and compatibility with the assistive technology they use.

As curb cuts become virtual, the curb cut effect's built-world origins likewise have given way to an increasingly prominent role in cyberspatial contexts, as the first section of this chapter details. And, as the second section explains, the curb-cut effect is often cited as a benefit or even a justification for innovation in assistive technology and disability law and policy.

But as the third section argues, the Effect's repeated invocation over the past several decades has resulted in erasure, to varying extents, of disabled people from innovation and disability law and policy, with serious harms to disabled people and their civil and human rights to accessibility. This chapter closes by endorsing, highlighting, and building on the work of disability and design scholars who have raised concerns about the potential harms of the curb-cut effect—the benefits of spillovers notwithstanding—and concludes that law and policy efforts at the intersection of disability and technology should be wary of invoking or relying on the effect.

THE CURB-CUT EFFECT, TECHNOLOGY, AND UNIVERSAL DESIGN

The curb-cut effect is especially widely observed in information and communications technology.[6] Famous early examples chronicled by Steve Jacobs include the typewriter—initially designed for blind writers; the telephone—initially designed as part of Alexander Graham Bell's work with deaf people and evolved as part of Bell Labs' work on a suite of sound technology including the hearing aid; teletypewriters (TTYs), real-time communications devices that paved the way for both ARPANET, the predecessor to the internet, and modern instant messaging technology; and many more.

An oft-cited modern example is closed captioning—designed to convey spoken dialogue on video programming for deaf and hard of hearing viewers, but also used to improve access in bars, restaurants, hospitals, and other public or quasi-public places where social norms around noise prevent anyone from hearing a television's audio or require it to be muted. Another is optical character recognition, initially designed to help transform books for blind and other print-disabled readers but later applied in a wide range of business and other contexts.

The curb-cut effect is not always purely utilitarian, and often materializes in cultural and aesthetic contexts.[7] In another modern example, the popular Netflix show *Bridgerton* contains graphic audio descriptions of sex scenes widely enjoyed by nondisabled "superfans" of the show in what the Wall Street Journal describes as a "saucier" version of the curb-cut effect.[8]

The curb-cut effect has also come to be closely associated with the "Universal Design" movement. Generally speaking, Universal Design converts the descriptive observation of the curb-cut effect into a normative edict: technology should be designed to be accessible and usable by disabled and nondisabled people alike—"the broadest possible range of users."[9] A "blue ribbon" report prepared by a panel of advocates, technologists, and industry members in 1994 boldly declared that "Universal Design Is The Solution" to the problematic barriers to technology access faced by disabled people.[10]

THE CURB-CUT EFFECT IN THE LAWS
OF THE BUILT WORLD AND CYBERSPACE

The appeal of the innovation spillovers of the curb-cut effect has become so well-trod over time that it is often invoked in law as a justification for legal and policy interventions to improve accessibility for disabled people. For example, the Department of Justice waxed specifically about the curb-cut effect in justifying the benefits of its regulations implementing Title II of the Americans with Disabilities Act, which bars discrimination on the basis of disability in state and local government services:

> *Use benefits accruing to persons without disabilities.* . . . Even though the requirements
> were not designed to benefit persons without disabilities, any time savings or easier
> access to a facility experienced by persons without disabilities are also benefits that
> should properly be attributed to that change in accessibility . . . and ideally, all should
> be part of the calculus of the benefits to society of the rule.[11]

The curb-cut effect likewise played a large role in early discourse around the application of disability law. In one foundational example, Paul Schroeder of the American Council of the Blind, testifying at a hearing in the lead-up to the

Telecommunications Act of 1996, urged Congress to "ensure that electronic curb cuts are built into the information highway" and described technology accessibility mandates as an "important first step toward universal design"—an approach he described as making technology "equally accessible to and usable by the vast majority of individuals, including people with disabilities."[12]

Though telecommunications law is often missing from cyberlaw discussions, the curb-cut effect has featured prominently in the vein of telecommunications law and policy directed at the accessibility communications and video technology. While many of these examples predate the internet, I join authors including Karen Peltz Strauss in emphasizing the critical foundation role of telecommunications law in ensuring the accessibility of the internet technologies more traditionally associated with cyberlaw.[13]

For example, advocacy in the lead-up to the closed captioning provisions of the Television Decoder Circuitry Act of 1990 (TDCA)[14] specifically focused on the benefits of closed caption as a tool to improve literacy, including reading comprehension, language retention, and word retention.[15] In the final version of the TDCA, Congress explicitly alluded to the curb-cut effect, including specific findings that "closed captioned television can assist both hearing and hearing-impaired children with reading and other learning skills among adults" and "assist those among our Nation's large immigrant population who are learning English as a second language with language comprehension."[16]

In more modern contexts, the FCC has also deployed this rhetoric to support internet accessibility measures. When the FCC extended the '96 Act's closed captioning requirements to internet-delivered programming under the Twenty-First Century Communications and Video Accessibility Act, Commission Mignon Clyburn declared that "when captioning becomes a part of universal design, everyone wins," noting that in the context of captions in education, "hearing students see how words are spelled, and the visual text reinforces the message that they hear," that "all of this helps them learn how to read and write."[17]

Though an exhaustive survey is beyond the scope of this chapter, these examples illustrate how the curb-cut effect—as well as Universal Design and other integralist notions—has been an implicit or explicit basis for a degree of both accessibility-focused technological activity and law and policy developments aimed at improving the accessibility of technology.

THE PERILS OF THE CURB-CUT EFFECT

While the curb-cut effect has, as a result, helped bolster a range of well-intended and sometimes essential accessibility efforts, disability and design scholars including Liz Jackson[18] and Alex Haagaard[19] have begun to question its invocation. The Effect's addictive quality, both to policymakers and technologists, is one that risks substantial harms to disabled people by systematically losing the disability forest for the accessibility trees, subordinating (albeit unintentionally) disabled people to nondisabled people—addressing the interests and needs of disabled people only to extent their interests converge.[20] The harms of unjustly relegating the interests of disabled people to the often-narrow bounds of this convergence—however inadvertent—is a series of denials of quality, individualized accommodations, marginalization of disabled designers, unavailability and unaffordability of accessible products for disabled users, and the fluid invocation and revocation of disabled users in narratives about policy, law, and innovation without their consent or consultation.

ACCESSIBILITY AND QUALITY

One critical area where valorization of the curb-cut effect can disserve disabled people is in fostering misperceptions about the quality of technology actually required to break down accessibility barriers, and leading to nominal improvements that don't adequately serve the needs of disabled people. As Haagaard notes, "when designs that were meant to serve disabled people become 'for everyone,' disabled people and their specific needs as users often end up getting erased."[21]

In one foundational example, Haagaard analyzes the built-world technology of actual curb cuts, noting that most nondisabled people taking advantage of curb cuts simply need a sloped surface, not "too steep . . . and free from large cracks, holes, or dramatically uneven tiles."[22] But wheelchair users, Haagaard explains, need a range of additional features, such as a level transition and no gaps between the bottom of a curb cut.[23]

Shifting to a cyberlaw context, Haagaard's example rhymes with the delay faced by the deaf and hard of hearing community in seeking rules improvements to the quality of closed captions for video programming. After the initial implementation of closed captions in the late 1990s and early 2000s, they were regularly beset with inaccuracies, missing portions, long delays, and other features that limited to some degree their utility to people actually relying on them to convey the ground truth of video programming content.[24]

Quality issues can go beyond the basic fitness for purpose of accessibility measures in cyberspace to implicate broader issues of erasure. For example, Thomas Reid notes that audio description—the insertion of aural descriptive narratives about visual components of video during pauses in the soundtrack—frequently omits visible details about the race, ethnicity, and skin color of on-screen characters unless they are deemed by the describer to be sufficiently integral to the plot of a program to warrant specific mention.[25] This literal imposition of "color blindness," as Reid describes it, harms blind viewers by denying them access to the implicit racial dimensions of content while simultaneously erasing the identity of on-screen actors in a way that exacerbates long-running efforts to ensure representation in film and television.[26] Yet leading guidance on audio description quality subordinates blind audiences' interest in knowing the visual characteristics of on-screen actors to the interests of content creators, emphasizing that "content creators have the discretion and final authority over the content of audio description . . . consistent with the First Amendment" and suggesting that individual characteristics of on-screen actors, including skin color (and visible disabilities), need be described only "as relevant to the content" and need not "be described in each and every circumstance."[27]

More generally, implicit in Haagaard's analysis is that the proliferation of accessible technology via innovation and disability law and policy often follows initial enthusiasm for universally designed features with implementation and enforcement fatigue or even skepticism that leave details critical to disabled people unaddressed because no justifying benefit to nondisabled people is driving momentum forward. These themes are especially likely to materialize in cyberspatial contexts where generativity facilitates initially enthusiastic development of nominally accessible technologies that falls by the wayside as the difficulty of improving its quality increases and the perceived spillovers decrease.

One response to this critique is that it positions the perfect as the enemy of the good. Indeed, the quality of technology does not always reduce to a binary question of accessible or not. The foregoing examples illustrate that quality often implicates questions of degree and line-drawing about what, exactly, adequacy entails. And as Elizabeth Emens has persuasively argued, there is critical normative and practical import to integralist notions of highlighting benefits of accessibility to nondisabled people.[28] Nevertheless, even in situations where spillovers bring accessibility forward to some degree, the limits of those improvements not only may fall short of serving the needs of disabled people, but politically and legally constrain the prospects of making necessary improvements that can't be justified by reference to spillovers.

DENIAL OF ACCOMMODATION

Emphasis on the curb-cut effect can have more binary, existential effects beyond quality. These effects can become particularly pronounced in scenarios where measures to overcome technological inaccessibility must become more individualized, customized, and justified by reference to anti-subordination goals, rather than Universal Design.

Haagaard has taxonomized accessibility barriers and measures spatially into (1) physical barriers, such as curbs, and measures such as ramps to overcome them; (2) sensory barriers, such as aural and visual formats, and measures such as closed captions to overcome them; (3) cognitive/psychological/cultural barriers such as complexity and measures such as plain language translations to overcome them; and (4) temporal barriers that prevent people from individually participating in activities at particular places and times, and measures such as flexible asynchronicity to overcome them.[29] Haagaard explains that institutions are far more likely to support measures to overcome and correct physical and sensory barriers; less likely to support measures to overcome cognitive/psychological/cultural barriers; and even less likely to support measures to overcome temporal barriers.[30]

It is no surprise, then, in Haagaard's taxonomy, that measures to address physical and sensory barriers that can be deployed in a relatively turnkey, universalized fashion with positive spillovers for nondisabled people are more likely to be supported—in the cyberspatial context, the deployment of closed captions or compliance with basic standards for web development, for example. It is likewise no surprise that institutions are less likely to support cognitive/psychological/cultural and temporal measures that must be individually customized or allow flexibility for smaller groups' or individuals' needs, and thus are less likely to yield obvious positive spillovers for nondisabled people.

On the spectrum of this taxonomy, commitment to accessibility declines as disabled people increasingly emerge from a generic backdrop of a hypothetical, heterogenous crowd who all might benefit from generic accessibility interventions and increasingly confront the institution with their individual disabilities and needs and identify barriers that are more specific to them.[31] What results is a decidedly nonuniversal commitment to accessibility, materializing in institutions undertaking accessibility efforts that maintain barriers to disabled people when removing them does not serve the institution's nondisabled constituencies.

DENIAL OF CREDIT AND SUPPLY-SIDE DESIGN

Basic dysfunctionality of technology for disabled people is not the only problem that flows from the curb cut effect's (and Universal Design's) risk of erasure—it cuts through policy to the broader innovation policy of cyberspace—with ableist (and often sexist and other discriminatory) results.

In the built world, Liz Jackson has detailed how universal design often reframes disabled people as "'inspiration' rather than active participants," writing their "integral [role in] design processes" out of historical narratives.[32] Jackson chronicles the example of OXO's universally designed housewares, some of which were conceived by Betsey Farber as hacks to make her kitchen tools easier to use with arthritis, but which were popularly credited to, as she described it, "the brilliance and kindness of [her husband] who made these tools for his poor crippled wife so she can function in the kitchen."[33] Jackson highlights examples of erasure in cyberspace, such as Wayne Westerman, an electrical engineer with repetitive stress syndrome that developed touch-screen technologies foundational to modern smartphones and tablets, including the iPhone.[34]

This erasure is likely to materialize in cyberspace as well. For example, discourse about digital innovation is likely to disregard or minimize the contributions of disabled people because of what feminist scholar Laura Forlano has described as disabled designers,' hackers,' and makers' (though they may not identify as such) complex "socio-technical engagement" with their own bodies.[35]

Jackson notes that the "unique experiences and insights" of disabled people "enable [them] to see what's available to make things accessible," but that their "contributions are often overshadowed or misrepresented" in favor of "a story with a savior as its protagonist."[36] Jackson suggests that properly attributing credit for their contributions is critical to "attract disabled people to design" in the first instance.[37] Chris Buccafusco relatedly notes that this credit is broadly important to the success of supply-side innovation policies, such as patent law, in spurring accessibility by establishing "signaling value" for disabled designers, both for purchasers of their products and themselves.[38] More broadly, Jackson and Haagaard identify how these dynamics can "flatten" and erase disabled cultures and histories, often in ways that especially harm people with invisible disabilities, and intellectual and developmental disabilities, and Black and indigenous disabled people.[39]

DENIAL OF DISTRIBUTION AND SUPPLY-SIDE USE

These supply-side problems of the curb-cut effect can affect disabled people not only as innovators, but as consumers of technology.

In one foundational example, Jackson and Jai Verdi describe the long-running phenomenon of "adaptive clothing" designed for—and often claimed to be designed in collaboration with—disabled users.[40] These designs include, for example, featured double fabric under the arms for users of crutches, stylish bags to store hearing aid batteries, undergarments with Velcro closures, and other designs.[41] But as these designs became appropriated by large clothing labels, marketing narratives began erasing disabled people out of their roles as designers of and users of "adaptive clothing," and of their inspiration for the designs, for which clothing labels often claimed to be the originator.

As Verdi and Jackson explain, this period of inspiration is followed by a shift toward optimizing for the "mass appeal" of these products and erasure of the disabled user—and even the word "disabled"—from the sale of the product.[42] Finally, the product is made inaccessible to disabled users—priced out of reach[43]—or sold in limited, inaccessible venues.[44]

WRITING DISABILITY AND DISABLED PEOPLE
OUT OF ACCESSIBILITY

The curb-cut effect—along with Universal Design and other techno-social-political phenomena, including the infamous "Disability Dongle"—perpetuate what Jackson, Haagaard, and Rua Williams describe as a process of "reiterating a spectral technology for a virtual or hypothetical user [with disabilities]," thereby "continually re-produc[ing] the virtual user as an idea that is consumed and shared by nondisabled audiences online."[45] Connor Scott-Gardner and Alexa Heinrich have identified examples of this phenomenon, including the coopting of alternative text fields initially designed to contain descriptions of images for screen reader users for other material, such as jokes[46] or copyright management information such as photo credits,[47] and aesthetically pleasing ramps that are not actually accessible to wheelchair users, which take the curb-cut effect so far that disabled people are ultimately removed from the calculus altogether.[48]

By providing a foundation for writing disabled users in and out of narratives as is convenient for broader political, policy, technical, or economic reasons, the curb-cut effect can ultimately facilitate accessibility law, policy, and innovation—in cyberspace as well as the built world—from which disabled people do not benefit (or do not benefit adequately). Put in economic terms, the curb-cut effect can ultimately result in the conversion of accessibility from the primary goal of economic and legal/policy activity—from which positive spillovers for nondisabled people flow—to a spillover itself. That is, the curb-cut effect converts accessibility into an externality of an activity whose actors are superficially interested in accessibility but which does not treat disabled people as its primary constituents, or perhaps even as constituents at all.

Finally, the curb-cut effect's fluid insertion and removal of virtual/hypothetical disabled users from policy, law, and innovation narratives can happen over time. One particularly salient example is that of the widespread proliferation of video-conferencing—and, more generally, remote work—in the wake of the COVID-19 pandemic.[49] Though remote work was a frequently requested accommodation of disabled employees—for example, with mobility disabilities—prior to the pandemic, the courts and the Equal Opportunity Employment Commission routinely were skeptical and dismissive of treating remote work as a reasonable accommodation under Title I of the Americans with Disabilities Act.[50] The needs of disabled people simply were rejected from the narrative of in-person work.

Yet as the pandemic progressed and remote work become a regular feature of American office culture, disabled people often were written back into the narrative, as glowing commentary of the benefits for disabled people of remote work proliferated.[51] Accessibility literally became the spillover of a social phenomenon—for example, remote work—that disabled people had long demanded as an accommodation. At the same time, the shift to remote work created a wide range of negative externalities for accessibility, introducing new barriers for deaf and hard of hearing people, who often faced participating in meetings without captioning and sign language interpretation—a community, again, largely written out of the narrative.[52] And as executives have begun to pivot back to the alleged merits of in-person work, disabled people are starting to be written back out of the story.[53]

. . .

The curb-cut effect persists as an appealing, addictive narrative for policymakers and innovators looking to justify accessibility interventions and investments by reference to benefits beyond accessibility and to nondisabled people. But disability and design scholars rightfully suggest skepticism of deploying or relying on the effect. Policymakers and advocates should stay focused on accessibility for the sake of the civil and human rights of disabled people, and properly credit and respect their agency in narratives about accessibility, design, innovation, law, and policy.

NOTES

The opinions expressed here are my own and do not necessarily reflect those of my clinic, clients, any institutional affiliation, or anyone else. Thanks to Liz Jackson for her extraordinary generosity with conversations that seeded and crystalized many of the insights in this chapter, and for her foundational work on the perils of the curb-cut effect and an array of related concepts at the intersection of disability, technology, and design, including with her coauthors and collaborators, Alex Haagaard, Jai Virdi, and Rua Williams, whose work I am likewise deeply grateful for. Liz and Alex, who are not institutionally affiliated, have experienced significant citational injustice toward their work. *See* Liz Jackson, Alex Haagaard, and Rua Williams, *Disability Dongle* (Apr. 19, 2022), https://blog.castac .org/2022/04/disability-dongle/. It is my great hope that this chapter both celebrates their work as scholars and draws attention to its import for cyberlaw/technology law and disability law and policy. In equal measure, my thanks to Amanda Levendowski and Meg Jones for helpful framing conversations and for the generous opportunity to participate in this volume, and to Karen Peltz Strauss, Rabea Benhalim, Kristelia Garcia, Margot Kaminski, Nadav Orian Peer, Scott Skinner-Thompson, Bernard Chao, Zahra Takhshid, Viva Moffat, and Doron Dorfman for helpful feedback along the way, and to all my coauthors in this volume for their collective dedication of time and spirit. All errors and omissions are my own.

1. As Natalie Wright concisely explains, across disability communities, "some may prefer identity-first language (e.g., 'disabled person'), or person-first language (e.g., 'person with a disability')." *Functional Fashions*, Milwaukee Art Museum (May 7, 2019), https://blog.mam.org/2019/05/07/functional -fashions/. Following Liz Jackson, Alex Haagaard, and Rua Williams, this chapter uses identity-first language consistent with usage in their scholarship (*see* Jackson, Haagaard, and Williams in acknowledgements at top of notes), but acknowledges the diverse range of perspectives on this topic and the preferences of others for person-first language.

2. *E.g.*, Angela Glover Blackwell, *The Curb-Cut Effect*, STANFORD SOCIAL INNOVATION REVIEW (Winter 2017), https://ssir.org/articles/entry/the_curb_cut_effect. Elizabeth Emens has lauded the importance of and provided a rich taxonomy of spillover benefits of disability law obligations in the context of ADA workplace accommodations. *See generally* Elizabeth F. Emens, *Integrating Accommodation*, 156 U. PA. L. REV. 839, 840 (2008).

3. *See generally* Julie E. Cohen, *Cyberspace As/and Space*, 107 COLUM. L. REV. 210 (2007).

4. *See generally* Department of Justice, *ADA Best Practices Tool Kit for State and Local Governments*, chap. 6, https://www.ada.gov/pcatoolkit/chap6toolkit.htm.

5. *E.g.*, 99% Invisible, *Curb Cuts*, https://99percentinvisible.org/episode/curb-cuts/ (quoting and citing Deb Kaplan, Ed Roberts, and Steve Brown).

6. *See generally* Steve Jacobs, *Section 255 of the Telecommunications Act of 1996: Fueling the Creation of New Electronic Curb Cuts* (1999), http://www.accessiblesociety.org/topics/technology /eleccurbcut.htm.

7. *Cf.* Jasmine E. Harris, *The Aesthetics of Disability*, 119 COLUM. L. REV. 895, 896 (2019).

8. Robbie Whelan, *"Bridgerton" Is About to Get Saucier*, WALL STREET JOURNAL (Mar. 25, 2022), https://www.wsj.com/articles/bridgerton-superfans-embrace-audio-option-that-narrates-steamy-on -screen-action-11648223396.

9. *See generally* Eric Bergman, Alistair Edwards, Deborah Kaplan, Greg Lowney, T.V. Raman, and Clayton Lewis, *Universal Design: Everyone Has Special Needs*, Computer-Human Interaction (CHI) Conference (Apr. 1996), https://dl.acm.org/doi/pdf/10.1145/257089.257893.

10. Deborah Kaplan and John De Witt, *Telecommunications and Persons with Disabilities: Building the Framework: The Second Report of The Blue Ribbon Panel on National Telecommunications Policy*, World Institute on Disability (1994), https://park.org/Guests/Trace/pavilion/framewr1.htm. Universal Design, and related concepts such as integralism, are often also framed in complementary—and sometimes adversarial—terms relative to the anti-subordination goals of disability law. *See generally* Ruth Colker, *Anti-Subordination Above All: A Disability Perspective*, 82 NOTRE DAME L. REV. 1415, 1416 (2007) (discussing the tensions and dynamics of integration and anti-subordination approaches). Liz Jackson has also critiqued the evolving concept of "inclusive design" along similar lines. @elizejackson (July 5, 2022), https://twitter.com/elizejackson/status/1544359749709447168. In consideration of ongoing precarity and reliability of Twitter, archives of this Tweet and others referenced in this chapter are on file with author.

11. Department of Justice, *Nondiscrimination on the Basis of Disability in State and Local Government Services*, Final Rule (Oct. 11, 2016), https://www.ada.gov/regs2010/titleII_2010/titleII_2010_regulations .htm (emphasis original).

12. *See* S. 1822, *The Communications Act of 1994: Hearing Before the S. Comm. on Commerce, Science, and Transportation*, 103rd Cong. 790 (1994) (emphasis added), http://archive.org/details /s1822communicatioounit.

13. *See generally* Karen Peltz Strauss, A NEW CIVIL RIGHT (2006); Blake Reid, *Two Paths for Digital Disability Law*, 65 COMMUNICATIONS OF THE ACM 36 (May 2022), https://cacm.acm.org /magazines/2022/5/260349-two-paths-for-digital-disability-law/fulltext.

14. Pub. L. 101–431 § 3 (Oct. 15, 1990) (TDCA) (codified at Section 303(u) of the Communications Act of 1934 (47 U.S.C. § 303(u)).

15. *See generally* Strauss, *supra* note 13 at 230 (2006).

16. TDCA § 2(5)-(6).

17. *Closed Captioning of Internet Protocol-Delivered Video Programming*, Report and Order, 27 FCC Rcd. 787, 897 (2012).

18. *E.g.*, Liz Jackson, @elizejackson (Nov. 17, 2021), https://twitter.com/elizejackson/status /1460970716912930816 (on file with author).

19. *E.g.*, Alex Haagaard (@alexhaagaard), Twitter thread (May 20, 2020), https://twitter.com /alexhaagaard/status/1263216724448612353 (on file with author).

20. Cf. Derrick A. Bell, Jr., *Brown v. Board of Education and the Interest-Convergence Dilemma*, 93 HARV. L. REV. 518 (1980), https://www.jstor.org/stable/1340546?seq=1.

21. Haagaard, *supra* note 19.

22. *Id.*

23. *Id.*

24. The Commission adopted quality standards in 2014, though it punted a range of complex issues to a further notice of proposed rulemaking. *See generally Closed Captioning of Video Programming*, Report and Order, Declaratory Ruling, and Further Notice of Proposed Rulemaking, 29 FCC Rcd. 2221, 2291–2312, ¶¶ 121–67 (Feb. 24, 2014).

25. Thomas Reid, *In Living Color: Audio Description Looks Past People of Color*, BITCH MEDIA (Nov. 1, 2021), https://www.bitchmedia.org/article/color-blind-audio-description-inaccessibility.

26. *Id.*

27. Recommendation of the Federal Communications Commission Disability Advisory Committee (Oct. 14, 2020), https://www.fcc.gov/file/19830/download.

28. Emens, *supra* note 2 at 840.

29. Alex Haagaard, *Notes on Temporal Accessibility* (Mar. 12, 2021), https://alexhaagaard.medium.com/notes-on-temporal-inaccessibility-28ebcdf1b6d6.

30. *Id.*

31. These confrontations may be mediated under the rubric of what Jasmine Harris has described as the complex "aesthetics of disability." *Cf.* Harris, *supra* note 7.

32. Liz Jackson, *We Are the Original Lifehackers*, NEW YORK TIMES (May 30, 2018), https://www.nytimes.com/2018/05/30/opinion/disability-design-lifehacks.html.

33. *Id.*

34. *Id.*

35. Laura Forlano, *Hacking the Feminist Disabled Body*, JOURNAL OF PEER PRODUCTION (Mar. 2016), http://peerproduction.net/issues/issue-8-feminism-and-unhacking-2/peer-reviewed-papers/issue-8-feminism-and-unhackingpeer-reviewed-papers-2hacking-the-feminist-disabled-body/.

36. Jackson, *supra* note 32.

37. *Id.*

38. Christopher Buccafusco, *Disability and Design*, 95 NYU L. REV. 952, 965 (2020).

39. DSI, *Welcoming Liz Jackson and Alex Haagaard: Designers in Residence for Fall 2020* (July 30, 2020), https://web.archive.org/web/20220712002702/https://dsi.sva.edu/blog/welcoming-liz-jackson-and-alex-haagaard-designers-in-residence/.

40. Liz Jackson and Jaipreet Verdi, *Beyond Functional: Unraveling the Long Line of Disability Fashion*, BITCH MEDIA (Nov. 1, 2021), https://www.bitchmedia.org/article/disability-fashion-history-access-issue.

41. *Id.*

42. Jaipreet Verdi and Liz Jackson, *Why Won't Nike Use the Word* Disabled *to Promote Its New Go FlyEase Shoe?*, SLATE (Feb. 5, 2021), https://slate.com/technology/2021/02/nike-go-flyease-shoe-disabled-design.html; *see also* Brendan Dunne, *Disabled People Question Nike Over FlyEase Shoes*, COMPLEX (May 5, 2021), https://www.complex.com/sneakers/nike-go-flyease-sneakers-for-disabled-people?utm_campaign=sneakerstw&utm_source=twitter.com&utm_medium=social; Connor Scott-Gardner, @CatchTheseWords, Twitter (June 11, 2022), https://twitter.com/catchthesewords/status/1535597029673541633 ("accessibility doesn't have to be cool or appealing to non-disabled people for us to talk about it") (on file with author).

43. *Id.* The problem of pricing accessible technology out of reach of its nominally intended audience is not a new one. *See generally* Strauss, *supra* note 13, at 217 (describing the high prices that deaf and hard of hearing viewers faced to acquire early closed caption decoders).

44. Liz Jackson and Jaipreet Verdi, *Olay's New Lid Was Made for Disabled People. Too Bad You Can't Find It in Stores*, FAST COMPANY (Nov. 15, 2021), https://www.fastcompany.com/90696611/olays-new-lid-was-made-for-disabled-people-too-bad-you-cant-find-it-in-stores (describing similar offerings from Olay, P&G, and LEGO).

45. Jackson, Haagaard, and Williams (see acknowledgments at top of notes).

46. This is a construct long-employed by the popular webcomic xkcd: xkcd.com (accessed June 16, 2022).

47. E.g. Alexa Heinrich, @HashtagHeyAlexa (June 4, 2022), https://twitter.com/HashtagHeyAlexa/status/1533208238736429061 (on file with author).

48. Scott-Gardner, *supra* note 42.

49. *See generally* Arlene S. Kanter, *Remote Work and the Future of Disability Accommodations*, 107 Cornell L. Rev. 1927 (2022); Blake E. Reid, Christian Vogler, and Zainab Alkebsi, *Telehealth and Telework Accessibility in a Pandemic-Induced Virtual World*, Colo. L. Rev. Forum (Nov. 9, 2020), https://lawreview.colorado.edu/digital/telehealth-and-telework-accessibility-in-a-pandemic-induced -virtual-world/.

50. *See generally* Kate Strickland, *Remote Work as a Reasonable Accommodation: Implications from the COVID-19 Pandemic*, Harvard Civil Rights-Civil Liberties Review (Nov. 4, 2021). Though this example focuses on remote work, similar examples abound in virtual education, telehealth, and other contexts. *See, e.g.*, Reid, Vogler, and Alkebsi, *supra* note 49.

51. *E.g.*, Marcy Klipfel, *How the New Normal of Remote Work Evens the Playing Field for Workers with Disabilities*, Forbes (Dec. 28, 2020), https://www.forbes.com/sites/forbeshumanresourcescouncil /2021/12/28/how-the-new-normal-of-remote-work-evens-the-playing-field-for-workers-with -disabilities/; Nicolle Liu, *Neurodiverse Candidates Find Niche in Remote Cybersecurity Jobs*, Wall Street Journal (Apr. 13, 2022), https://www.wsj.com/articles/neurodiverse-candidates-find-niche -in-remote-cybersecurity-jobs-11649842380.

52. *See* Reid, Vogler, and Alkebsi, *supra* note 49.

53. *E.g.*, Aria Bendix, *Musk Is Pushing Staff Back to the Office, but the Research Is Only Partly on His Side*, NBC News (June 8, 2022), https://www.nbcnews.com/news/us-news/elon-musk-staff-back -office-research-mixed-rcna32136. Doron Dorfman describes how suspicion of remote work has arisen during the progression of the pandemic as a version of what he calls "the disability con." Doron Dorfman, *Pandemic 'Disability Cons'*, 49 Journal of Law, Medicine & Ethics 401 (2021). Jasmine Harris more optimistically argues that the shift toward remote work will require employers to change their approach to accommodations. *See* Erin Prater, *Long COVID Is a New Disability Affecting Millions of Workers—and a 'Moment of Essential Innovation' for Employers, One Lawyer Contends*, Fortune (June 5, 2022), https://fortune.com/well/2022/06/05/long-covid-new-disability-moment-essential-innovation -for-employers-lawyer-contends/.

9

———

Uncovering Online Discrimination
When Faced with Legal Uncertainty
and Corporate Power

Esha Bhandari

Imagine an increasingly common scenario: you apply for a job through an online platform that connects employers to jobseekers. You send your materials into the void and then never hear back. You might assume this was because you didn't meet the criteria for the job or because the company was overwhelmed with applicants who did. You might be perturbed to learn that a human never reviewed your application—a computer determined you weren't qualified—but perhaps you're resigned to that reality. But how would you react if you knew that the jobs platform used a ranking algorithm that systematically ranked women lower than equally qualified men applying for the job, and that's why the employer never interviewed you?[1]

As upsetting as it would be to learn that you were discriminated against in the job-seeking process, it is in fact more likely that you would never find that information out at all. Most people using websites and mobile applications have no information about the hidden automated processes that are used to determine who gets certain opportunities online. Companies that run platforms don't generally reveal details about the algorithms they use or whether those algorithms discriminate on the basis of race, gender, age, disability, or other protected class status under civil rights laws—including because they have self-interested reasons not to voluntarily provide information that could render them liable for discrimination. Uncovering this type of discrimination therefore often requires some form of adversarial testing by researchers or journalists, using techniques designed to assess the workings of automated processes online.

117

But there is a barrier to a robust environment of online accountability research and journalism. The United States continues to have an uncertain legal environment for adversarial civil rights testing and research online due to outdated computer crime laws that fail to accommodate and encourage digital-era research techniques.[2] These laws are focused on antiquated notions of "hacking" into closed computer systems and do not map neatly onto the online environment of today. Furthermore, the legal environment has given outsize power to corporations to control how and when their actions are evaluated for discrimination. Corporate terms of service, which are one-sided and drafted with the company's interests in mind, often prohibit using the techniques necessary for adversarial testing. The US Supreme Court's recent decision in *Van Buren v. United States* has gone a long way to clearing the threat posed by the federal Computer Fraud and Abuse Act (CFAA), a computer crime law that had long created the risk of federal criminal prosecution for those engaged in civil rights testing online in violation of website terms of service.[3] But even with that welcome advance, there remain state laws on the books that could pose a barrier to robust research. And corporate terms of service that are hostile to independent testing and research continue to create ambiguity in a legal landscape sorely in need of clarity.

For every researcher or journalist willing to conduct important research in the face of such uncertainty, there are likely untold numbers of others who would engage in such work but cannot in light of the risks attached—including those very members of communities most likely to be harmed by online discrimination, such as people of color. Others who may be deterred are researchers without tenure or graduate students on student visas, or independent journalists without the backing of a large newsroom with a legal team. Anyone potentially revealing wrongdoing by powerful corporations online must contend with the legal tools that could be used against them. Despite these concerns, there are promising developments in the law. Courts are increasingly recognizing the legitimacy of certain common online research techniques. And federal regulatory bodies are stepping up enforcement of civil rights laws online, which serves to encourage even more research into online discrimination.

This chapter argues that independent research and journalism is needed to address the growing problem of unchecked online discrimination, which is often invisible to the people affected by it. The chapter then examines the legal barriers that computer crime laws such as the CFAA have posed to independent testing of online platforms. It argues that while there have been promising legal developments, further clarity in the law is needed to assure researchers and journalists that they need not fear liability for their work. Lastly, the chapter notes that there are privacy considerations that should inform online research and journalism, and that efforts to address privacy concerns should proceed alongside efforts to clear away the legal hurdles to independent, adversarial online testing.

ADDRESSING THE PROBLEM
OF ONLINE DISCRIMINATION

The online world, for all its promise of greater access to knowledge and economic opportunities, has also ushered in a new era of discrimination. The structural inequalities of the real world are being replicated online, turbocharged by ubiquitous data collection and surveillance practices. Private companies have amassed vast amounts of data about online user behavior, much of it using methods that have given users no meaningful control over their information. The data can reveal particularly sensitive information about people, including their race, gender, sexual orientation, or disability status. And this sensitive information can, in turn, be used to determine which opportunities people are given.[4] Increasingly, some of the most important decisions that shape people's lives are mediated by algorithms and data in online settings.[5] Long-standing discriminatory practices in housing, credit, and employment are often replicated, and in some instances exacerbated, by internet services. Not long ago, many of these discriminatory decisions were made only after someone physically went to a bank, a rental company, or a job fair. But today, these activities have largely migrated online. Accordingly, if the promise of our civil rights laws are to be realized, we must understand how these online services—including websites and mobile applications—operate. Only by first uncovering discrimination online can we do something about it, including by robustly enforcing existing federal and state antidiscrimination laws in the digital realm, and designing additional laws and regulations to target new forms of digital-era discrimination.

We are a long way from the time when the internet held the promise of mitigating certain long-standing and persistent structural inequities in society. While early studies of the internet suggested that the anonymity of online transactions would close the gap for women and other groups who were historically discriminated against in the "real world" marketplace, that promise has faded away.[6] Now, corporations have amassed vast amounts of data about individuals, much of it through tracking our online activities. Online interactions are losing much of their anonymity, as tracking technologies allow websites and platforms to access all kinds of information about visitors, including information that may reveal race, gender, age, and sexual orientation.[7] Companies that operate commercial websites have access to massive amounts of data about internet users and can employ algorithms to analyze that data. Such "big data analytics" enables behavioral targeting, meaning that websites can steer individuals toward viewing different content on the internet.[8] Most critically for purposes of civil rights concerns, online targeting allows platforms to steer housing or credit offers or jobs on the basis of protected class status, such as race, age, or gender.[9] Behavioral targeting opens up vast potential for discrimination against marginalized communities.

The risks of discrimination can arise in a variety of contexts. Online ad targeting, for example, can be used to exclude users from seeing certain ads on the basis of race, gender, age, or other protected characteristics, as well as on the basis of proxies for those categories. Sometimes the ad targeting is done through choices on the part of the advertiser or the platform to select (or exclude) users with particular characteristics.[10] But other times the ad targeting occurs through an ad delivery algorithm or automated system that determines which users should see which ads—and those delivery systems can end up discriminating on the basis of protected characteristics. In the latter cases, ad delivery algorithms can discriminate in who sees an ad because of large skews in underlying metrics that inform the algorithm.[11] For example, an ad delivery system that shows ads to users based on whether they share characteristics with existing employees in a certain industry could replicate the bias in that industry—systematically showing the ad to fewer women and nonbinary people, for example, for technology or engineering jobs because of long-standing underrepresentation in those fields.[12] This discrimination in ad delivery might occur even if the employer is not aware of and does not want such discriminatory ad delivery.[13]

Discrimination in ads online is particularly pernicious because users will rarely, if ever, be aware of what ads they were not shown. In the offline world, a woman might see a job ad for "Men Only" and be able to raise a complaint of discrimination. But online, that same woman might never see the job opportunity that an advertising platform showed only to men, and never know she was discriminated against. After all, we seldom have a way to identify the ads we're *not* seeing online.[14] That this discrimination is invisible to the excluded user makes it all the more difficult to stop.

Another example of online discrimination is when hiring platforms serve a matching function between employers and jobseekers. These platforms can use automated systems, or algorithms, to rank candidates for jobs, or even to eliminate candidates from eligibility.[15] Individual applicants using such a system might never know why they didn't get the job, let alone whether the ranking algorithm systematically discriminates against people on the basis of a protected class status. In such cases, even the employers might not know that the platform they are using is discriminating in the candidates it highlights for them.

These examples are not exhaustive, but illustrative of the larger problem of identifying discrimination online, where individual users may not even be aware of the systems that are operating to deny them opportunities. And all of this discrimination has been fueled by business practices in which individuals have had no meaningful choice in the information they give up to online services, nor any control over whether that information ends up in the hands of other companies or potential landlords, realtors, or employers.[16]

These discriminatory practices persist despite increasing enforcement of antidiscrimination laws against online platforms in recent years. Meta (formerly Facebook), for example, has faced multiple lawsuits and federal enforcement action regarding its online ad targeting and delivery system, for violating the federal Fair Housing Act and other civil rights laws, leading to major changes to its ad platform.[17] These lawsuits were enabled by the work of journalists and researchers who uncovered discrimination in the platform's ad system.[18] But despite such recent enforcement actions raising the prospect of potential liability, the industry is slow to change, and there is a need for much more research into a wider variety of platforms and actors in the online ecosystem.[19]

PROGRESS IN RESOLVING LEGAL BARRIERS TO CIVIL RIGHTS TESTING ONLINE

The problem of rampant and unchecked online discrimination requires robust accountability research and journalism to hold platforms accountable. This type of civil rights testing has long been common in the offline world, and yet online civil rights testing faces unjustified barriers because of an uncertain legal environment. These barriers include open questions about how computer crime laws intersect with common online research techniques, including creating tester accounts with fictitious user information or scraping data. Scraping is a method of collecting information from the internet that generally involves programming automated queries to retrieve content, without using a web browser or application programming interface. Scraping allows for efficient collection of large amounts of information that might be impracticable for someone to record manually.[20]

In the offline world, adversarial testing has long been used to enforce the guarantees of civil rights laws, such as the federal Fair Housing Act, Title VII of the Civil Rights Act (which prohibits discrimination in employment), the Age Discrimination in Employment Act, and the Equal Credit Opportunity Act. A method called audit testing, for example, has long been recognized as a crucial way to uncover racial discrimination in housing and employment. This technique involves pairing individuals of different races to pose as home- or job-seekers to determine whether they are treated differently.[21] A correspondence test can involve auditors submitting two job applications for fictional applicants who vary only with respect to racial or gender signifiers, and comparing results.[22] The law has protected the ability to engage in such misrepresentation in the offline world during the course of civil rights testing, regardless of whether businesses would rather not deal with applicants who are not real.[23]

In the online world, however, conducting the same kind of audit testing generally violates websites' terms of service, which often prohibit providing false information, creating multiple user profiles, or using automated methods of recording the information displayed for different users, such as scraping. Yet there is often no way to conduct systematic testing of online platforms for discrimination without doing these things—such as creating tester accounts with fictitious user information that varies by gender or race, searching for jobs online through those accounts to see how results differ for each fictional user, and recording those results efficiently through scraping. Some terms of service simply prohibit any uses not specifically allowed by the platform, thereby targeting not any one particular technique but effectively banning all testing whatsoever.[24]

Computer crime laws, most notably the CFAA, have long served as a deterrent to such testing because they could render violations of website terms of service into criminal violations. The CFAA is a federal anti-hacking law from the 1980s that has proven ill-suited to the modern internet. For many years, the federal government and some courts interpreted its prohibition on "exceed[ing] authorized access" to a computer to prohibit visiting a website and violating its terms of service— even though such terms are unilaterally imposed, self-serving conditions written by companies (and largely unread by most internet users).[25] This interpretation risked turning everyday internet behavior, such as using a pseudonym on social media, into a crime.[26] And it meant that anyone conducting adversarial research, journalism, or testing of a platform for discrimination had to worry about whether they could be subject to prosecution or civil liability for going against a company's terms of service in doing so. Unsurprisingly, some researchers, especially those who are themselves marginalized or vulnerable in the face of legal threats, understandably chose to forgo investigations they might have otherwise undertaken.[27]

This is why the Supreme Court's decision in 2021 in *Van Buren v. United States* was a welcome step in easing one of the major hurdles to such research. At first glance, the case does not seem obviously related to civil rights enforcement. It concerned a police officer who searched for information about a license plate in a law enforcement database in exchange for money.[28] The officer was criminally charged with "exceed[ing] authorized access" under the CFAA because he violated his employer's computer use policies. The Supreme Court held that the CFAA should not be read to criminalize violations of computer use policies alone. Instead it should be read to prohibit behavior that is akin to breaking and entering—such as in the course of accessing parts of a computer that someone does not have authority to access at all.[29] By narrowing the scope of the CFAA, the decision has cleared the way for researchers and journalists to use common investigative techniques online without worrying that violating terms of service alone will subject them to liability under the CFAA.

The *Van Buren* decision came after a lower court decision that had explicitly considered the claims of civil rights researchers. The federal district court in *Sandvig v. Barr* held that the CFAA should not be read to criminalize terms of service violations, in a lawsuit brought by academic researchers who argued that they had a First Amendment right to conduct their discrimination testing online, including through creating fictitious tester accounts. Such fictitious accounts would allow the

researchers to test how platforms treat similar users who vary only by a controlled variable, such as race, gender, or age.[30] The court concluded that the CFAA did not apply to barring the researchers' proposed online testing activities, and thus did not need to reach their claim that the First Amendment protected those activities.

Even with the Supreme Court's decision in *Van Buren*, however, questions remain about various legal issues affecting adversarial online discrimination testing. All fifty states have computer crime laws, many of which are analogous to their federal counterpart and have been interpreted consistently with the CFAA.[31] While *Van Buren* should prove persuasive in similarly limiting application of those computer crime laws to violations of terms of service, there remains ambiguity absent definitive constructions of those laws in state courts. And the courts have also been inconsistent on the enforceability of website terms of service in contract, which can also act as a deterrent to research.[32]

There also remain questions about the application of the CFAA and other computer crime laws to research techniques where the threatened liability does not stem from violations of terms of service, but rather from whether the particular research technique might be deemed the equivalent of "breaking and entering" a system (for example, through the use of password sharing for user accounts or bypassing Internet Protocol [IP] address barriers).[33] One of the challenges of adversarial testing online is that platforms may implement technical barriers to prohibit scraping and other common research methods. Platforms might also suspend or remove specific accounts they identify as researcher accounts.[34] While these challenges might inhibit or prevent testing of certain platforms, in other cases they may spur innovation in research techniques, as a result of the adversarial back-and-forth between independent testers and the platforms that seek to shut them out. For this reason, it is important that courts provide more definitive guidance on the types of technical barriers that researchers can bypass without running afoul of computer crime laws that are focused on notions of trespass.

And yet, courts have been slow to address the legality of particular research methods online even as data journalism, online auditing, and other digital-era research methods have adapted to keep pace with the systems they are studying. A recent decision by a federal district court, for example, held that the South Carolina State Conference of the NAACP had stated a First Amendment claim to scrape public housing court records in order to efficiently reach tenants in eviction proceedings to provide them with services to fight those evictions.[35] That decision denying a motion to dismiss the case is one of the few in which courts have explicitly considered the legality of scraping as a research technique, despite the fact that the practice is exceedingly common, both for research and commercial purposes.[36]

Recent caselaw concerning the First Amendment limitations on laws restricting access to agricultural facilities for the purpose of undercover investigations— so called "ag-gag" laws—may prove relevant to securing the right to engage in online research. Courts have struck down some laws that restrict the ability to record in agricultural facilities, or to provide misleading information about one's intent in gaining access to such facilities, in part because they are targeted only at critics of those facilities.[37] These cases may provide support for the claims of online civil rights testers, particularly because platforms (in a manner similar to agricultural facility owners) often assert rights of property ownership or control to prohibit adversarial researchers from accessing or recording information on their platforms that is available to other users.

Finally, there are, of course, privacy considerations that online civil rights testing, research, or journalism in the public interest must consider. This tension is not new to the digital era—even offline efforts at antidiscrimination testing and research have privacy implications, particularly when they involve collecting sensitive data on protected class status such as race, sexual orientation, or disability. The tensions between individual privacy considerations and the need for research data to advance equality have existed for a long time, and merit special consideration in the digital era. Never before has so much data about so many people been potentially available. With the mission to advance the public good through adversarial platform research also comes a heavy responsibility for the people doing that work. It is beyond the scope of this piece to outline specific policies, ethical guidelines, or security best practices that should be adopted by online civil rights researchers. But others are engaged in that endeavor, which should proceed simultaneously with efforts to clear away legal barriers to such research.[38]

CONCLUSION

Much of what we know about the world of online discrimination today is thanks to researchers, academics, and journalists who have conducted online testing and research to which the subject companies did not consent. This critically important work must continue in order for the promise of our civil rights laws to be realized online, and in order for us to adapt our laws and policies to the new world of discrimination enabled by the digital era. While the Computer Fraud and Abuse Act has long posed a significant hurdle to online civil rights testing by creating the risk of criminal prosecution for necessary research techniques, the legal environment is shifting slowly in the direction of greater clarity, so that researchers don't have to bear the burden of potential liability for their work that serves the public good.

NOTES

Thank you to Rachel Goodman and Galen Sherwin for collaborating on developing the ideas reflected in this piece, to Mitra Ebadolahi for her comments, and to Amanda Levendowski for shepherding the project.

1. Such a hypothetical is not fanciful. Amazon stopped developing an automated hiring tool that was demonstrating bias against female job candidates. *See* Jeffrey Dastin, *Amazon Scraps Secret AI Recruiting Tool That Showed Bias against Women*, REUTERS (Oct. 18, 2018), https://www.reuters.com/article/us-amazon-com-jobs-automation-insight/amazon-scraps-secret-ai-recruiting-tool-that-showed-bias-against-women-idUSKCN1MK08G.

2. *See, e.g.*, 18 U.S.C. § 1030 *et seq.* (Computer Fraud and Abuse Act); *see generally* Orin S. Kerr, *Norms of Computer Trespass*, 116 COLUM. L. REV. 1143 (2016) (arguing that courts have struggled to interpret computer trespass laws, with some imposing liability for trivial wrongs such as violating website terms of service).

3. *Van Buren v. United States*, 141 S. Ct. 1648 (2021).

4. *See generally* Solon Barocas & Andrew D. Selbst, *Big Data's Disparate Impact*, 104 CALIF. L. REV. 671 (2016).

5. *See generally* Safiya Umoja Noble, ALGORITHMS OF OPPRESSION: HOW SEARCH ENGINES REINFORCE RACISM (2018); Virginia Eubanks, AUTOMATING INEQUALITY: HOW HIGH-TECH TOOLS PROFILE, POLICE, AND PUNISH THE POOR (2018).

6. *See, e.g.*, Fiona Scott Morton, et al., *Consumer Information and Discrimination: Does the Internet Affect the Pricing of New Cars to Women and Minorities?*, 1 QUANTITATIVE MARKETING AND ECONOMICS 65–92 (2003), https://doi.org/10.1023/A:1023529910567.

7. Characteristics such as race, or perceived race, can be inferred even when users do not explicitly provide that information. Pioneering early studies have demonstrated the persistence of racial bias online. *See, e.g.*, Latanya Sweeney, *Discrimination in Online Ad Delivery*, 11 ACM QUEUE 1 (2013); Benjamin Edelman, et al., *Racial Discrimination in the Sharing Economy: Evidence from a Field Experiment*, 9 AM. ECON. J. APPLIED ECON. 1 (2017).

8. Beginning as far back as 2014, the federal government released a series of reports highlighting the discriminatory potential in the era of "big data." *See* Exec. Office of the President, *Big Data: Seizing Opportunities, Preserving Values* (2014); Fed. Trade Comm'n, *Big Data: A Tool for Inclusion or Exclusion?* (2014); Exec. Office of the President, *Big Data: A Report on Algorithmic Systems, Opportunity, and Civil Rights* (2016).

9. *See, e.g.*, Samuel Gibbs, *Women Less Likely to Be Shown Ads for High-Paid Jobs on Google, Study Shows*, THE GUARDIAN (July 8, 2015), https://www.theguardian.com/technology/2015/jul/08/women-less-likely-ads-high-paid-jobs-google-study; Byron Spice, *Questioning the Fairness of Targeting Ads Online*, CARNEGIE MELLON UNIVERSITY NEWS (July 7, 2015), https://www.cmu.edu/news/stories/archives/2015/july/online-ads-research.html.

10. *See* Julia Angwin, et al., *Facebook (Still) Letting Housing Advertisers Exclude Users by Race*, PROPUBLICA (Nov. 21, 2017).

11. *See* Muhammad Ali, et al., *Discrimination through Optimization: How Facebook's Ad Delivery Can Lead to Biased Outcomes*, Proceedings of the ACM on Human-Computer Interaction (2019), available at arXiv:1904.02095.

12. *See* Rachel Goodman, *Why Amazon's Automated Hiring Tool Discriminated against Women*, ACLU NEWS AND COMMENTARY (Oct. 12, 2018), https://www.aclu.org/blog/womens-rights/womens-rights-workplace/why-amazons-automated-hiring-tool-discriminated-against.

13. Piotr Sapiezynski, et al., *Algorithms That "Don't See Color": Comparing Biases in Lookalike and Special Ad Audiences*, Proceedings of the 2022 AAAI/ACM Conference on AI, Ethics, and Society (Dec. 17, 2019), https://arxiv.org/abs/1912.07579.

14. Aaron Rieke and Miranda Bogen, *Help Wanted: An Examination of Hiring Algorithms, Equity, and Bias*, UPTURN (Dec. 10, 2018), https://www.upturn.org/work/help-wanted/ ("The complexity and opacity of digital advertising tools make it difficult, if not impossible, for aggrieved jobseekers to spot discriminatory patterns of advertising in the first place").

15. *Id.*

16. *See* Rick Edmonds, *People Don't Want to Trade Privacy for Targeted Ads*, POYNTER (Jan. 14, 2016), https://www.poynter.org/business-work/2016/people-dont-want-to-trade-privacy-for-targeted-ads.

17. *See* US Dep't of Justice, *Justice Department and Meta Platforms Inc. Reach Key Agreement as They Implement Groundbreaking Resolution to Address Discriminatory Delivery of Housing Advertisements* (Jan. 9, 2023), https://www.justice.gov/opa/pr/justice-department-and-meta-platforms-inc-reach-key-agreement-they-implement-groundbreaking; Ariana Tobin & Ava Kofman, *Facebook Finally Agrees to Eliminate Tool That Enabled Discriminatory Advertising*, PROPUBLICA (June 22, 2022), https://www.propublica.org/article/facebook-doj-advertising-discrimination-settlement; US Dep't of Justice, *Justice Department Secures Groundbreaking Settlement Agreement with Meta Platforms, Formerly Known as Facebook, to Resolve Allegations of Discriminatory Advertising* (June 21, 2022), https://www.justice.gov/opa/pr/justice-department-secures-groundbreaking-settlement-agreement-meta-platforms-formerly-known; Esha Bhandari & Galen Sherwin, *Facebook Settles Civil Rights Cases by Making Sweeping Changes to Its Online Ad Platform*, ACLU NEWS AND COMMENTARY (Mar. 19, 2019), https://www.aclu.org/news/womens-rights/facebook-settles-civil-rights-cases-making-sweeping.

18. Ariana Tobin & Ava Kofman, *Facebook Finally Agrees to Eliminate Tool That Enabled Discriminatory Advertising*, PROPUBLICA (June 22, 2022), https://www.propublica.org/article/facebook-doj-advertising-discrimination-settlement.

19. *See* Jeremy B. Merrill, *Google Has Been Allowing Advertisers to Exclude Nonbinary People from Seeing Job Ads*, THE MARKUP (Feb. 11, 2021), https://themarkup.org/google-the-giant/2021/02/11/google-has-been-allowing-advertisers-to-exclude-nonbinary-people-from-seeing-job-ads.

20. *See* Andrew Sellers, *Twenty Years of Web Scraping and the Computer Fraud and Abuse Act*, 4 B.U. J. Sci. & Tech. L. 372, 372, 381–88 (2018).

21. *See, e.g.*, US Dep't of Housing and Urban Development, Office of Policy Development and Research, *Housing Discrimination against Racial and Ethnic Minorities* 2012 xi, http://www.huduser.gov/portal//Publications/pdf/HUD-514_HDS2012.pdf (government-sponsored study used paired-testing methodology in twenty-eight metropolitan areas and found that Black, Latino, and Asian testers were told about and shown fewer homes than white testers); US Dep't. of Justice, *Fair Housing Testing Program* (Mar. 5, 2019), https://www.justice.gov/crt/fair-housing-testing-program-1; Diane K. Levy, et al., *A Paired-Testing Pilot Study of Housing Discrimination against Same-Sex Couples and Transgender Individuals*, URBAN INST. (2017), https://www.urban.org/sites/default/files/publication/91486/2017.06.27_hds_lgt_final_report_report_finalized_0.pdf.

22. *See* Devah Pager & Bruce Western, *Identifying Discrimination at Work: The Use of Field Experiments*, 68 J. OF SOCIAL ISSUES 221, 223 (2012).

23. *See Havens Realty Corp v. Coleman*, 455 U.S. 363, 373 (1982) (testers have standing to sue for Fair Housing Act violations). Courts regularly acknowledge the importance of testing to enforce the Fair Housing Act, *see, e.g., Smith v. Pac. Properties & Dev. Corp.*, 358 F.3d 1097, 1102 (9th Cir. 2004); *Richardson v. Howard*, 712 F.2d 319, 321 (7th Cir. 1983); and Title VII, *see, e.g., Kyles v. J.K. Guardian Sec. Servs., Inc.*, 222 F.3d 289, 292 (7th Cir. 2000); *Fair Employment Council of Greater Washington, Inc. v. BMC Marketing Corp.*, 28 F.3d 1268, 1277–78 (D.C. Cir. 1994).

24. *See, e.g.*, Esha Bhandari & Rachel Goodman, *Data Journalism and the Computer Fraud and Abuse Act: Tips for Moving Forward in an Uncertain Landscape*, Northwestern Computation and Journalism Symposium (2017), https://cj2017.northwestern.edu/documents/data-journalism-cj2017-paper-23.pdf; Alex Abdo, *Facebook Is Shaping Public Discourse. We Need to Understand How*, THE GUARDIAN (Sept. 15, 2018), https://www.theguardian.com/commentisfree/2018/sep/15/facebook-twitter-social-media-public-discourse (discussing terms of service restrictions on Facebook and Twitter that impede digital journalism and research).

25. The Ninth Circuit Court of Appeals was one notable court to hold that the CFAA does not encompass mere violations of computer use policies. *See United States v. Nosal*, 676 F.3d 854 (9th Cir.

2012); *see also* Uri Benoliel & Shmuel I. Becher, *The Duty to Read the Unreadable*, 60 B.C. L. REV. 2255, 2296 (2019) (noting that the unilaterally imposed terms of most online services "permit online firms to contract with millions of users, with no negotiation, and without verifying that the contract was read [let alone understood]").

26. The federal government prosecuted someone under the CFAA for lying about her age to create a fictitious account on MySpace, in violation of that website's terms of service. Although the defendant allegedly used the account to cyberbully a minor, who subsequently died by suicide, the CFAA misdemeanor charges were for terms of service violations alone. The district court overturned the jury's guilty verdicts on those charges. *See United States v. Drew*, 259 F.R.D. 449 (C.D. Cal. 2009). For a critique of CFAA reform advocacy for failing to recognize that overcriminalization of everyday behavior is not a phenomenon limited to the Internet, *see* Kendra Albert, *Not a Crime: The CFAA and Respectability Politics*, TECH POLICY PRESS (Jan. 3, 2022), https://techpolicy.press/not-a-crime-the-cfaa-and-respectability-politics.

27. D. Victoria Baranetsky, *Data Journalism and the Law*, TOW CENTER FOR DIG. JOURNALISM (Sept. 19, 2018), https://www.cjr.org/tow_center_reports/data-journalism-and-the-law.php ("No journalists to date have been sued or prosecuted under the Computer Fraud and Abuse Act, but there's evidence that stories have been hindered or held from publication for the threat of penalty"); Ellen Nakashima, *First Amendment Advocates Urge Change in Facebook Platform Rules*, WASHINGTON POST (Aug. 7, 2018), https://www.washingtonpost.com/world/national-security/first-amendment-advocates-urge-change-in-facebook-platform-rules/2018/08/06/ddaa4180-99dc-11e8-8d5e-c6c594024954_story.html; Surya Mattu & Kashmir Hill, *Facebook Wanted Us to Kill This Investigative Tool*, GIZMODO (Aug. 7, 2018), https://gizmodo.com/ facebook-wanted-us-to-kill-this-investigative-tool-1826620111; Letter from Alex Stamos, et al., to Congress and Members of the Senate and House Committees on the Judiciary (Aug. 1, 2013), https://www.eff.org/files/dc_bh_letter_f4.pdf ("The mere risk of litigation or a federal prosecution is frequently sufficient to induce a researcher . . . to abandon or change a useful project. Some of us have jettisoned work due to legal threats or fears").

28. *Van Buren v. United States*, 141 S. Ct. 1648, 1653 (2021). Although the police officer was the subject of a sting operation, he believed he was conducting the search for a friend to be able to identify a woman he had recently met, with no seeming regard for her safety.

29. *Id.*, at 1661–62.

30. *See Sandvig v. Barr*, 451 F. Supp. 3d 73 (D.D.C. 2020). The author of this piece was counsel for the plaintiffs in *Sandvig*.

31. *See* National Conference of State Legislatures, *Computer Crime Statutes* (May 4, 2022), https://www.ncsl.org/technology-and-communication/computer-crime-statutes#:~:text=All%2050%20states%2C%20Puerto%20Rico,and%20ransomware%2C%20as%20shown%20below; *see also Facebook, Inc. v. Power Ventures*, 844 F.3d 1058, 1069 (9th Cir. 2016) (noting that the analysis of the reach of California's computer crimes law, the Comprehensive Computer Data Access and Fraud Act, Penal Code § 502, is similar to the CFAA).

32. *See hiQ Labs v. LinkedIn*, No. 17-cv-03301-EMC (N.D. Cal. Nov. 4, 2022) (finding hiQ Labs liable for breach of contract when it scraped LinkedIn's public facing site in violation of LinkedIn's terms of service).

33. *See, e.g., Facebook v. Power Ventures*, 844 F.3d 1058 (9th Cir. 2016); *see also* Orin S. Kerr, *Norms of Computer Trespass*, 116 COLUM. L. REV. 1143, 1167–69 (2016).

34. In August 2021, Facebook suspended the accounts of NYU researcher Laura Edelson and two colleagues after the NYU team's research revealed that over half of the US political ads on Facebook in a particular period violated the platform's own rules on transparency. *See* Mark Scott, *Facebook's Attempt to Ban Academics Runs Into Trouble*, POLITICO (Aug. 5, 2021), https://www.politico.eu/article/facebook-nyu-laura-edelson-political-ads. This incident led to the formation of the Coalition for Independent Technology Research, a group of organizations and individuals across civil society,

journalism, and academia committed to advancing independent research into technology companies. *See* Coalition for Independent Technology Research, *Founding Document* (Oct. 12, 2022), https://independenttechresearch.org/coalition-for-independent-technology-research-founding-document.

35. *NAACP v. Kohn*, No.: 3:22–01007-MGL (D.S.C. Jan. 10, 2023). The author of this piece is counsel for the plaintiff in *Kohn*.

36. The litigation between LinkedIn and hiQ has been significant in developing the law around scraping, albeit in a context involving commercial scraping for business purposes. The Ninth Circuit held, in the posture of a preliminary injunction, that scraping a public website does not likely violate the CFAA. *See hiQ Labs v. LinkedIn*, 31 F.4th 1180 (9th Cir. 2022). But following that decision, the district court held that hiQ had committed breach of contract in scraping LinkedIn's website in violation of terms of service. *See hiQ Labs v. LinkedIn*, No. 17-cv-03301-EMC (N.D. Cal. Nov. 4, 2022).

37. *See, e.g., Animal Legal Def. Fund v. Kelly*, 9 F.4th 1219 (10th Cir. 2021), *cert. denied*, 142 S. Ct. 2647 (2022) (holding that Kansas' ag-gag law was viewpoint discriminatory in violation of the First Amendment because it operated only to restrict critics of agricultural facilities from gaining access and recording there); *Animal Legal Defense Fund v. Wasden*, 878 F.3d 1184 (9th Cir. 2018) (concluding that Idaho's criminalization of using misrepresentations to enter a production facility and ban on audio and video recordings of a production facility's operations violated the First Amendment); *see also People for the Ethical Treatment of Animals, Inc. v. N. Carolina Farm Bureau Fed'n, Inc.*, 60 F.4th 815 (4th Cir. 2023) (enjoining North Carolina from enforcing its law prohibiting, among other things, employees from surreptitiously recording information to breach their duty of loyalty to their employer, but only insofar as the law would interfere with newsgathering activities).

38. Caitlin Vogus & Emma Llansó, Center for Democracy and Technology, *Making Transparency Meaningful: A Framework for Policymakers* (Dec. 14, 2021), https://cdt.org/insights/new-cdt-report-provides-guide-for-policymakers-on-making-transparency-meaningful (including guidance on protecting researcher data from law enforcement access).

Dobbs Online

Digital Rights as Abortion Rights

Elizabeth E. Joh

Even when legal, safe abortions have not been easy to obtain. Poverty, distance, youth, and domestic violence have all posed barriers.[1] But even so, the guarantee of a constitutionally protected right to legal abortion provided a bulwark against outright prohibition. That is why the Supreme Court's 2022 decision in *Dobbs v. Jackson Women's Health Organization* was a "jolt to the legal system."[2] The Court not only upheld a Mississippi state ban on abortions after fifteen weeks, it used the *Dobbs* case as an opportunity to overturn the nearly fifty-year-old constitutional right to legal abortion in the United States.

Dobbs has been called a turning back on the clock for abortion rights, women's rights, and pregnant people's rights. But that is not quite accurate. The Court has decided *Dobbs* at a time when unprecedented amounts of digital data about us now exist thanks to an enormous surveillance infrastructure. These digital trails we all leave everywhere are ripe for criminal investigation. And those trails may also be useful now that abortion can be a crime. The Supreme Court's decision in *Dobbs* doesn't just spell the loss of control over women's bodies. *Dobbs* reminds us of how little control we have over our digital selves, and emphasizes how digital rights are also reproductive rights.

The first place to begin is *Dobbs* itself. In 1973, the Supreme Court first recognized a woman's fundamental right to a legal abortion, grounded in the Fourteenth Amendment's "concept of personal liberty," and part of a family of rights including marriage, procreation, birth control, family relationships, and childrearing.[3] Despite numerous calls to overturn that decision, the Court reaffirmed the *Roe* right in its 1992 decision in *Planned Parenthood v. Casey*.[4] The ability to choose abortion was linked to those matters "central to personal dignity and autonomy," and thus "central to the liberty protected by the Fourteenth Amendment."[5] After *Roe* and *Casey*, states could not ban abortion outright, although they could impose bans after the point of fetal viability, so long as there were exceptions to preserve the pregnant woman's life or health.[6]

Dobbs upended this framework. The *Dobbs* court overruled both *Roe* and *Casey*, with the observation that the "Constitution makes no reference to abortion."[7] Although the *Dobbs* majority acknowledged that the liberty referred to in the Fourteenth Amendment's due process clause protected some fundamental but unexpressed rights, abortion was, in its view, different. According to the Court, abortion is not "deeply rooted in the Nation's history and tradition."[8] Abortion is also distinct from marriage, sexual relationships, and birth control because it "uniquely involves what *Roe* and *Casey* termed 'potential life.'"[9]

The *Dobbs* majority claimed to be returning the issue of abortion to "the people and their elected representatives."[10] Put differently, after *Dobbs*, states are free to criminalize abortion—completely. Some states had passed "trigger laws" intended to ban or severely restrict abortion if the Court overturned *Roe* and *Casey*. Other states with abortion bans that existed before the Court decided *Roe* in 1973 may now enforce those laws.[11] Other states may soon see laws passed that similarly restrict or ban abortion outright. Some states will continue to permit access to legal abortion,[12] but in at least half of the states, legal abortion will be practicably unavailable.[13]

The post-*Roe* world has begun to take shape, but one thing is clear. When abortion is a crime, either by criminalizing the provision of abortion or by targeting pregnant people themselves, the ordinary mechanisms of criminal justice apply. That includes today's digital surveillance infrastructure.

We leave streams of sensitive personal digital data everywhere in our browser searches, online chats and emails, browser searches, and even our physical movements captured by surveillance technology. This surveillance economy often operates without our practical knowledge, our meaningful consent, or robust legal protections. All of that data supplies the enormous and vastly underregulated marketplace where data brokers can buy information on millions of American.[14] The initial motivation to create this digital surveillance infrastructure may have been to sell us ads, but today that surveillance infrastructure powers authoritarian governments abroad.[15] That surveillance economy also aids ordinary criminal investigations at home.

While most pre-*Roe* bans targeted those who provided abortion services, after *Dobbs* nothing bars the passage of state laws targeting those who seek abortions themselves.[16] States could create new crimes that specifically allow the criminal punishment of abortion patients.[17] Others might classify abortion as a traditional criminal homicide.[18] The scope of these laws may extend beyond conventional abortion. A state's declaration that legal personhood begins at fertilization might criminalize the use of contraceptive IUDS and emergency contraception.[19]

Such laws may even lead to bans on IVF technologies to help couples become parents at all.[20]

And when abortion is a crime, the massive amounts of digital data we produce every day become potential criminal evidence. Period tracking apps, which can document a sudden change in your menstrual cycle, are ready-made sources of potentially incriminating information.[21] But a focus on specialized fertility or health apps overlooks the many other forms of digital data that police and prosecutors can turn to for evidence. Online searches for medication abortions, geolocation data (from cell phone towers, apps, or license plate readers) tracing movements to suspected abortion providers, online conversations, and even the use of DNA databases to identify fetal remains may support criminal prosecutions.[22]

Ordinary criminal investigations already take advantage of the massive amount of data that "shows the whole pattern of life."[23] Consider some of the tools. A reverse location or "geofence" warrant tries to identify every person who has been within a certain geographic area at a time and place. This technique takes advantage of the nearly constant location data collected from Google users and the company's storage of that information. Investigators may eventually narrow down a pool of suspects, but only after identifying hundreds, or perhaps thousands of innocent people who are unlucky targets of ubiquitous data collection practices. If police use these tools to investigate the theft of $650 worth of stolen tires, they will surely apply them to some abortion investigations as well.[24] In the first half of 2021 alone, Google reported that it received more than forty-five thousand subpoenas and search warrants for subscriber information by the government.[25]

In other cases, the government does not even face the hurdle of a seeking a subpoena or search warrant. The location data marketplace is large, lucrative, and open to both private and government customers. Federal agencies have purchased access to cell phone location data for use in immigration enforcement.[26] In the murky world of data brokers, information from seemingly unrelated cell phone apps for weather or recreation can have their users' location sold, repackaged, and resold in data products, including patterns of travel to and from abortion services providers.[27] In 2022, one journalist bought a week's worth of location data of those traveling to more than six hundred Planned Parenthood offices for just over $160.[28] The company providing this data claims it can identify "how often people visit, how long they stay, where they came from, where else they go, and more."[29]

Even internet searches can become incriminating evidence. Federal investigators successfully identified the person responsible for a 2019 arson through the use of a "keyword warrant": asking Google for information on any "users who had searched the address of the residence close in time to the arson."[30] If these searches supported a prosecution, so too could searches for home abortion methods, underground providers, and appeals for help in states where abortion is a crime. Text messages, emails, payment data are part of the many streams of data available, too.

We can predict that this information will drive prosecutions because some prosecutors have already aggressively investigated women who have experienced miscarriages or stillbirths as potential criminal homicides or feticides.[31] The most infamous pre-*Dobbs* case involved the prosecution of Purvi Patel, whom hospital employees suspected of having induced her own abortion although she claimed that she had had a miscarriage.[32] Prosecutors charged Patel under Indiana's laws criminalizing feticide as well as child neglect for attempting to have a medication abortion. Key evidence included text messages in which Patel told a friend about ordering abortion medication from a Hong Kong pharmacy, her browsing history—including a website about abortion—and her emails from an online pharmacy where abortion medications could be ordered without a prescription.[33]

The digital net becomes wider still when we consider criminal law's traditional doctrines. If abortion is a crime, then attempts, aid, and agreements to aid all become part of the prosecutor's toolbox. The crimes of attempt and conspiracy can be completed even if the contemplated act never takes place. If the criminal law can punish the half-hearted thief or a bank robbery lookout with a negligible role, then it can also punish the pregnant woman who buys abortion medication but does not takes it, or the person who texts that they will drive a pregnant woman to an underground abortion provider.

The initial advice after *Dobbs* to people in states where abortion will be banned or practically unavailable has taken the form of digital self-defense. Privacy advocates have urged that anyone who might ever seek an abortion to delete period tracking apps, erase browsing and location history, forgo health tracking devices, "properly" erase files, and use encrypted channels for communication.[34] Other varieties of advice include using a "burner" phone (one not connected to an ordinary cell phone account), turning to virtual private networks, or even leaving phones and other digital devices at home.[35] Others might advise abortion seekers to engage in anti-surveillance techniques, such as obscuring facial features to thwart facial recognition programs[36] or, like pro-democracy protestors in Hong Kong, vandalizing the technologies that would collect information in the first place.[37]

But these solutions aren't practical ones at all when we consider the realities of abortion in the United States. The typical abortion patient is in her late twenties, is unmarried, and is poor.[38] Abortion access was a hurdle even before *Dobbs*. In states where there were few, or just one, abortion services provider,[39] traveling for an abortion meant finding childcare, taking time off work, and the costs associated with travel: all of which are high hurdles and will be higher still for women who can, in theory, travel to other states where abortion remains legal, but whose biggest hurdle is poverty.[40]

Asking low-income people to engage in digital self-help to avoid abortion prosecutions ignores the "matrix of vulnerabilities" they face.[41] While we are all subject to the pervasive forms of private and public surveillance around us, poor people have always faced particularly intense forms of surveillance.[42] The acceptance of government benefits often requires accepting close scrutiny of one's personal habits. Receiving food stamps leads to monitoring of spending habits.[43] Signing up for state sponsored prenatal care may require divulging everything from the identities of partners, experiences with substance use or abuse, mental health problems, and personal finances.[44] A call to a hotline about a suspected case of neglect or abuse may lead to a predictive risk assessment that includes factors heavily correlated to poverty like sustained reliance on government benefits and exposes a parent to a potential investigation.[45]

Poor people not only experience greater surveillance over their lives, they also face greater hurdles when it comes to protecting their privacy. Here too we can point to the byzantine corporate privacy policies and the lack of a general data protection scheme faced by all Americans, but poverty exacerbates these problems.[46] Being poor often means buying a (cheaper) phone with less privacy protective features,[47] having less "digital literacy" to identify and take appropriate privacy protective steps,[48] and lacking the means to pay for apps or other services that might afford greater privacy.[49]

Greater surveillance and fewer privacy protections means that poor women—the typical abortion patients—are ill-served by a tool kit of digital self-help. Such advice proceeds as if individual digital responsibility and risk assumption were the primary or even sufficient policy choice for limitless intrusions upon our privacy and the ability to control our information. In states were abortion providers, patients, and their families and friends are potential suspects, digital evidence will be easy to find. Law enforcement officials will be able to rely on the lack of individual control and choice over personal information embedded into the structure of digital life itself.

Structural solutions are the answer to structural problems. For reproductive rights, the initial responses may come from the private sector. Platforms can delete sensitive location data connecting users to abortion service providers and other now suspicious places.[50] Or they can stop from collecting the information in the first place, from everyone.[51] A federal administration supportive of reproductive rights can decline to assist state and local law enforcement agencies in abortion related prosecution, such as providing technology and personnel to analyze digital evidence.[52] Congress could shore up digital protections that have been flagged for years, including the government's current ability to buy digital information in the marketplace like any other customer. Further still, Congress could provide a statutory right to abortion that would apply nationwide. The Supreme Court decided that the structure of the Constitution would not protect reproductive rights. Pregnant people must now find a protective framework elsewhere.

NOTES

1. *See, e.g.*, Lindsay E. Clark, et al., *Reproductive Coercion and Co-occurring Partner Violence in Obstetrics and Gynecology Patients*, 210 AM. J. OBSTET. GYNECOL. 42 (2014)(reporting prevalence of "male behavior to control contraception and pregnancy outcomes of female partners" including "birth control sabotage and forcing unwanted pregnancy); Jonathan M. Bearak, et al., Disparities and Change over Time in Distance Women Would Need to Travel to Have an Abortion in the USA: A spatial Analysis, 2 THE LANCET 493 (2017) (reporting results of 2017 study showing that some women in South Dakota traveled more than three hundred miles to obtain a legal abortion).

2. 142 S.Ct. 2288, 2316 (2022)(Roberts, C.J., concurring in judgment)("The Court's decision to overrule *Roe* and *Casey* is a serious jolt to the legal system—regardless of how you view those cases").

3. 410 U.S. 113, 153 (1973).

4. 505 U.S. 833 (1992).

5. 505 U.S. at 852.

6. 505 U.S. at 879 ("We also reaffirm *Roe*'s holding that 'subsequent to viability, the State in promoting its interest in the potentiality of human life may, if it chooses, regulate, and even proscribe, abortion except where it is necessary, in appropriate medical judgment, for the preservation of the life or health of the mother").

7. 142 S.Ct. at 2242.

8. *Id.*, at 2253.

9. *Id.*, at 2280.

10. *Id.*, at 2259.

11. *See, e.g.*, Ken Paxton, Updated Advisory on Texas Law Upon Reversal of *Roe v. Wade* (July 27, 2022), https://texasattorneygeneral.gov/sites/default/files/images/executive-management/Updated%20Post-Roe%20Advisory%20Upon%20Issuance%20of%20Dobbs%20Judgment%20(07.27.2022).pdf (observing "local prosecutors may choose to immediately pursue criminal prosecutions based on violations of Texas abortion prohibitions predating *Roe* that were never repealed by the Texas Legislature"); *cf.* Karen Brooks Harper, *Abortion-Rights Groups Sue Texas AG, Prosecutors to Protect Ability to Help Pregnant Texans Seek Legal Abortions in Other States*, TEXAS TRIBUNE (Aug. 23, 2022), https://www.texastribune.org/2022/08/23/abortion-funds-lawsuit-texas-travel/.

12. *See, e.g.*, Officer of Governor Gavin Newsom, *West Coast States Launch New Multi-State Commitment to Reproductive Freedom, Standing United on Protecting Abortion Access* (June 24, 2022), https://www.gov.ca.gov/2022/06/24/west-coast-states-launch-new-multi-state-commitment-to-reproductive-freedom-standing-united-on-protecting-abortion-access/ (publishing commitment of governors in California, Oregon, and Washington states to "defend access to reproductive healthcare, including abortion and contraceptives").

13. Amy Schoenfeld Walker & Allison McCann, *How State Abortion Laws are Changing*, NEW YORK TIMES (June 24, 2022), https://www.nytimes.com/2022/06/20/us/how-state-abortion-laws-are-changing.html (observing that "about half of states are expected to ban or further restrict access to abortion following the Supreme Court's decision to overturn Roe v. Wade").

14. *See, e.g.*, Stuart A. Thompson & Charlie Warzel, *Twelve Million Phones, One Dataset, Zero Privacy*, New York TIMES (Dec. 19, 2019), https://www.nytimes.com/interactive/2019/12/19/opinion/location-tracking-cell-phone.html ("In the United States, as in most of the world, no federal law limits what has become a vast and lucrative trade in human tracking").

15. *See, e.g.*, Paul Mozur & Aaron Krolik, *A Surveillance Net Blanket's China's Cities, Giving Police Vast Powers*, NEW YORK TIMES Dec. 17, 2019, https://www.nytimes.com/2019/12/17/technology/china-surveillance.html

16. Safia Samee Ali, *Prosecutors in States Where Abortion Is Now Illegal Could Begin Building Criminal Cases against Providers*, NBC News, June 24, 2022, https://www.nbcnews.com/news/us-news/prosecutors-states-abortion-now-illegal-begin-prosecute-abortion-provi-rcna35268 (noting that "a path has been cleared for at least 13 states -those with 'trigger laws'-to begin penalizing and prosecuting people who violate abortion bans").

17. Even before *Dobbs*, there have been several cases of prosecutions of pregnant women for violating state laws against self-induced abortions, harm to fetuses, and expansive interpretations of other criminal laws. *See, e.g. If/When/How, Roe's Unfinished Promise: Decriminalizing Abortion Once and For All* (Nov. 28, 2017)(noting that even as of 2017 that there were "7 states with laws directly criminalizing self-induced abortions, 10 states with laws criminalizing harm to fetuses that lack adequate exemptions for the pregnant person, and 14 states with criminal abortion laws that have been and could be misapplied to people who self-induce").

18. Veronica Stracqualursi, et al., *Louisiana Lawmakers Pull Back from Classifying Abortion as Homicide*, CNN (May 13, 2022), https://www.cnn.com/2022/05/13/politics/louisiana-abortion-bill-criminalize-women/index.html (describing Louisiana House Bill 813 which allowed for "women to be criminally charged for terminating their pregnancies").

19. Greg Hilburn, *Louisiana Wants to Make Abortion a Crime of Murder. Supporters Even Say It's Unconstitutional* (May 5, 2022), https://www.usatoday.com/story/news/nation/2022/05/05/louisiana-abortion-bill-would-make-crime-murder/9656102002/ ("Opponents argued the bill would not only put the mother and doctor at risk of murder prosecution, but criminalize in vitro fertilization and perhaps some forms of birth control").

20. *See, e.g.*, Jan Hoffman, *Infertility Patients and Doctors Fear Abortion Bans Could Restrict I.V.F.*, NEW YORK TIMES (July 5, 2022), https://www.nytimes.com/2022/07/05/health/ivf-embryos-roe-dobbs.html (observing that "many fear that regulations on unwanted pregnancies could, unintentionally or not, also control people who long for a pregnancy").

21. Hannah Norman and Victoria Knight, *Should You Worry about Data from Your Period-Tracking App Being Used Against You?*, KAISER HEALTH NEWS (May 13, 2022), https://khn.org/news/article/period-tracking-apps-data-privacy/.

22. *See, e.g.*, Russell Brandom, *Police Are Using DNA Testing to Track Down a Fetus's Mother*, THE VERGE (May 10, 2018), https://www.theverge.com/2018/5/10/17340666/dna-testing-georgia-fetus-codis-abortion-genetics-investigation (reporting Georgia case of discovered fetal remains sent for testing to compare to state DNA database and to identify woman involved).

23. Jennifer Valentino-DeVries, *Tracking Phones, Google Is a Dragnet for the Police*, NEW YORK TIMES (Apr. 13, 2019), https://www.nytimes.com/interactive/2019/04/13/us/google-location-tracking-police.html (quoting deputy police chief Mark Bruley of Brooklyn Park, Minn.).

24. Tony Webster, *How Did the Police Know You Were Near a Crime Scene? Google Told Them*, MPR NEWS (Feb. 7, 2019), https://www.mprnews.org/story/2019/02/07/google-location-police-search-warrants.

25. Google, Global Requests for User Information (Jan. 2021–June 2021), https://transparencyreport.google.com/user-data/overview?user_requests_report_period=series:requests,accounts;authority:US;time:2021H1&lu=user_requests_report_period.

26. Byron Tau and Michelle Hackman, *Federal Agencies Use Cellphone Location Data for Immigration Enforcement*, WALL STREET JOURNAL (Feb. 7, 2020), https://www.wsj.com/articles/federal-agencies-use-cellphone-location-data-for-immigration-enforcement-11581078600 (reporting that "the Trump administration has bought access to a commercial database that maps the movements of millions of cellphones in American and is using it for immigration and border enforcement").

27. Joseph Cox, *Data Broker Is Selling Location Data of People Who Visit Abortion Clinics*, VICE (May 3, 2022), https://www.vice.com/en/article/m7vzjb/location-data-abortion-clinics-safegraph-planned-parenthood

("Often app developers install code, called software development kits (SDKs), into their apps that sends users' location data to companies in exchange for the developer receiving payment. Sometimes app users don't know that their phone—be that via a prayer app, or a weather app—is collecting and sending location data to third parties").

28. *Id.*

29. *Id.*

30. Isobel Asher Hamilton, *Documents from an Arson Attack Linked to the R Kelly Investigation Show How Google Hands "Keyword" Search Data to Police*, BUSINESS INSIDER (Oct. 9, 2020), https://www.businessinsider.com/google-can-give-police-keyword-data-from-search-histories-2020-10; see also Nina Pullano, *R. Kelly Associate Get 8 Years for Setting Fire Outside a Victim's Home*, COURTHOUSE NEWS (June 29, 2022), https://www.courthousenews.com/r-kelly-associate-gets-8-years-for-setting-fire-outside-a-victims-home/ (noting that in defendant's search history, federal agents also "found that he Googled how fertilizer and diesel fuel bombs work, where to buy a custom machine gun, and laws related to federal witness intimidation").

31. Cat Zakrewski, Pranshu Verma & Claire Parker, *Texts, Web Searches about Abortion have Been Used to Prosecute Women*, WASHINGTON POST (July 3, 2022), https://www.washingtonpost.com/technology/2022/07/03/abortion-data-privacy-prosecution/.

32. *See, e.g.*, Mary Ziegler, *Some Form of Punishment: Penalizing Women for Abortion*, 26 WILLIAM & MARY BILL OF RIGHTS J. 735, 774–75 (2018) (recounting details of Patel prosecution).

33. Emily Bazelon, *Purvi Patel Could Be Just the Beginning*, NEW YORK TIMES MAGAZINE (Apr. 1, 2016), https://www.nytimes.com/2015/04/01/magazine/purvi-patel-could-be-just-the-beginning.html. Patel's conviction was later overturned on appeal. Associated Press, *Purvi Patel Is released after Feticide Conviction Overturned*, INDY STAR (Sept. 2, 2016), https://www.indystar.com/story/news/crime/2016/09/01/purvi-patel-releases-feticide-conviction-overturned/89707582/.

34. *See, e.g.*, Heather Kelly, Tatum Hunter & Danielle Abril, *Seeking an Abortion? Here's How to Avoid Leaving a Digital Trail*, WASHINGTON POST (June 26, 2022), https://www.washingtonpost.com/technology/2022/06/26/abortion-online-privacy/ (providing advice on encrypting messaging, secure internet browsing, etc.).

35. *See, e.g.*, Daly Barnett, *Security and Privacy Tips for People Seeking An Abortion*, Electronic Frontier Foundation (June 23, 2022), https://www.eff.org/deeplinks/2022/06/security-and-privacy-tips-people-seeking-abortion; *see also* Sarah Emerson & Emily Baker-White, *In a Post-Roe America, Googling "Abortion" Could Put You at Risk. Here's How to Protect Yourself*, BUZZFEEDNEWS (May 4, 2022), https://www.buzzfeednews.com/article/sarahemerson/abortion-digital-privacy-guide (suggesting the use of professional deletion services).

36. *See, e.g.*, Radhamely De Leon, *Researchers Defeated Advanced Facial Recognition Tech Using Makeup*, VICE (Sept. 17, 2021), https://www.vice.com/en/article/k78v9m/researchers-defeated-advanced-facial-recognition-tech-using-makeup (reporting that researchers "have found a new and surprisingly simple method for bypassing facial recognition software using makeup patterns").

37. Sidney Fussell, *Why Hong Kongers Are Toppling Lampposts*, THE ATLANTIC (Aug. 30, 2019), https://www.theatlantic.com/technology/archive/2019/08/why-hong-kong-protesters-are-cutting-down-lampposts/597145/ (noting that protestors have been cutting down "smart" lampposts out of fear that they contain sensors and cameras); *see also* Alex Lee, *This Ugly T-shirt Makes You Invisible to Facial Recognition Tech*, WIRED (Nov. 5, 2020), https://www.wired.co.uk/article/facial-recognition-t-shirt-block (reporting that researchers have designed shirt with "a design that can confuse the AI network's classification and labelling system").

38. Margot Sanger-Katz, Claire Cain Miller & Quoctrung Bui, *Who Gets Abortions in America?*, NEW YORK TIMES (Dec. 14, 2021), https://www.nytimes.com/interactive/2021/12/14/upshot/who-gets-abortions-in-america.html.

39. The respondent in *Dobbs*, Jackson Women's Health Organization, was the *only* abortion services provider in the state. *See How Mississippi Ended Up with One Abortion Clinic and Why It Matters*, Washington Post (Nov. 30, 2021), https://www.washingtonpost.com/dc-md-va/2021/11/30/abortion-mississippi-closed-clinics/; *see also* Jolie McCullough, *After Losing Battle to Preserve Roe v. Wade, Mississippi's Last Abortion Clinic Is Moving to New Mexico*, Texas Tribune (June 29, 2022), https://www.texastribune.org/2022/06/29/mississippi-abortion-new-mexico/ (reporting that respondent clinic in *Dobbs* has relocated to Las Cruces, New Mexico).

40. *See* Sanger-Katz, *supra* note 38 ("About half of women who had an abortion in 2014 were below the poverty line, with another quarter very close to poverty"); *Dobbs*, 142 S.Ct., at 2345 (2022)(Breyer, Sotomayor, and Kagan, J.J., dissenting)("In States that bar abortion, women of means will still be able to travel to obtain the services they need. It is women who cannot afford to do so who will suffer most").

41. Marry Madden, et al., *Privacy, Poverty, and Big Data: A Matrix of Vulnerabilities for Poor Americans*, 95 Wash. U. L. Rev.53, 122 (2017)(discussing "a matrix of overlapping vulnerabilities that low-income communities face in the big data era").

42. Michele Gilman & Rebecca Green, *The Surveillance Gap: The Harms of Extreme Privacy and Data Marginalization*, 24 N.Y.U. Rev. L & Social Change 253, 255 (2018).

43. Madden, *supra* note 41, at 63.

44. Khiara M. Bridges, The Poverty of Privacy Rights 4–5 (2017).

45. Virginia Eubanks, Automating Inequality: How High-Tech Tools Profile, Police, and Punish the Poor 127–73 (2017)(describing use of Allegheny Family Screening Tool by Allegheny County, PA Office of Children, Youth, and Families).

46. *See, e.g.*, Geoffrey A. Fowler, *"I Tried to Read All My App Privacy Policies. It Was 1 Million Words,"* Washington Post (May 31, 2022), https://www.washingtonpost.com/technology/2022/05/31/abolish-privacy-policies/ ("There's a big little lie at the center of how we use every website, app and gadget. We click "agree," saying we've read the data policy and agree to the terms and conditions. Then, legally speaking, companies can say we've given them consent to use our data"); Nuala O'Connor, *Reforming the U.S. Approach to Data Protection and Privacy*, Council on Foreign Relations (Jan. 30, 2018), https://www.cfr.org/report/reforming-us-approach-data-protection ("The United States lacks a single, comprehensive federal law that regulates the collection and use of personal information.").

47. Madden, *supra* note 41, at 62 ("Poor Americans are considerably less likely to use Apple phones, which provide more robust encryption and are generally less susceptible to being hacked compared to their less expensive Android counterparts").

48. Digital literacy here refers to the set of "technical, cognitive, and sociological skills" people need "in order to perform tasks and solve problems in digital environments." Madden, *supra* note 41, at 117.

49. *See, e.g.*, Heather Kelly, *How to Scrub Yourself from the Internet, the Best That You Can*, Washington Post (June 24, 2022), https://www.washingtonpost.com/technology/2022/06/24/delete-yourself-online/ (noting "paid services that . . . are a good option if you're worried about your personal [digital] safety").

50. Jen Fitzpatrick, *Protecting People's Privacy on Health Topics*, Google (July 1, 2022), https://blog.google/technology/safety-security/protecting-peoples-privacy-on-health-topics/ (announcing that Google intends to delete entries from its Location History from "abortion clinics, fertility centers," etc., soon after users visit); *see also* Alexandra Kelley, *2 Data Brokers Pledge to Halt Location Data Collection after Abortion Ruling*, Nextgov (July 7, 2022), https://www.nextgov.com/analytics-data/2022/07/2-data-brokers-pledge-halt-location-data-collection-after-abortion-ruling/373944/ (reporting that Safegraph and Placer.ai pledged to stop selling user location regarding abortion clinic visits).

51. Geoffrey Fowler, *Okay, Google, To Protect Women, Collect Less Data about Everyone*, Washington Post (July 1, 2022), https://www.washingtonpost.com/technology/2022/07/01/google-privacy-abortion/ (outlining steps Google could take to "build civil rights into its products").

52. *See, e.g.* Riana Pfefferkorn, *Federal Government Will Help States Punish Abortion—Using Our Phones*, THE HILL (July 1, 2022), https://thehill.com/opinion/criminal-justice/3543721-federal-government-will-help-states-punish-abortion-using-our-phones/ (noting that the federal government often provides equipment, technology, training, and personnel help to state and local law enforcement for digital evidence gathering).

11

Digital Security
and Reproductive Rights

Lessons for Feminist Cyberlaw

Michela Meister and Karen Levy

Reproductive rights in the United States are under threat, and the threat is growing more serious by the day. The 2022 Supreme Court opinion in *Dobbs v. Jackson Women's Health Organization*,[1] overturning the fundamental right to abortion enshrined in *Roe v. Wade*,[2] cast into danger the lives and livelihoods of millions of people. Alongside (and quite clearly related to) the decimation of reproductive rights in courts and legislatures are an increasing number of ideologically driven attacks on abortion seekers, providers, and clinics. Clinics have been the targets of bombings, blockades, and invasions. Day to day, providers and their clients face picketers, protesters, online harassment, stalking, and doxing designed to intimidate clients into ceasing to exercise what reproductive rights they still have, and to dissuade providers from providing essential health services.

The rise of digital technologies has exacerbated these threats in multiple ways, and digital threats have a marked impact on abortion access. Abortion is a common experience in the United States—almost one in four women will have an abortion in her lifetime[3]—and these threats are clearly designed to chill and punish access to care for people seeking abortions. While much has been written about the impact of violence and harassment on abortion services, the relationship between these threats and digital privacy and security is only beginning to be fully appreciated.[4] Given the impact that digital attacks have on abortion across all levels—from the individual patient experience to providers, to clinics, and to the legality of abortion across the nation—this attention is long overdue.

Threats to reproductive rights are of paramount importance to people interested in the gendered relationship between law and technology. But they also offer a case study in what a feminist viewpoint provides to cyberlaw even beyond abortion. In this chapter, we offer three lessons for feminist cyberlaw in the wake of *Dobbs*. We show how a feminist perspective—one that acknowledges "contexts, bodies, and legacies," as articulated by this volume's coeditor Meg Leta Jones[5]—offers a fuller view of how digital security and privacy intrusions are embedded in social ecosystems, can result in grave physical and mental harms, and are impossible to understand or prevent in isolation from broader patterns of surveillance. These lessons are applicable not only in the critical context of reproductive rights, but across many arenas in which cyberlaw operates.

SILOES AND DEAD BODIES

Dobbs and its aftermath hit home a lesson that feminist security scholars have consistently highlighted: that a good deal of contemporary security research tends to understand digital security threats in relative isolation, devoid of broader context. Academic security scholarship often highlights novel, technically sophisticated digital attacks, yet sometimes neglects the social contexts in which everyday people experience insecurity, and the real, lived consequences of those threats. A new wave of feminist security research has countered this trend, calling explicit attention to the social and relational aspects of digital insecurity—and showing how even technically unsophisticated attacks (which might not traditionally garner much interest among academic security researchers) can be both immensely harmful and extremely difficult to protect against, largely because of their social complexity.

Much of this feminist security scholarship focuses particularly on the context of technology-mediated abuse, an extremely widespread phenomenon which is very likely the most frequent context in which digital insecurity is inexperienced by everyday people.[6] One in three women and one in four men in the United States experiences intimate partner violence, stalking, or rape at some point during their lives, and transgender people are about twice as likely as cisgender people to experience intimate partner violence;[7] digital technologies play a prominent role in abuse contexts, providing means by which attackers can control, stalk, and harass their targets.[8] In this context, the vectors of attack for abuse may be technically very simple and require no special technical expertise—even something as basic as looking over a partner's shoulder or perusing search history on a shared device can be sufficient to glean intimate personal data.[9]

A core insight of this line of work is that digital security, while often siloed in academic analysis, is in reality inextricably linked to physical, emotional, sexual, and economic security. Analyzing digital security threats in isolation from other vectors of attack is necessarily incomplete, and often mischaracterizes or understates the potential risks and consequences of digital security breach. For example, traditional digital security research is unlikely to account for the physical proximity of an attacker and a target (which can facilitate involuntary information-sharing, as in shoulder-surfing), the ways in which a target may be have a preexisting relationship with the attacker (giving the attacker access to resources like the answers to common security questions), or the ways in which threats to digital security can go hand-in-hand with threats to other forms of security (for example, an attacker may threaten physical violence if one takes steps to protect one's digital data from access).[10] Feminist thinkers describe how conventional security threat modeling that focuses on digital access in isolation can neglect broader questions about safety and justice for marginalized people.[11]

A similar question of focus arises in legal privacy scholarship. Privacy is sometimes described as having a "dead body problem": many privacy violations lack harms that are readily cognizable as such, making it difficult to address and prevent them through tort law.[12] Targeted ads based on internet tracking, for example, may give one an uneasy feeling of being watched; shoddy privacy practices that result in disclosure of personal information may cause embarrassment or impinge on one's sense of dignity. But unease and humiliation are not concrete harms, and tend not to be readily compensable via tort law. The "dead body problem" in privacy, as it's described, is that there aren't any: the nature of harm is diffuse and abstract, making it difficult to seek legal redress for harms and to marshal the political will to address privacy problems in the policy realm.[13]

Yet feminist thinkers retort: if you can't find any dead bodies in privacy law, you just aren't looking very hard. Feminist legal thinkers have long highlighted in their scholarship the dire, violent, and often life-or-death consequences of privacy and security violation, particularly for women, the LGBTQ community, and communities of color.[14] Perhaps the most direct confrontation between feminist legal thought and "mainline" privacy scholarship arose in 2006, when Ann Bartow wrote an essay reviewing Daniel Solove's *A Taxonomy of Privacy*.[15] Solove's taxonomy, published that same year, has since become one of the most influential and heavily cited articles in all of privacy law; in it, Solove attempts to bring order to the notoriously slippery concept of "privacy" by categorizing privacy violations into sixteen types (aggregation, appropriation, breach of confidentiality, etc.).[16] In her review, Bartow asserts that Solove's taxonomy "suffers from too much doctrine, and not enough dead bodies";[17] that his "dry, analytical"[18] approach "fail[s] to sufficiently identify and animate the compelling ways that privacy violations can negatively impact the lives of living, breathing human beings beyond simply provoking feelings of unease."[19] The diminishment of reproductive rights is one of the chief examples Bartow brings to bear in her critique, noting presciently that "the prospect that women will either forgo sexual relationships or possibly even bear unwanted children as a consequence of inadequate information privacy is the sort of harm Solove's taxonomy could have taken greater notice of."[20]

Solove countered Bartow's critique in a subsequent article,[21] responding that "most privacy problems lack dead bodies."[22] He acknowledges as aberrations ("exceptional cases"[23]) a few situations in which women were murdered by stalkers after the stalkers obtained the women's physical addresses from government and commercial sources—but dismisses what he decries as "Bartow's quest for horror stories"[24] as counterproductive.[25] In Solove's view—one that has become as authoritative as that of any contemporary privacy scholar—highlighting the most visceral and violent privacy harms (it must be noted, those suffered in these cases by women) could serve to obscure other pervasive privacy harms that accrete more gradually and less egregiously. Solove is, of course, correct in assessing that not all privacy harms need to rise to the level of stalking, rape, murder, or forced childbirth to constitute real harms worth addressing. Yet the scholarship also has a performative effect: dismissing these harms as "sensationalistic," as Solove does, sidelines them as distractions from apparently more pressing issues. [26] And it is incontrovertible that the mine run of privacy scholarship has for decades focused a great deal more energy on issues related to consumer protection than it has on issues related to bodily autonomy and physical safety. In part, deciding which harms to name and to most closely associate with the term "privacy" is a question of political strategy, with both benefits and drawbacks; but it certainly bears notice that at least one such drawback is reduced focus, from both scholars and policymakers, on centering reproductive and bodily integrity as a core privacy issue.

The aftermath of *Dobbs* illustrates the inseparability of digital and physical security, and the production of "dead bodies" as a consequence of privacy violation, with stark clarity. Digital vulnerabilities—say, location tracking of one's visit to a reproductive health clinic, or search results demonstrating information-seeking around abortion access—are life-or-death scenarios: they bear directly on the ability to seek lifesaving medical care and to have autonomy over one's own body and future. Digital privacy *is* physical safety in these scenarios, and to isolate it in analysis, without fully accounting for its broader context and effects, necessarily impoverishes both our research and our law. A feminist approach ameliorates this shortcoming through a focus on the inextricability of the digital and the physical, and attention to visceral and violent harm as a key outcome produced by insecurity.

TILES AND MOSAICS

In Fourth Amendment jurisprudence, "mosaic theory" refers to the idea that courts, in determining whether a search is constitutional, should take a collective, holistic approach—considering the aggregation of police information-gathering as a whole to evaluate whether that activity constitutes a search, rather than focusing on any discrete information-gathering action in isolation.[27] Mosaic theory relies on the insight that pervasive data collection is more than the sum of its parts—that individual pieces of data, like the tiles of a mosaic, may reveal information about a person's life that becomes clear only when the pieces are viewed in the context of one another, as a whole picture.

This insight has a corollary important in the post-*Dobbs* era, with crucial implications for privacy protection. It's true that some insights only emerge given the arrangement of individual data points into a more coherent whole. But it's similarly true that once a mosaic is in view—once the full picture is visible—the removal of any one tile tends not to have a substantial effect on the image's interpretation. A mosaic of a horse still looks pretty much like a horse even if it's missing a few tiles. In the context of privacy, this leads to an important implication: protecting any particular data point from view may not be enough to substantially reduce what can be inferred about a person given the totality of data points available.[28]

After the leak of the initial *Dobbs* draft (and again after the release of the full opinion), well-meaning individuals took to the internet to share advice about how to protect one's privacy around abortion and reproductive care. A common suggestion was to delete digital period trackers, which are used by many people to track periods of fertility and menstruation—and which, it might be assumed, could be a source of critical evidence in any legal action based on termination of a pregnancy.[29] Another common approach was for people in states with abortion access to offer aid to abortion seekers from other states, using coded language—offering, for instance, to take out-of-state visitors "camping" as code for helping them obtain abortion services.[30] And immediately following the *Dobbs* ruling, some Big Tech firms altered internal policies as well: Google, for example, announced plans to automatically delete location-tracking data from trips to abortion clinics, domestic violence shelters, and addiction treatment facilities, among other places.[31] Each of these developments was intended to provide some degree of privacy around particularly sensitive data involving abortion-seeking.

But feminist writers—notably Cynthia Conti-Cook, Kendra Albert, Maggie Delano, Emma Weil, and Elizabeth Joh (in this volume)—offered a more realistic view that demonstrated that these efforts, though well-meaning, were ultimately misguided and of limited utility in protecting the privacy of abortion seekers.[32] Cynthia Conti-Cook's clear-eyed analysis of the "digital abortion diary" demonstrates that search histories and communication logs (e.g., text messages) are much more likely to be used in prosecutions than is something like a period tracker.[33] Efforts to rely on coded messages among networks of untrained volunteers could expose abortion seekers to myriad risks poorly understood by those seeking to help. And Google's deletion of location data logs, while perhaps a step in the right direction, is of limited effect in the context of amassed search query data, text messages, license plate tracking, and easily purchased data from data brokers.[34]

Essentially, these efforts aim to remove a tile from the mosaic of ubiquitous surveillance—but doing so doesn't obscure the full picture from view. There's very little that individual abortion seekers, medical providers, or allies can do in the face of generalized surveillance from which inferences of all types (including, but not limited to, abortion-seeking behavior) can be drawn from general communications, search, and behavioral data. A targeted focus on technologies specific to reproductive tracking is a natural point of focus, but largely symbolic in the broader context.[35]

ECOSYSTEMS AND ENTANGLEMENTS

Threats to reproductive rights are multiplex. They originate from many points, including statehouses, intimate partners, and religious and political ideologues. They have many vectors of attack, including both digital surveillance and physical intimidation—as well as the propagation of misinformation and other behaviors not always immediately understood as privacy threats. The targets of attack include not only abortion seekers, but clinics, individual health care providers, and allies who might aid abortion seekers in obtaining care. This complexity implies that vulnerabilities at any point, from any attacker, against any target can effectively impede reproductive care—and demands that we adopt a broad *ecosystemic* approach to reproductive privacy and security protection.

To illustrate, consider the following three threats (among many): the 2015 misinformation campaign against Planned Parenthood, online "hit lists" of abortion providers, and the digital surveillance of abortion seekers.

A Massive Misinformation Campaign

In July 2015, the Center for Medical Progress, an anti-abortion group, promoted a massive misinformation campaign against Planned Parenthood which incited a wave of attacks against abortion clinics.[36] The campaign centered around the use of fetal tissue, a key component for a variety of areas in medical research, such as in developing vaccines and studying diseases like ALS, cancer, and HIV. Some clinics allow people having abortions to donate the fetal tissue to medical research; however, the donation is always voluntary and the tissue is never sold.[37] The main claim of the misinformation campaign was that Planned Parenthood sells the fetal tissue from abortions.

This campaign involved a high degree of espionage and took place over the course of two years. Members of the Center for Medical Progress set up a fake company, BioMax, which they claimed works to bring fetal tissue to research labs. Under the guise of this fake company, attackers set up meetings with Planned Parenthood officials, where they used hidden cameras to secretly record hundreds of hours of meetings. They then edited these videos to imply that Planned Parenthood sells fetal tissue.[38]

The implications were drastic. Millions of people viewed the manipulated videos. The doctors and staff depicted in the videos were subjected to both digital and physical harassment and death threats. The effects were not only felt by the doctors and staff in the videos, but by abortion clinics nationwide. Threats to Planned Parenthood clinics around the country skyrocketed and have remained at higher levels ever since.[39]

Bounties and "Wanted" Lists

Abortion providers endure daily harassment, political stigma, and at times physical violence. Online databases created by anti-abortion extremists are a serious threat to providers. These sites display photos and personal information about abortion providers. The first such website was created in the mid-1990s with the name "The Nuremberg Files," a reference to the Nuremberg Trials through which Nazi war criminals were tried after World War II. The site, which was eventually forced off the internet by its ISP, included personal information about providers, including names, photos, home addresses, license plate numbers, information about their families, and even the addresses of churches they attend. The site also included "Wanted" posters for certain doctors and operated like a "hit list": after a doctor was injured, their name was grayed out, and after a doctor was murdered, their name was drawn with a strike through it.[40]

Currently, the anti-abortion group Operation Rescue maintains a website called AbortionDocs.org. The site contains dossiers about (at the time of this writing) 1,479 individual abortion providers and hundreds of clinics, comprising tens of thousands of documents in total.[41] Each provider (which the site calls an "Abortionist") has a page which often includes their photo, the clinic where they work (which the site calls the "Abortion Mill"), an inset Google map of the clinic, and any other available documents on the provider, such as their medical license, social media profiles, personal pictures, malpractice suits against them, and relevant news articles.

The policy of the site is to only post publicly available information and not to post private information, like home addresses or photos of family members.[42] The site specifically states that its purpose is to simply provide information; it claims to "denounce acts of violence against abortion clinics and providers in the strongest terms."[43] However, given the history of the Nuremberg Files, it is clear that such a public repository of information about providers poses a significant threat by providing a centralized resource to people wishing to target abortion providers.

"Vigilante" laws like Texas's SB8 augment the threat from anti-abortion advocates by incentivizing motivated individuals to enforce state laws privately. These laws provide a monetary "bounty" to people willing to bring private civil actions against abortion providers (as well as others who aid abortion seekers in receiving care)—up to $10,000 under Texas's law.[44] Private enforcement mechanisms not only effectively circumvent certain forms of legal challenge (since the state is not a direct actor in preventing care) but can provide motivation for individuals ideologically opposed to abortion to both surveil and sue those suspected of providing or assisting with abortions. Websites like prolifewhistleblower.com offer means through which people can provide tips on abortion providers (though the website has had trouble maintaining consistent hosting).[45]

Threats Faced by People Seeking Abortions

People seeking abortions (or information about abortions) face a variety of threats, including harassment, surveillance, and targeted misinformation. Some threats, of course, may come directly from the state in jurisdictions where abortion is criminalized. But many threats are closer to home. Given the immense stigma surrounding abortion, abortion seekers may wish to keep their abortions secret from family members or partners, particularly (though not exclusively) in cases of abuse. A common fear is that a family member or partner might learn of an abortion, for example, from the search history on an abortion-seeker's phone or computer, or because of the time they are away to have the procedure.[46]

Another set of threats comes from anti-abortion advocacy groups, who employ strategies like digital marketing campaigns to target abortion seekers at clinics via geofencing. For example, the anti-abortion marketing group Choose Life helps anti-abortion groups implement geofencing to target people sitting in abortion clinics with anti-abortion ads.[47] To enter an abortion clinic, clients must often walk past crowds of picketers, who may verbally harass clients, disseminate misinformation about abortions, or attempt to physically block clients from entering clinics. Anti-abortion protesters have also been known to take photos of clients entering clinics and record license plate numbers. For example, in one case in Texas, an anti-abortion group matched license plates with car registration information and sent mass emails to a local college about people they suspected were seeking abortions.[48]

These three threats are, of course, far from the only difficulties people and organizations face in seeking or providing abortion care; our aim here is not to provide a complete threat model of all potential vulnerabilities to reproductive privacy and security, and new threats are very likely to arise as the legal and technology landscapes continue to change over time. However, a few important analytic points arise from considering these three scenarios.

First, we see—again—the entanglement of the digital and the physical, as digital threats often have physical consequences. Misinformation campaigns and sites such as AbortionDocs.org both enable violence against providers. People who are unable to receive a wanted abortion, either because of misinformation they read online, or fear of harassment or stigma, are forced to undergo the life-changing process of being pregnant and bearing a child. All these threats can pose a chilling effect: simply the threat of a family member finding out about an abortion can prevent someone from seeking one. Similarly, harassment and threats to providers may dissuade doctors from providing abortion care.

Second, the role of misinformation as a component of privacy and security threat is often underappreciated. Misinformation researchers Claire Wardle and Hossein Derakhshan characterize both misinformation and "mal-information" (a category including hate speech, harassment, and disclosure of private information) as interconnected elements of a broader phenomenon, which they term *information disorder*.[49] Combatting misinformation about abortion is vital to helping people make informed decisions about their health—both through the prevention of highly orchestrated campaigns like the Center for Medical Progress's expose of Planned Parenthood, and through ensuring accurate information is readily available online without risk or manipulation. (For example, lawmakers have recently urged Google to improve its search results about abortion services, which often divert abortion seekers to "crisis pregnancy centers" that dissuade them from receiving abortion care.)[50]

Finally, the nature of reproductive care requires that we approach privacy and security through an *ecosystemic* lens. Threats to abortion providers' privacy *are* threats to abortion seekers' reproductive rights. Targeted misinformation campaigns about Planned Parenthood can (and are designed to) motivate attacks against unaffiliated abortion providers and people seeking abortion care. In considering how to defend against privacy and security threats to reproductive rights, it's not enough to focus on strengthening the defenses of a single target—be it an abortion seeker, an individual provider, or a clinic; threats to each affects the other parties. This interdependence is yet another reason why individualized solutions, like deleting a period tracker app, are insufficient for robust reproductive privacy protection.

. . .

As we've seen, feminist perspectives offer a clear-eyed view of the nature of threats to reproductive privacy. They illustrate that privacy threats indeed lead to physical harms and "dead bodies," if you prioritize looking for them; they show the insufficiency of protecting discrete pieces of particularly sensitive data while continuing to collect massive amounts of other more general data; and they emphasize the entanglements and interdependence of multiple kinds of vulnerabilities, multiple kinds of attacks, and multiple kinds of targets. Recognizing these characteristics shows an appreciation for the complexity of the problem—a first step toward devising adequate solutions to protect the lives and livelihoods of abortion seekers and providers in the post-*Dobbs* era.

NOTES

1. 597 U.S. ___ (2022).
2. 410 U.S. 113 (1973).

3. *See* Guttmacher Institute, *Abortion Is a Common Experience for U.S. Women, Despite Dramatic Declines in Rates*, https://www.guttmacher.org/news-release/2017/abortion-common-experience-us -women-despite-dramatic-declines-rates (Oct. 19, 2017).

4. *See, e.g.*, Center for Reproductive Rights, *Defending Human Rights: Abortion Providers Facing Threats, Restrictions, and Harassment* (2009), https://reproductiverights.org/sites/default/files /documents/DefendingHumanRights_0.pdf.

5. Meg Leta Jones, *Cyberlaw, But Make it Feminist, in* FEMINIST CYBERLAW (Meg Leta Jones and Amanda Levendowski, eds., 2024) (distinguishing the feminist cyberlaw perspective from the cyberlaw canon due to its focus on these dimensions). *See also* Amanda Levendowski, *Defragging Feminist Cyberlaw*, 37 BERKELEY TECH. L.J. __ (2023) (describing the reliance of cyberlaw on core feminist values of consent, accessibility, and safety).

6. *See generally* Diana Freed, et al., *"A Stalker's Paradise": How Intimate Partner Abusers Exploit Technology*, PROC. ACM CONF. ON HUMAN FACTORS IN COMPUTING SYSTEMS (CHI) Article 667 (2018); Diana Freed, et al., *Digital Technologies and Intimate Partner Violence: A Qualitative Analysis with Multiple Stakeholders*, PROC. ACM CONFERENCE ON HUMAN-COMPUTER INTERACTION (CSCW) Article 46 (2017); Karen Levy & Bruce Schneier, *Privacy Threats in Intimate Relationships*, 6 J. CYBERSECURITY 1 (2020); Tara Matthews, et al., *Security and Privacy Experiences and Practices of Survivors of Intimate Partner Abuse*, 15 IEEE SECURITY & PRIVACY 76 (2017); Julia Slupska, *Safe at Home: Towards a Feminist Critique of Cybersecurity*, 15 ST. ANTONY'S INT'L REV. 83 (2019); Julia Slupska and Leonie Maria Tanczer, *Threat Modeling Intimate Partner Violence: Tech Abuse as a Cybersecurity Challenge in the Internet of Things, in* EMERALD INTERNATIONAL HANDBOOK OF TECHNOLOGY-FACILITATED VIOLENCE AND ABUSE 663 (Jane Bailey, Asher Flynn, and Nicola Henry, eds., 2021); Emily Tseng, et al., *The Tools and Tactics Used in Intimate Partner Surveillance: An Analysis of Online Infidelity Forums*, 29 PROC. USENIX SECURITY SYMPOSIUM 1893 (2020).

7. Domestic Violence Statistics, National Domestic Violence Hotline, https://www.thehotline.org /stakeholders/domestic-violence-statistics/; Sarah M. Peitzmeier, et al., *Intimate Partner Violence in Transgender Populations: Systematic Review and Meta-Analysis of Prevalence and Correlates*, 110 AM. J. PUB. HEALTH e1, e1 (2020).

8. Freed et al., *Stalker's Paradise, supra* note 6, at 1.

9. Freed et al. describe the nature of the attack in this context as often coming from a "UI-bound adversary" without specialized technical knowledge—that is, "an authenticated but adversarial user of a victim's device or account who carries out attacks by interacting with the standard user interface [UI], rather than through the installation of malicious or sophisticated software tools." *Id.*

10. *See id.*; Levy & Schneier, *supra* note 6.

11. *See* Angelika Strohmayer, Rosanna Bellini, and Julia Slupska, *Safety as a Grand Challenge in Pervasive Computing: Using Feminist Epistemologies to Shift the Paradigm from Security to Safety*, IEEE PERVASIVE COMP. 1 (July 14, 2022); Tactical Technology Collective, *The Holistic Security Manual*, https://holistic-security.tacticaltech.org/index.html.

12. *See, e.g.*, Gideon Lewis-Kraus, *Facebook and the "Dead Body" Problem*, NEW YORK TIMES MAGAZINE (Apr. 24, 2018), https://www.nytimes.com/2018/04/24/magazine/facebook-and-the-dead -body-problem.html.

13. *See, e.g.*, TransUnion LLC v. Ramirez, 594 U.S. __ (2021) (demonstrating the difficulty of establishing concrete harm).

14. *See, e.g.*, Anita Allen and Erin Mack, *How Privacy Got Its Gender*, 10 N. ILL. U. L. REV. 441 (1991); Alvaro M. Bedoya, *Privacy as Civil Right*, 50 NEW MEXICO L. REV. 301 (2020); KHIARA BRIDGES, THE POVERTY OF PRIVACY RIGHTS (2017); SIMONE BROWNE, DARK MATTERS: ON THE SURVEILLANCE OF BLACKNESS (2015); Danielle Keats Citron, *Sexual Privacy*, 128 YALE L.J. 1870 (2018); Karen Levy, *Intimate Surveillance*, 51 IDAHO L. REV. 679 (2015); SCOTT SKINNER-THOMPSON, PRIVACY AT THE MARGINS (2021); Kristen Thomasen, *Beyond Airspace Safety: A Feminist Perspective on Drone Privacy Regulation*, 16 CANADIAN J. L. & TECH. 307 (2018); Ari Ezra Waldman, *Law, Privacy, and Online Dating: "Revenge Porn" in Gay Online Communities*, 44 L. & SOC. INQUIRY 987 (2019).

15. Ann Bartow, *A Feeling of Unease About Privacy Law*, 155 U. PA. L. REV. PENNumbra 52 (2006).

16. Daniel J. Solove, *A Taxonomy of Privacy*, 154 U. PA. L. REV. 477 (2006).

17. Bartow, *supra* note 15, at 52.

18. *Id.*

19. *Id.*

20. *Id.*, at 62.

21. *See* Daniel J. Solove, *"I've Got Nothing to Hide" And Other Misunderstandings of Privacy*, 44 SAN DIEGO L. REV. 745 (2007).

22. *Id.*, at 768.

23. *Id.*

24. *Id.*, at 769.

25. Note, however, that in later work typologizing privacy harms, Solove—writing with Danielle Keats Citron—did highlight physical violence as a salient type of harm that could result from privacy violation. *See* Danielle Keats Citron and Daniel J. Solove, *Privacy Harms*, 102 B.U. L. REV. 793, 831–34 (2022).

26. Solove, *Nothing to Hide, supra* note 21, at 769.

27. *See* Orin S. Kerr, *The Mosaic Theory of the Fourth Amendment*, 111 MICH. L. REV. 311 (2012).

28. This point is aligned with analyses of deanonymization, which demonstrate that the removal of particularly sensitive "personally identifiable information" does little to mitigate the risk of reidentification since so much other information is available. *See, e.g.*, Arvind Narayanan and Vitaly Shmatikov, *Myths and Fallacies of "Personally Identifiable Information,"* 53 COMM. ACM 24 (2010).

29. Kashmir Hill, *Deleting Your Period Tracker Won't Protect You*, NEW YORK TIMES (June 30, 2022), https://www.nytimes.com/2022/06/30/technology/period-tracker-privacy-abortion.html.

30. Kaitlyn Tiffany, *What Are Abortion Code Words Even For?*, THE ATLANTIC (July 17, 2022), https://www.theatlantic.com/technology/archive/2022/07/abortion-code-words-social-media-activism/670521/.

31. Jen Fitzpatrick, *Protecting People's Privacy on Health Topics*, Google Keyword blog (July 1, 2022), https://blog.google/technology/safety-security/protecting-peoples-privacy-on-health-topics/.

32. *See* Hill, *supra* note 29; Cynthia Conti-Cook, *Surveilling the Digital Abortion Diary*, 50 U. BALT. L. REV. 1 (2020); Kendra Albert, Maggie Delano, and Emma Weil, *Fear, Uncertainty, and Period Trackers*, MEDIUM (June 28, 2022), https://medium.com/@Kendra_Serra/fear-uncertainty-and-period-trackers-340ab8fdff74. Within this volume, Elizabeth Joh's chapter also hits home this point—explaining in detail the multitude of readily available data sources that obviate the need for reliance on something like a period tracker to establish an inference that a person is seeking an abortion. Elizabeth Joh, *Dobbs Online: Digital Rights as Abortion Rights, in* FEMINIST CYBERLAW (Meg Leta Jones and Amanda Levendowski, eds., 2024). Joh further notes that "digital self-help" strategies are unlikely to be of much utility for poor women, who comprise the majority of abortion seekers. *Id.*

33. In corroboration of Conti-Cook's point, a prominent case in Nebraska a few weeks after the *Dobbs* ruling demonstrated the inefficacy of narrow privacy protection for abortion-seeking. In this case, police investigated a seventeen-year-old and her mother after receiving a tip that the women had purchased medication to induce abortion and had buried the fetus. Police submitted a search warrant to Meta (Facebook's parent company) and were able to obtain private direct messages between the teenager and her mother discussing the situation, which provided critical evidence. Both the teenager and her mother were charged with several felonies. *See* Jason Koebler and Anna Merlan, *This Is the Data Facebook Gave Police to Prosecute a Teenager for Abortion*, MOTHERBOARD (Aug. 9, 2022), https://www.vice.com/en/article/n7zevd/this-is-the-data-facebook-gave-police-to-prosecute-a-teenager-for-abortion.

34. *See* Abby Ohlheiser, *Anti-Abortion Activists Are Collecting the Data They'll Need for Prosecutions Post-Roe*, MIT TECH. REV. (May 31, 2022), https://www.technologyreview.com/2022/05/31/1052901/anti-abortion-activists-are-collecting-the-data-theyll-need-for-prosecutions-post-roe/; Alfred Ng, *Data Brokers Resist Pressure to Stop Collecting Info on Pregnant People*, POLITICO (Aug. 1, 2022), https://www.politico.com/news/2022/08/01/data-information-pregnant-people-00048988.

35. This point echoes a similar issue in analyses of the privacy risks of "sex tech": the tendency to focus on the "sexiest" and most novel examples of potential privacy breach (e.g., connected sex toys) to the exclusion of the quotidian, generalized avenues through which most intimate surveillance occurs (e.g., email, search). *See* Karen Levy, *The Phallus-y Fallacy: On Unsexy Intimate Tracking*, 18 AM. J. BIOETHICS 22 (2018).

36. Sharmila Devi, *Anti-Abortion Groups Target Funding of Planned Parenthood*, 386 LANCET 941 (2015).

37. Center for Medical Progress v. Planned Parenthood Federation of Am., 551 F. Supp. 3d 320, 324 (S.D.N.Y. 2021).

38. Jackie Calmes, *Planned Parenthood Videos Were Altered, Analysis Finds*, NEW YORK TIMES (Aug. 27, 2015), https://www.nytimes.com/2015/08/28/us/abortion-planned-parenthood-videos.html.

39. The National Abortion Federation collects detailed data about the frequency of different types of violence and disruption propagated against providers, and has done so since 1977. Its most recent available statistics show significant year-on-year increases in stalking, blockades of abortion facilities, suspicious packages, vandalism, invasions, and assault and battery. *See* National Abortion Federation, *2021 Violence and Disruption Statistics*, https://prochoice.org/wp-content/uploads/2021_NAF_VD_Stats_Final.pdf. In 2015, the year of the Center for Medical Progress misinformation campaign, there were marked increases in death threats and threats of harm to providers, picketing, hate mail, and other forms of disruption. *See* National Abortion Federation, *2015 Violence and Disruption Statistics*, https://prochoice.org/wp-content/uploads/2015-NAF-Violence-Disruption-Stats.pdf.

40. *See* Michael Vitiello, *The Nuremberg Files: Testing the Outer Limits of the First Amendment*, 61 OHIO ST. L.J. 1175 (2000); Rene Sanchez, *Abortion Foes' Internet Site on Trial*, WASHINGTON POST (Jan. 15, 1999), https://www.washingtonpost.com/archive/politics/1999/01/15/abortion-foes-internet-site-on-trial/a284d05f-f83b-4eae-ad57-61985b66eaae/.

41. AbortionDocs.org, https://abortiondocs.org/.

42. AbortionDocs.org *Disclaimer*, https://abortiondocs.org/disclaimer/.

43. *Id.*

44. *See* Emma Bowman, *As States Ban Abortion, The Texas Bounty Law Offers a Way to Survive Legal Challenges*, NPR (July 11, 2022), https://www.npr.org/2022/07/11/1107741175/texas-abortion-bounty-law.

45. *See* Meryl Kornfield, *A Website for 'Whistleblowers' To Expose Texas Abortion Providers Was Taken Down—Again*, WASHINGTON POST (Sept. 6, 2021), https://www.washingtonpost.com/nation/2021/09/06/texas-abortion-ban-website/.

46. *See* Digital Defense Fund, *Keep Your Abortion Private and Secure*, https://digitaldefensefund.org/ddf-guides/abortion-privacy.

47. *All About Geofencing*, Choose Life Marketing, https://www.chooselifemarketing.com/all-about-geofencing/.

48. *See* Center for Reproductive Rights, *supra* note 4.

49. Claire Wardle and Hossein Derakhshan, *Information Disorder: Toward an Interdisciplinary Framework for Research and Policy Making*, Council of Europe Report No. DGI(2017)09 (Sept. 27, 2017), https://rm.coe.int/information-disorder-toward-an-interdisciplinary-framework-for-researc/168076277c, at 20–22.

50. Kim Bellware, *Lawmakers Urge Google to Fix Abortion Searches Suggesting "Fake Clinics,"* WASHINGTON POST (June 18, 2022), https://www.washingtonpost.com/health/2022/06/18/google-abortion-clinic-searches-fake/. *See also* Yelena Mejova, et al., *Googling for Abortion: Search Engine Mediation of Abortion Accessibility in the United States*, 2 J. QUANTITATIVE DESCRIPTION 1 (2022) (describing the frequency of listings for crisis pregnancy centers vs. abortion clinics in response to search queries).

PART III

Governance × Feminism

12

The Rise, Fall, and Rise
of Civil Libertarianism

Hannah Bloch-Wehba

In 2012, I spent the summer working as a legal intern at the Electronic Frontier Foundation (EFF). Then headquartered in a dim and cavernous former pornography studio in San Francisco's Mission District, the organization was in the process of finalizing its move to an erstwhile Planned Parenthood clinic that it had recently acquired near the Tenderloin. One day EFF staffers took me and my fellow interns to the new building, where we appreciatively gushed over the square footage and rifled around the metal storage cabinets that had been left behind in examination rooms that had been abandoned but not yet cleared out.

A decade later, the occupation of a former women's health clinic by a technology advocacy organization seems a fitting metaphor for Silicon Valley's social and political ambitions. Nearly every contemporary social and political conflict touches, or is touched by, networked technologies in some way. Protests against police brutality are organized online and surveilled by law enforcement using social media monitoring. Amid a global pandemic that has killed over 6 million people to date, networked technologies enable contact tracing and permit public health disinformation to flourish. And the criminalization of pregnancy wrought by the Supreme Court's decision in *Dobbs* has brought to fruition both a new era of social mobilization and a new era of surveillance, as Elizabeth Joh's contribution to this volume shows.

At the time, EFF's move to its new building seemed like a harbinger of a promising future in which the organization could move from the fringes of the legal community to a position nearer to its center, while maintaining some of its iconoclasm. Though perhaps a little too on-the-nose, EFF's move is also an apt symbol of cyberlaw's maturation. From the outset, cyberlaw was characterized by a moral panic over sexual speech, pornography, and the protection of children familiar to First Amendment scholars. Important civil libertarian victories recognized that sexual speech and pornography were constitutionally protected from state intervention. The civil libertarian approach advanced by EFF, the ACLU, and others cautioned against government efforts to expand surveillance and weaken encryption. The civil libertarian paradigm saw government regulation as the primary threat to free speech online, the marketplace as the more appropriate mechanism for regulating expression, and courts as the rightful arbiters of these disputes.

But while civil libertarians successfully rolled back much regulatory intervention to enforce moral codes online, their successes came at a price: the legitimation of private power over speech. Though the civil libertarian tradition would theoretically protect sexual speech, it has in practice shifted the locus of power over speech from public to private hands.[1] Today, private speech enforcement is far broader than what the state could accomplish through direct regulation.

Using sexual speech as its focal point, this chapter explores the ambiguous legacy of cyber civil liberties and the ascent of alternative paradigms for digital freedom. Civil libertarians won important initial cyberlaw victories against early efforts by states to sanitize the Web and to surveil its users. These victories, coupled with an expansive interpretation of free speech in the courts, have resulted in a growing industry of private speech enforcement and control. The result is a form of "market" ordering that is nominally private but that, in fact, reflects the entrenched power and influence of conservative cultural politics. In turn, this burgeoning private authority has prompted both political and cultural realignments (the "techlash") and a broader turning away from the civil libertarian approach to speech. But in a moment of challenge to sexual freedom and equality, cyber civil libertarianism might yet find another foothold.

CYBER CIVIL LIBERTIES

In many respects, cyberlaw inherited the First Amendment civil libertarian tradition and its anti-regulatory stance. At the core of the civil libertarian tradition is the metaphor of the marketplace of ideas. Initially articulated by thinkers including John Milton and John Stuart Mill, the "marketplace" denotes "the metaphorical space in civil society in which ideas are espoused, debated, and refined."[2] In his famous dissent in *Abrams v. United States*, Justice Oliver Wendell Holmes rearticulated the marketplace concept, calling for "free trade in ideas" and making the market a permanent fixture in First Amendment jurisprudence.[3]

Notwithstanding the rhetoric of *laissez faire*, the notion of a free marketplace for ideas was almost immediately challenged by the conviction that some kinds of ideas were not worth trading in. For example, obscenity was seen as lacking any First Amendment value or protection.[4] Excluding obscenity from the marketplace of ideas aptly illustrates a basic legal realist insight: no market is truly "free" from regulation.[5] The apparent simplicity of obscenity's categorical exclusion from constitutional protection also belied a more complicated struggle to articulate a workable test for identifying "obscene" material. Even as the test for obscenity was narrowed and refined, the Court continued to permit states to regulate sexual expression—pornography, nude dancing, and adult businesses, to name a few—in ways that they could not regulate nonsexual speech.[6]

"Cyberspace," like the "marketplace," was similarly envisioned as both a quasi-physical space and a philosophical metaphor. In the heady early days of the commercial internet, its enthusiasts imagined cyberspace as a unique new "place" distinct from any "territorially based sovereign."[7] In one of the earliest and most influential formulations, *A Declaration of the Independence of Cyberspace*, John Perry Barlow, one of EFF's cofounders, articulated the utopian, libertarian ideal of the internet as a self-governing community in which "anyone, anywhere may express his or her beliefs, no matter how singular, without fear of being coerced into silence or conformity."[8]

The bar was set unattainably high. Like the "marketplace of ideas," the romantic vision of "cyberspace" as a world open to equal participation by all and governed from the bottom up has not lived up to its idealized formulation. From the start, the terrain of cyberspace was shaped by legal, political, and cultural currents that sought to confront a perceived flood of pornography, sanitize online speech, and push sexual speech to the margins. These efforts to sanitize the Web were nothing new; indeed, fights over online pornography reprised decades-old debates about free speech, feminism, and the protection of children.

In the 1980s, Catharine MacKinnon and Andrea Dworkin argued that pornography subordinates women and constitutes legally cognizable sex discrimination.[9] MacKinnon and Dworkin advanced an anti-pornography civil rights ordinance that defined "the graphic sexually explicit subordination of women through pictures or words" as sex discrimination.[10] The effort to bar pornography through civil rights law ultimately failed: the versions of the statute adopted in Indianapolis and Bellingham were struck down as viewpoint-based distinctions in violation of the First Amendment.[11]

The failure of the anti-pornography civil rights ordinance was not the end of the battle against pornography. Over the decades, lawmakers and regulators have repeatedly based attempts to regulate sexual speech on the grounds that it is harmful to minors. In 1968, the Supreme Court upheld a New York statute that barred the sale of nonobscene nude pictures to minors even though they were constitutionally protected for adults.[12] The Court deferred to the state's determination that exposure to sexual speech could "impair the ethical and moral development of our youth."[13] Similar assertions about sexual speech's adverse effects on children repeatedly resurfaced in other contexts. Cities used the "harmful to minors" argument to justify using zoning laws to limit where adult businesses could operate.[14] In one case, the city of Jacksonville, Florida, attempted to prohibit drive-in movie theaters from showing films with nudity by arguing (unsuccessfully) that the ordinance was necessary to protect children.[15] The FCC's authority to sanction a radio station for airing George Carlin's "seven dirty words" monologue rested in large part on the finding that it was broadcast at a time when children could hear it.[16]

Compared to the anti-subordination argument, the notion that porn was "harmful to minors" was less objectionable on First Amendment grounds. In *American Booksellers Association v. Hudnut*, the Seventh Circuit had rejected the anti-pornography civil rights ordinance because it singled out for regulation "speech that subordinates women," whereas "speech that portrays women in positions of equality is lawful, no matter how graphic the sexual content."[17] Writing for the court, Judge Easterbrook brushed aside the argument that pornography silenced women, infamously castigating the ordinance as impermissible "thought control."[18] In contrast, courts had always considered whether sexual speech was "harmful to minors," or whether it caused any of an array of antisocial effects, as a content- and viewpoint-neutral inquiry.

The "harmful to minors" argument thus proved a more potent justification for restrictions on sexual speech than the subordination of women. As Robin West notes, however, the feminist anti-pornography movement gave rise to political realignments: liberals and "anti-censorship feminists," on the one hand, who argued that pornography constituted protected speech with some social value, and conservatives and "anti-pornography feminists," on the other, who argued that pornography could be highly regulated or even banned, consistent with constitutional principles.[19] Those political realignments gave the anti-pornography movement an established position in domestic politics.

The introduction and commercialization of the Web made debates over sexual speech salient once again. Regulatory efforts to limit sexual speech reflected the "political pressure produced by the dramatic and rapid mainstreaming of pornography in our culture."[20] As Amy Adler illustrates, changing technological and cultural mores yielded innumerable attempts to control the flow of sexual content, typically oriented around the protection of children.

For example, the "cyberporn panic of 1996" gave rise to the Communications Decency Act (CDA), which made it a crime to knowingly send "obscene or indecent" messages to people under 18.[21] The CDA also made it a crime to display any message that "depicts or describes, in terms patently offensive as measured by contemporary community standards, sexual or excretory activities or organs."[22] The CDA provided an affirmative defense to websites that took steps to restrict access to minors or that employed age verification techniques.

So it is no surprise that the CDA's drafters cited sexual speech's potential harmful effects on minors as a reason to control the rapidly commercializing World Wide Web. The Supreme Court struck the CDA down in *Reno v. American Civil Liberties Union*, rejecting the argument that the imperative of protecting children justified broad, vague, content-based penalties for online speech.

Shortly after *Reno v. ACLU*, Congress tried again with the Child Online Protection Act (COPA). COPA restricted the posting of material "harmful to minors" for "commercial purposes," unless the poster used some means to verify that viewers were above legal age. Again, the Court struck the statute down on First Amendment grounds. Because COPA affected at least some protected speech, and because it employed means that were broader than necessary, the Court held that it was unconstitutional.[23]

THE RISE OF PRIVATE CENSORSHIP

What is slightly more surprising, however, is that a widespread crackdown on sexual speech occurred *even in spite of* the victories in *Reno v. ACLU* and *Ashcroft v. ACLU*. Pressure to suppress pornography migrated from the halls of Congress to the conference rooms of Silicon Valley, where it was embedded into content policies, community standards, and automated enforcement techniques.

First, *Reno v. ACLU* left intact intermediary immunity rules that shielded platforms from liability for user-generated content and allowed companies to make and enforce their own rules and standards to limit the kinds of content that they would host.[24] Section 230I(1) infamously immunizes online websites from liability for information posted by third parties. Section 230I(2), the "Good Samaritan" provision, protects online providers from liability when they take action "in good faith" to block or filter "obscene, lewd, lascivious, filthy, excessively violent, harassing or otherwise objectionable" material from their services.[25]

Section 230's survival meant that the internet did not become a "digital cesspool," as some had feared.[26] Instead, the internet was preserved as a domain for private ordering rather than public regulation. And the incentive to moderate online content set by Section 230's Good Samaritan provision aligned directly with conservative attacks on pornography and "indecency." As a result, even when attempts to regulate were not directly successful, what Alice Marwick calls "technopanics" often led private entities to voluntarily constrain speech in ways that reflected the dominant cultural and political milieu.[27]

So while platforms were not required to screen out pornography, nudity, or sexual content from their services, many—particularly the major social media platforms—have promised to do so. In short, as Ari Waldman has argued, online platforms have adopted the same kind of "moralistic discourse" about sexual speech and the need to protect children that lawmakers advanced around the CDA.[28] For example, YouTube bars all explicit content that is "meant to be sexually gratifying."[29] Facebook likewise bars nudity and "sexual activity," citing concerns about users who might be "sensitive."[30] The desire to maximize advertising revenue provides further justification for suppressing what platforms define as sexual speech. Indeed, YouTube explicitly defines "adult content" as "not advertiser-friendly."[31]

As platforms grew and commercialized, they also developed technological methods to moderate online content, including for adult content and nudity. Technology firms began to use hash-matching tools to monitor content for unlawful child sexual abuse imagery and terrorist content.[32] Using machine learning and artificial intelligence, platforms broadened their efforts to make content-related decisions rapidly and at scale.[33] Automated techniques remain a vital mechanism for platforms to be able to detect violations of their community standards. But despite a popular veneer of objectivity and perfect enforcement, they are frequently wrong. When the blogging site Tumblr announced that it would no longer host adult content, it rolled out an AI system to moderate posts that immediately began to flag "vases, witches, fishes, and everything in between" as impermissible sexual content.[34]

Intolerance of sexual speech has only grown more pronounced during the four years since the passage of the Allow States and Victims to Fight Online Sex Trafficking Act (FOSTA). FOSTA expanded federal criminal liability for sex trafficking and for intentionally promoting or facilitating prostitution through interactive computer services.[35] As Kendra Albert documents, although FOSTA has had little real-world impact on criminal and civil liability, it has incentivized large "general purpose" platforms to crack down on sexual content. Small platforms were "deterred by the possibility of federal criminal investigation;" many "niche, free, and queer" websites shut down.[36] FOSTA has had a particularly dramatic effect on sex workers, who have been harmed by the law's effort to eliminate sites that facilitate sex work and simultaneously "deplatformed" by the major platforms.[37]

As Waldman points out, the mainstream online platforms' sexual content policies disproportionately affect queer content and reinforce social media as a "straight space."[38] FOSTA doubled down on these policies, as Albert notes, both because "fear of queerness and non-normative sexuality is intimately tied to whorephobia, and because a huge number of transgender people, primarily transgender women of color and transfeminine people of color, trade sex."[39]

To understand the stakes, compare these two examples. Over the years, Facebook has repeatedly taken down photographs of women breastfeeding their children as violative of the firm's policy against nudity.[40] When asked, Facebook asserted that breastfeeding photos were permitted and that most of these takedown decisions were erroneous. The company's public position was that breastfeeding was "natural and beautiful" and so photographs of breastfeeding were permitted.[41] In contrast, Facebook's Oversight Board recently announced that it will consider an appeal from a decision to remove two pictures of a transgender, nonbinary couple with captions explaining that one member was planning to undergo top surgery and that the couple was raising funds to support their surgery and recovery. Facebook took the photos down because they violated the company's policy on sexual solicitation, and refused to reinstate them even after the couple appealed.[42]

The convergence of formally "private" incentives with public policy provides a powerful new avenue for suppression of sexual speech. In theory, platforms' decisions about adult content are entirely private. In fact, however, the "private" rules of content moderation operate within a political context in which government is a powerful stakeholder. This political context renders platforms vulnerable to government pressure, despite formal independence.[43] With governments unable to enforce anti-pornography laws directly, platforms became particularly apt at policing undesirable speech.

Sexual speech thus presents a rejoinder to the idealized image of openness and democratic participation in the "marketplace of ideas" and in its virtual instantiation, "cyberspace." Indeed, at the core of the internet's democratic promise is the idea that it lowers the barriers to participation in public discourse. With widely distributed communicative technology, as the Court in *Reno v. ACLU* put it, "any person with a phone line can become a town crier with a voice that resonates farther than it could from any soapbox."[44] Even, in theory, a sex worker.

But the emergence of large online platforms blunted these possibilities. Instead, as online platforms emerged and commercialized, the preference for what Barlow applauded as "natural anarchy" and social ordering collapsed into a preference for private or market ordering.[45] Online communities developed rules and enforcement methods.[46] The growth of commercial platforms meant that the individual speech that was at the core of the libertarian tradition grew increasingly reliant on technological infrastructure in private hands.[47] As those private entities grew increasingly powerful, it became clear that their preferences for online speech aligned in significant part with those of cultural conservatives who opposed sexual content and, in particular, the flourishing of sexual minorities. The approach to content regulation jettisoned in *Reno v. ACLU* came back, this time originating in Silicon Valley.

CONFRONTING ONLINE HARMS
AND PLATFORM POWER

For nearly thirty years, the dominant mode of thinking about online speech has been libertarian in outlook. But faced with the seemingly innumerable challenges of digital culture and politics today—disinformation, misinformation, weaponized harassment, extractive surveillance capitalism, to name just a few—the cyber civil libertarianism that EFF espouses and, in many ways, pioneered, is on the decline.[48]

First, a growing consensus holds that much online speech causes significant harms, and that the internet industry has largely failed to address those harms. Perhaps the sharpest critique of cyber civil libertarianism comes from Danielle Citron, who offers an alternative paradigm in her germinal work on cyber civil rights. Citron paints a disturbing picture of a flood of online mobs, harassment, and abuse. She argues that civil rights law is an appropriate response to patterns of behavior that can "extinguish the self-expression of another" while evading accountability for harmful speech.[49] Citron contends that online attacks and abuse rarely implicate the kinds of interests that free speech doctrine is meant to protect. In particular, she rejects the notion that online threats, doxing, and harassment contribute to the "marketplace of ideas."[50] In fact, as she shows, online attacks frequently have the effect of silencing women and people of color.[51]

In her book *Algorithms of Oppression*, Safiya Umoja Noble offers a distinct, but parallel critique of search engines' "corporate control over personal information."[52] In a chapter on the right to be forgotten, Noble describes how Google has resisted legal obligations to erase information about individuals, even when it causes significant harm. Under the First Amendment's protections for publishing truthful information, Google has the better of these arguments.[53] But they come at a high cost. Noble focuses on several anecdotes about women who were fired, bullied, and harassed after past work in the porn industry was discovered online.[54] As Noble describes it, the interest in concealing one's past is in tension with Google's position that its search engine preserves "the cultural record of humanity."[55] Noble aptly describes how Google's dominance has wrested control over reputation, history, and information away from institutions and individuals.

Firms' invocation of robust expressive freedom to shield themselves from regulation has also invited scrutiny.[56] As Julie Cohen puts it, "a campaign has been underway to insulate all forms of commercial information processing from regulatory oversight by invoking the First Amendment's protection for freedom of speech."[57] The result is that the countercultural origins of cyber civil libertarianism have faded while the modern libertarian approach benefits behemoths such as Verizon and Google. To put it another way, the "winners" of First Amendment cases are "more likely to be corporations and other economically and politically powerful actors" than individuals, movement groups, or activists.[58] Tech giants promise to use their First Amendment rights to fight for their users, but whether they do so is ultimately left to their discretion.

To a progressive, then, it looks increasingly like platforms' First Amendment freedoms are running headlong into the expressive, dignitary, and reputational interests of their users. But cultural conservatives are also, once again, seeking to regulate the internet, making arguments (often in bad faith) about social media "censorship" that they argue disproportionately silences conservative viewpoints.

Contemporary confrontations with platform power directly challenge the libertarian tradition in surprising and internally contradictory ways. As evelyn douek and Genevieve Lakier have put it, political conservatives are raising "concern about the threat that private corporate power poses to freedom of speech," while liberals are defending private governance.[59] Meanwhile, progressives see the role of private firms in what Jack Balkin calls the "Second Gilded Age" as a roadblock to democracy.[60] To some extent, these reconfigured political alignments echo the shifts that took place during the feminist anti-pornography movement, when political conservatives and anti-porn feminists joined forces in support of censorship.

Today, however, even the "anti-censorship" coalition is anti-sexual speech. Conservative majorities in Texas and Florida have enacted "must-carry" legislation that prohibit "censorship" by social media firms. At the time of writing, courts have struck down both statutes as unconstitutional. Anti-censorship groups have pointed out that these laws are so broad that they would prohibit online platforms from removing pornography. For example, the Texas statute prohibits any censorship on the basis of viewpoint. When pressed in litigation, however, the state argued that platforms could still exclude pornography as a "content category," as if doing so raises no problem for free expression.[61] The Florida law does not permit platforms to "censor, deplatform, or shadow ban" a "journalistic enterprise" unless that enterprise posts content that meets the legal standard of obscenity. As the Eleventh Circuit pointed out, "The provision is so broad that it would prohibit a child-friendly platform like YouTube Kids from removing—or even adding an age gate to—soft-core pornography posted by PornHub."[62]

Could civil libertarianism be revived? I think so, with caveats. The first wave of cyber civil libertarianism pitted the interests of the state against the interests of the users of a nascent World Wide Web, a classic First Amendment clash between state and speaker. With the reversal of *Roe v. Wade* and the widespread criminalization of abortion, the same kind of danger arises once again: criminalizing and obstructing information about effectuating what was, until late June 2022, a constitutional right.

Indeed, "anti-censorship" conservatism is increasingly difficult to square with a political and cultural agenda that seeks to reverse hard-won gains for sexual freedom and equality. Shortly after *Dobbs*, South Carolina introduced the "Equal Protection at Conception—No Exceptions—Act," which would ban almost all abortions in the state. In addition, the statute has a provision making it unlawful to "aid or abet" a violation of the abortion ban. In particular, the law criminalizes "providing information . . . regarding self-administered abortions" and "providing access to a website . . . purposefully directed to a pregnant woman who is a resident of this State that provides information on how to obtain an abortion" if the provider knows that the information will be or is reasonably likely to be used to procure an abortion.[63]

For civil libertarians, laws like South Carolina's are a classic example of government overreach: direct state meddling with free expression. Like the anti-porn efforts rejected in *Reno v. ACLU* and *Ashcroft v. ACLU*, the "Equal Protection at Conception—No Exceptions—Act" pits law enforcement's interests against those of internet platforms, and their users: old wine in new bottles.

Amid attacks on women's health, privacy, equality, and autonomy, it is tempting to look to online platforms as guardians of these values and defenders of First Amendment traditions. But as legal theorists have long understood, this is not the exclusive way to imagine free speech. For over a century, it has been apparent that even *laissez faire* ordering is "in reality permeated with coercive restrictions of individual freedom."[64] To put it another way, "Market ordering is only neutral if one takes power off the table."[65] In 2022, after the Supreme Court opinion in *Dobbs*, Facebook and Instagram began to delete social media posts offering to send mifepristone through the mail. The posts, the platform said, violated their rules against "regulated goods."[66] Sexual expression has been effectively marginalized through both law and private action; will abortion-related speech suffer the same fate?

Putting porn at cyberlaw's center illustrates how the libertarian battles to ensure that the state could not censor sexual speech set the stage for the rise of platform power. Once the prime exemplar of free speech battles, today sexual speech is so off limits that even advocates of must-carry legislation believe that pornography need not find a home online. Abortion, now the subject of widespread criminalization and crackdown, may become even more difficult to discuss. In our cultural, political, and legal imagination, private platforms are bulwarks against censorship. But this vision was naïve from the start. If one lesson of the current political moment is that the Supreme Court won't save us, surely a second is that neither will Silicon Valley.[67]

NOTES

1. Scott Skinner-Thompson, *The First Queer Right*, 116 MICH. L. REV. 881, 886 (2018) (describing LGBTQ challenges to obscenity law); Jack M. Balkin, *Free Speech Is a Triangle*, 118 COLUM. L. REV. 2011 (2018).

2. G. S. Hans, *Changing Counterspeech*, 69 CLEV. ST. L. REV. 749, 759 (2021).

3. 250 U.S. 616, 630 (1919) (Holmes, J., dissenting).

4. Genevieve Lakier, *The Invention of Low-Value Speech*, 128 HARV. L. REV. 2166, 2175 (2015).

5. Mary Anne Franks, *Fearless Speech*, 17 FIRST AMEND. L. REV. 294 (2019).

6. David Cole, *Playing by Pornography's Rules: The Regulation of Sexual Expression*, 143 U. PA. L. REV. 111 (1994).

7. David R. Johnson & David Post, *Law and Borders—The Rise of Law in Cyberspace*, 48 STAN. L. REV. 1367, 1375 (1996).

8. John Perry Barlow, *A Declaration of the Independence of Cyberspace*, EFF (Feb. 8, 1996), https://www.eff.org/cyberspace-independence.

9. Catharine A. MacKinnon, *Pornography, Civil Rights, and Speech*, 20 HARV. C.R.-C.L. L. REV. 1 (1985).

10. Am. Booksellers Ass'n, Inc. v. Hudnut, 771 F.2d 323, 324 (7th Cir. 1985), aff'd, 475 U.S. 1001 (1986).

11. *Hudnut*, 771 F.2d 323; Village Books v. City of Bellingham, No. C88–1470D (W.D. Wash. Feb. 9, 1989).

12. Ginsberg v. New York, 390 U.S. 629 (1968).

13. *Ginsberg* at 641.

14. City of Renton v. Playtime Theaters, Inc., 475 U.S. 41, 51 (1986).

15. Erznoznik v. City of Jacksonville, 422 U.S. 205, 212–13 (1975).

16. F.C.C. v. Pacifica, 438 U.S. 726, 732–33 (1978).

17. *Hudnut*, 771 F.2d at 328.

18. *Id.*

19. Robin West, *The Feminist-Conservative Anti-Pornography Alliance and the 1986 Attorney General's Commission on Pornography Report*, 12 Am. B. Found. Res. J. 681 ([American Bar Foundation, Wiley] 1987).

20. Amy Adler, *All Porn All the Time*, 31 N.Y.U. Rev. L. & Soc. Change 695, 707 (2007).

21. Alice E. Marwick, *To Catch a Predator? The MySpace Moral Panic*, First Monday (May 2008).

22. Reno v. ACLU, 521 U.S. 844 (1997).

23. Ashcroft v. ACLU, 542 U.S. 656, 667 (2004)

24. Jeff Kosseff, The Twenty-Six Words that Created the Internet (2019).

25. 47 U.S.C. § 230(c).

26. John Perry Barlow, *Passing the Buck on Porn*, EFF, https://www.eff.org/pages/passing-buck-porn.

27. Marwick, *supra* note 21.

28. Ari Ezra Waldman, *Disorderly Content* 26 (Aug. 5, 2022), https://papers.ssrn.com/sol3/papers.cfm?abstract_id=3906001.

29. YouTube, Nudity and Sexual Content Policies, https://support.google.com/youtube/answer/2802002#zippy=.

30. Facebook Community Standards, Adult Nudity and Sexual Activity, Meta (2022), https://transparency.fb.com/policies/community-standards/adult-nudity-sexual-activity/.

31. YouTube, Advertiser-friendly content guidelines, https://support.google.com/youtube/answer/6162278#Adult.

32. Hannah Bloch-Wehba, *Content Moderation as Surveillance*, 36 Berkeley Tech. L.J. 132–33 (2022).

33. Hannah Bloch-Wehba, *Automation in Moderation*, 53 Cornell Int'l L.J. 41, 56 (2020).

34. Shannon Liao, *Tumblr Will Ban All Adult Content on December 17th*, The Verge (Dec. 3, 2018, 12:26 PM), https://www.theverge.com/2019/1/30/18202474/tumblr-porn-ai-nudity-artificial-intelligence-machine-learning.

35. Eric Goldman, *The Complicated Story of FOSTA and Section 230*, 17 First Amend. L. Rev. 279, 284 (2018).

36. Kendra Albert, *Five Reflections from Four Years of FOSTA/SESTA* at 13–14, Cardozo Arts & Entm't L.J., https://papers.ssrn.com/sol3/papers.cfm?abstract_id=4095115.

37. *Id.*, at 14.

38. Waldman, *supra* note 28.

39. Albert, *supra* note 36 at 5.

40. Caitlin Dewey, *Facebook Is Embroiled in Yet Another Breastfeeding Photo Controversy*, Washington Post (Feb. 26, 2015), https://www.washingtonpost.com/news/the-intersect/wp/2015/02/26/facebook-is-embroiled-in-yet-another-breastfeeding-photo-controversy/.

41. Facebook Help Center, *Does Facebook allow photos of mothers breastfeeding?* https://www.facebook.com/help/340974655932193.

42. Oversight Board, Gender Identity and Nudity (2022–009-IG-UA & 2022–010-IG-UA), https://oversightboard.secure.force.com/apex/VisualAntidote__HostedFastForm?f=DlyKO4pHoat13HNLhYmFwHF%2BcJ%2FsGkgPHMtAlFocqhDuu5bWsZsfCIoZCRFu2%2Brl.

43. Seth F. Kreimer, *Censorship by Proxy: The First Amendment, Internet Intermediaries, and the Problem of the Weakest Link*, 155 U. Pa. L. Rev. 11 (2006); Derek E. Bambauer, *Against Jawboning*, 100 Minn. L. Rev. 51 (2015).

44. Reno v. ACLU, 521 U.S. at 870.

45. Bloch-Wehba, *supra* note 33 at 51 (quoting Barlow).

46. *Id.*, at 54–55.

47. Jack M. Balkin, *Digital Speech and Democratic Culture: A Theory of Freedom of Expression for the Information Society*, 79 N.Y.U. L. Rev. 1, 6 (2004).

48. *See, e.g.*, Danielle Keats Citron & Neil M. Richards, *Four Principles for Digital Expression (You Won't Believe #3)*, 95 Wash. U. L. Rev. 1353 (2018).

49. Danielle Keats Citron, *Cyber Civil Rights*, 89 B.U. L. Rev. 61, 98 (2009).

50. *Id.*, at 103.

51. *Id.*, at 69–81.

52. Safiya Umoja Noble, Algorithms of Oppression: How Search Engines Reinforce Racism 121 (2018).

53. Hannah Bloch-Wehba, *Global Platform Governance: Private Power in the Shadow of the State*, 72 S.M.U. L. Rev. 27, 58 (2019).

54. Noble, *supra* note 52 at 119–20.

55. *Id.*, at 128.

56. Sam Lebovic, *The Conservative Press and the Interwar Origins of First Amendment Lochnerism*, 39 L. & Hist. Rev. 539 (2021).

57. Julie E. Cohen, Between Truth and Power: The Legal Constructions of Informational Capitalism 93 (2019).

58. Genevieve Lakier, *Imagining an Antisubordinating First Amendment*, 118 Colum. L. Rev. 2117, 2118 (2018).

59. evelyn douek & Genevieve Lakier, *First Amendment Politics Gets Weird: Public and Private Platform Reform and the Breakdown of the Laissez-Faire Free Speech Consensus*, U. Chi. L. Rev. Online (June 6, 2022), https://lawreviewblog.uchicago.edu/2022/06/06/douek-lakier-first-amendment/.

60. *See, e.g.*, Matt Stoller, Goliath: The 100-Year War between Monopoly Power and Democracy (2020).

61. NetChoice, LLC v. Paxton, Prelim. Inj. Mot. at 21, No. 1:21-cv-00840-RP (W.D. Tex. filed Nov. 22, 2021), ECF 39.

62. NetChoice, LLC v. Att'y Gen., Fla., 34 F.4th 1196, 1229 (11th Cir. 2022).

63. S. 1373, 124th Sess. (S.C. 2022).

64. Robert Hale, *Coercion and Distribution in a Supposedly Non-Coercive State*, 38 Pol. Sci. Q. 470 (1923).

65. Jedediah Britton-Purdy, et al., *Building a Law-and-Political-Economy Framework: Beyond the Twentieth-Century Synthesis*, 129 Yale L.J. 1784, 1823 (2020).

66. Associated Press, *Instagram and Facebook Begin Removing Posts Offering Abortion Pills*, NPR (June 28, 2022), https://www.npr.org/2022/06/28/1108107718/instagram-and-facebook-begin-removing-posts-offering-abortion-pills.

67. Chase Strangio, *The Courts Won't Free Us—Only We Can*, Them.com (July 1, 2022), https://www.them.us/story/chase-strangio-supreme-court-queer-rights.

13

Artificial Intelligence, Microwork, and the Racial Politics of Care

Iván Chaar López and Victoria Sánchez

"We are where artificial intelligence [AI] meets human ingenuity," Leila Janah told a packed audience at the 2018 meeting of The Next Web (TNW) in Amsterdam. TNW describes itself as "the heart of tech," a space where "digital thought leaders" connect with an audience of tech entrepreneurs, investors, and policymakers looking to be inspired, explore new opportunities, and build relationships.[1] The "human ingenuity" Janah referred to could be found at the heart of her organization, then known as Samasource.[2] That ingenuity was the capacity to tackle the "problem" of poverty "with technology and AI to create jobs for the bottom of the pyramid." Samasource integrated marginalized workers from depletion zones (most in the Global South) into the making of the modern world. And Janah pitched her project for an "ethical AI supply chain" to a room full of actors invested—metaphorically and literally—in tech. Yet her pitch was to have them invest in people, to "give work rather than aid."[3]

Since its founding in 2008, Janah committed Samasource to a unique model of philanthropy that was not concerned with providing displaced and marginalized populations with access to goods or services. Instead, it enacted an altruistic mode of care by incorporating these populations into the global labor market. The outsourcing nonprofit was organized around the premise that "talent is equally distributed, but opportunity is not."[4] The only way to bring people out of poverty was to give them higher paying jobs and, through these, create new opportunities. Samasource's intervention was informed by and partially funded through what the Rockefeller Foundation calls "impact sourcing"—a purportedly inclusive employment practice to hire and provide career development opportunities to populations excluded from the digital economy. Samasource would expand a tech company's worker network by tapping into a rich supply of labor in places like Kenya, Uganda, Haiti, and poor communities in the United States where jobs could help increase income. In doing so, it constructed and operated a micro-work supply chain—a network of production and circulation connecting datasets to data processing and validation centers, and to organizations powered by this rich supply of predominantly Black workers so that it's "purpose-built for impact."[5]

This chapter tackles the tensions inherent to Samasource's racial politics of care in relation to labor by analyzing the organization's plans (e.g., corporate materials and Janah's statements interpreting their efforts), its relations with benchmark tech companies, and its experimental practices with philanthropic policymaking groups. Reading alongside feminist thinkers in science and technology studies (STS) on the politics of care, we ask what kinds of ethics emerge when engaging with the affordances of Samasource's plans for a microwork supply chain? How is Black/non-white labor entrenched as the invisible infrastructure of AI, often times through practices of repair work, and what are the ramifications of this sociotechnical arrangement?[6] First, we unsettle dominant understandings of the politics of care by tracing relations not as necessarily beneficial but as potentially detrimental. Attention to asymmetry leads us next to account for the making of unequal arrangements of care.

We argue that Samasource's impact sourcing enacted neoliberal logics of self-government with a feminist sensibility toward repair work. The organization sought to repair the broken relations excluding many from the global market economy by instituting an outsourcing program that trained and integrated those on its margins. To care for the excluded was to bring them into the fold of global capital. Given the data- and labor-intensive aspects of AI or machine learning, this approach consolidated the place of microwork as integral for AI development and the tech industry in general. But even while Samasource sought to construct a "sociotechnical organization of 'humans-as-a-service,'" this was not a universal project.[7] Instead, it was a tightly defined one whereby already vulnerable populations (i.e., often Black/non-white migrant refugees and underrepresented communities) were locked into precarious labor arrangements that undermined their access to better wages and labor rights.[8] Through Samasource's training program and user interface, microworkers were made to care for informational systems and a tech industry that conscripted them as invisible labor. Their repair work maintains information infrastructures and the profit margins of the industry even as their participation falls to the background. Analyzing Samasource's ethical AI supply chain through the framework of racial politics of care helps draw out asymmetries in care work all the while grappling with its ambivalence.

Writing on microwork requires a feminist critical race analytics. Human-machine configurations are made through complex situations that cannot be neatly bounded as strict technical procedures. Elements of a situation become embedded in such configurations just as much as configurations shape elements of the situation. To that end, we draw on what Patricia Hill Collins calls "matrix of domination" to understand how microwork is constituted by and constituting intersecting oppressions. The labor force providing Silicon Valley with its extensive microwork supply chain is made through situated oppressive relations, relations organized by/through race, gender, class, sexuality, and ability.[9] As the case of Samasource shows, their racial politics of care operated through the integration of predominantly Black/non-white workers as AI's invisible labor. But such labor had to first be made available and able to work in AI development. As new laws and policies seek to regulate the growing gig economy, we must contend with the material infrastructure of the tech industry, differential impacts on labor, and what possibilities exist in this conjuncture for a feminist politics of care.

"ETHICAL AI": LABOR AND UNSETTLING CARE

With proliferating cases of (infra)structural injustice and wider mobilizations challenging structural oppression, researchers and actors in industry identified bias, fairness, transparency, accountability, privacy, and responsibility as the key issues in ethical AI.[10] Many of these actors prioritize correcting biased systems, smoothing over their hard edges. However, corrections rarely tackle the underlying rationale of AI or of its deployment in a range of contexts where they either institute or maintain asymmetrical social, economic, and political relations. This chapter builds on work questioning the effects of AI operations on marginalized communities and the data technopolitics embedded in these systems.[11] We open the black box of AI by focusing on the human labor that makes and maintains it.

Attention to labor opens room to question the relations made possible by and through AI. Of import is the hidden labor embedded in AI operations. Jenna Burrell and Marion Fourcade, for example, suggest that a society of algorithms emerges through the organization of specialized data labor. A wide swath of institutions pairs massive datasets with computer methods to sort, organize, extract, and mine them. This pairing relies on the articulation of what they call a "code elite" and a "cybertariat"—the first holds and controls data and software while the latter is tasked with producing, refining, and working the data fed through algorithms. The cybertariat is essential to the very operation of the society of algorithms as technicians are often confronted with the computational limits of automation.[12] The human labor of the cybertariat is inseparable from AI.

Caring for low-wage labor, as Janah's presentation at TNW 2018 stressed, is a matter of concern. In addressing the politics of care, feminist STS scholars ask who cares, why do they or we care, and how to care. They invite their interlocutors to trace and interrogate material relations formed by and through ethico-political obligations.[13] To care is to tend to something or someone, to notice and work in relation to them. Concern, feminist STS thinkers contend, "is an affectively charged sensibility," a practice or way of doing things "characterized by worry, attentiveness, and thoughtfulness."[14] Care is commonly enacted in ordinary fashion, in everyday practices that are life-sustaining and life-repairing. People's quotidian concern and attunement to relational well-being, or care, has often been construed in gendered terms as feminized, overlooked, and devalued labor. As a result, the politics of caring are, as María Puig de la Bellacasa argues, "at the heart of concerns with exclusions and critiques of power dynamics in stratified worlds."[15] To examine the articulations of care beckons an ethical disposition to question invisible arrangements that enforce, reify, and maintain unequal relations.

Tending to the politics of care means not falling into the trap of conflating it with a moral good. This is what Martin et al. call "care's darker side: its lack of innocence and the violence committed in its name." Care does not automatically nor inherently lead to a virtuous result. It is often implicated in reinforcing the practices and logics of capital and imperial formations, as they grow concerned with their own maintenance, reproduction, and perpetuation. Hence, these scholars and others like Michelle Murphy propose "situated critiques of care and its politics." The politics of care invite a critical accounting of raced, sexed, and classed violence, of dispossession, displacement, and exploitation.[16] Murphy's retelling of feminist self-help efforts in the 1970s shows how these scholars and activists grappled with differential arrangements enrolling some populations into asymmetrical relations. Care was not an intrinsic good but a practice that perpetuated precarity. Asymmetrical relations maintained and ensconced the privileged positions of few all the while undermining the capacities of exploited women workers to care for their own.[17] Precarity was embedded within these differential arrangements, rendered through invisible modes of repair work.

The privilege maintained by care work is at the heart of the "digital depletion economy." Such an economy emerges, the Precarity Lab suggests, through the space-making dialectics of "enrichment zones" and "depletion zones." The former comprises those spaces containing resources, labor, and raw materials extracted from the latter.[18] Enriching zones are ever-unfolding entanglements constituted through their capacities to finance, extract, and coordinate relations of dispossession and exploitation. Depletion zones are simultaneously life-sustaining and life-debilitating for the people whose labor constitute them as much as for the inhabitants of enriching zones. This does not mean that everyone is on the same life-preserving/life-weakening boat. Situated analysis shows that these zones are not homogeneous, but they do work toward homogenization. They consolidate the distribution of resources, discriminate between bodies and the value their labor generates, and conserve intersecting axes of domination to safeguard relations of dispossession and exploitation.

Enrichment and depletion zones are different yet repeating arrangements in the *longue durée* of racial capital.[19] The dialectics of differentiation worked through race as "the rationalization for the domination, exploitation, and/or extermination" of non-Europeans and non-whites.[20] The digital depletion economy hinges on persistent practices of distinction and discrimination that posit some bodies, some communities, and some places as extractable matter.[21] These practices follow logics of exception making possible "the combination of managerial and labor regimes in transnational networks that carve striated spaces—or 'latitudes'—shaped by the coordination of systems of governmentality and regimes of labor incarceration."[22] The racial politics of care work weave together enrichment and depletion zones through the veil of matters of concern—a concern that follows logics of differentiation or exception governing unequal arrangements.

Approaching care work through a racial politics of care also means to examine the articulation of an interlocking matrix of domination. Differentiation does not unfold through singular pathways but is the product of co-constituting, multipronged, and multi-sited forces. Care for the Other, especially when animated by notions of (economic) development, does not immediately undo systems of oppression. They can quite as easily exacerbate them because, as the following pages show, political recognition of the Other is premised on the idea that bodies and their labor ought to be productive. The Other, which in most instances here is a Black working person, is politically legible as worthy of concern insofar as they add value to artificial intelligence-as-commodity and intelligence-as-information infrastructure. Looking after racial politics of care fleshes out how matters of concern might undo some relations while reifying others.

UNEQUAL ARRANGEMENTS OF CARE

Samasource's plans to build an "ethical AI supply chain" enact a racial politics of care in two senses. Its care work for the poor means providing them with higher paying data-processing jobs, or attending to the life conditions of dispossession generated by modern capital. Such care work builds on techno-optimistic visions, or the long-standing belief that technological production and use, innovation, and human improvement are tightly bound together.[23] Samasource's plans seek to integrate the poor in predominantly Black/non-white countries and their vitality as an infrastructural appendage of Silicon Valley. As a result, the Black/non-white poor and their vitality are inscribed as racialized labor, or extractable and productive matter for capital. The other sense is the care work these worker's perform for AI. Their work, which Samasource calls "microwork," supports AI by allowing it to operate in a seemingly unobstructed manner. The labor of these workers is necessary to maintain the systems that are imagined as making up modern life; logically, modern life is dependent on the invisible AI care work of Samasource workers. They are the "ghost work" that operationalizes AI and sanitizes a vast range of websites by removing graphic, violent, and hateful content.[24]

When she founded the nonprofit organization Samasource in 2008, Janah set out to disrupt the philanthropic and outsourcing models. As she reflected years later in an essay on social entrepreneurialism, "the actual problem [of poverty] is access to opportunity—and the often deeply entrenched, systemic barriers that deny hard-working people the chance to build a future."[25] Charity did not transform root causes of poverty, and international aid packages, she concluded, were insufficient. A techno-optimistic solution was in the offing. Tapping into the wealthy outsourcing market, Samasource redirected some of its capital to address this lack of opportunity by hiring low-wage and unemployed workers to perform data service labor. Their jobs would, Janah often told captive audiences in the startup and tech worlds, improve their lives and the lives of those who relied on their source of income. A white paper by MIT economists concluded 40 percent of workers who received training and a job referral from Samasource went on to higher paying jobs and reported lower unemployment rates than their control group.[26] Relying on the company's internal worker surveys, Janah claimed that, prior to employment with Samasource, workers reported an average daily income of $2.20 with many living in improvised housing and maintaining unhealthy diets (e.g., eating sugar cane as a main source of caloric intake). After employment with Samasource, workers earned on average $8.15 a day which led to improvements in diets, education, and housing. "This is the power of work over charity."[27] Or this is Janah and Samasource's articulation of the first sense of racial politics of care, a care toward people in the Global South meant to protect them by enrolling their labor in the making of the modern technological world. A second sense requires further elaboration.

Samasource's "ethical AI supply chain" combines microwork with impact sourcing. Animating Janah's approach to microwork was her interest of "tapping into the brainpower of the poor."[28] Microwork breaks down big data projects such as the AI and machine learning models powering self-driving cars into smaller actions. Samasource workers, who must be literate and know how to use a computer, are enrolled in cognitive labor by annotating images and video to build training datasets subsequently fed into AI algorithms.[29] Annotators identify objects such as cars parked and moving, or lane location and change, and people and their pose (e.g., standing, sitting, walking, running) by drawing polygons around them as well as by labeling them. Samasource's in-house interface Samahub, meanwhile, allows real-time quality assurance to assess the accuracy and reliability of worker data inputs. The services offered by the company are not so dissimilar to those Lilly Irani studied in Amazon's Mechanical Turk. Microwork at Samasource assembles "cognitive pieceworkers in service of employers and their computer systems. The pieceworkers work on tasks in batches; the employers can put these batches out automatedly through computer work code they write."[30] Microwork, as Irani deftly shows, helped produce the distinction between innovative and menial labor—a crucial distinction in the articulation of value and of those bodies/minds imagined to represent such value. Scholars in new media studies expressed concerns and questions about the ethics of microwork and crowdsourcing soon after they became experimental sociotechnical arrangements.[31] A key difference lies in the company's commitment to "impact sourcing," which means the establishment of a sustained labor supply chain with Samasource playing a permanent intermediary, coordinating, and repairing role.

Toward the end of the 2000s, concerned with growing global economic inequality, the Rockefeller Foundation sought to transform the outsourcing industry through a new supply chain model called "impact sourcing."[32] The foundation and some of its partners saw impact sourcing as an "inclusive employment practice" whereby "companies in global supply chains intentionally hire and provide career development opportunities to people who otherwise would have limited prospects for formal employment."[33] Impact sourcing requires the articulation of an ecosystem comprising outsourced workers, the worker's immediate community, outsourcing organizations, and outsourcing clients. As proposed in a range of Rockefeller-funded reports, impact sourcing is meant to benefit all elements of this ecosystem via a developmentalist vision. First, it provides higher-income employment and access to new opportunities for these workers. Workers can then dispose of this income in their wider community and, thereby, create a ripple effect of economic and social activities. After all, these workers, from the purview of policy makers, often live in "rural areas of developing countries or in slums," lack access to secondary or tertiary education, or, despite having some education, find themselves in areas with high unemployment. Outsourcing organizations fulfilled the demands of its clients while managing and investing in jobs and skills development that benefit workers and their communities. Lastly, outsourcing clients meet cost savings and growth objectives all the while developing corporate social responsibility goals.[34]

Impact sourcing is a neoliberal political strategy imbued with a racial politics of care. It is an ethical commitment toward the excluded other through a moral calculus of worth. Human value as well as practices, lifestyles, and visions of the good are tightly understood in relation to the market. And the market is positioned as the privileged allocator of public resources; it is a technology of subjection through which to "differently regulate populations for optimal productivity," especially via the spatial practices of market forces.[35] Companies subscribing to impact sourcing enact modes of governing populations that follow differentiating logics of efficiency and optimization. These logics position some populations as prime targets for subjection, for their capacity to maximize values produced through exploitation, dispossession, and extraction. Impact sourcing also institutes knowledge and expert systems, as Samasource attests, that induce in workers self-animation and self-government through the attainment of skills, the pursuit of entrepreneurial endeavors, and more. And it was in the digital economy that the Rockefeller Foundation identified an immediate potential for the development of impact sourcing.

From work training and discipline to work assessments, Samasource is responsible for the smooth operation of its sourcing ecosystem. Janah developed her labor sociotechnical arrangement by testing it in 2009 in a few computer centers in the refugee camp of Dadaab in Kenya. She taught a small group of refugees in the camp how to do microwork for Microsoft and an outsourcing company in Silicon Valley. The high quality of the work convinced her that this microwork model could be expanded. Samasource began to work with nongovernmental organizations (NGOs) to "aggregate workers and recruits." These NGOs sent them to one of the company's partner organizations on the ground in Kenya and Uganda, to name two countries where it runs operations. Partner organizations are responsible for running data "delivery centers"; oftentimes these had been Internet cafés but were now reorganized to deliver Samasource with training data for its clients.[36] Microworkers at Samasource do not pick the small "batches" they want to work on, but instead are trained to perform repetitive tasks during six- to eight-hour sessions every day with most workers staying with the company for eight months.

The kind of labor performed by Samasource's workers in Kenya, Uganda, and Haiti is a somewhat permanent kind of "patch work." It is patch work in the computing sense that they are preempting errors in a system by providing it with accurate and reliable data to address existing or future problems. It is patch work in a repairing sense. Microworkers in depletion zones are enrolled to enact relations of repair and maintenance of information infrastructures designed to extract value. Artificial intelligence and machine learning algorithms are dependent on the training data produced by the cognitive labor of microworkers. This is how the "brainpower of the poor" fuels the machines of late capitalism in enrichment zones. Their care for these systems means the drawing out of a stable labor supply chain of contradictory ethical commitments and precarious labor arrangements in the digital depletion economy, especially through gig work.

Not content with organizing a microwork supply chain in the Global South, Samasource sought to bring its outsourcing philosophy into the United States by disrupting the gig economy. The gig economy has given rise to a new category of worker and raised important questions for researchers as well as for law and policymakers who have sought to protect and care for gig workers.[37] Gig work is similar to microwork in its short duration, its contingency, and the common treatment of workers as independent from the tech company responsible for allocating the work. Intent on intervening in this area as well, Samasource created a training program in 2013 known as Samaschool to "help low-income individuals become successful freelancers in today's changing job landscape."[38] With an online curation of modules, quizzes, and in-depth community discussion boards, the online training program was Samasource's commitment to teach poor and marginalized workers in the United States to "thinking gig." Schools were established in San Francisco, rural Arkansas, and New York City, with curriculum covering everything from how to manage professional communication on gig economy apps like TaskRabbit and Uber, to negotiating contracts, and upleveling on career skills like resume and LinkedIn writing.[39] The program hoped to provide training that met market needs while advocating for social change. Samaschool called on policy and lawmakers to intervene in the creation of new laws and policies to protect gig workers.[40] In this sense, Samasource's efforts in creating an "ethical AI supply chain" was entangled with promoting the gig economy. Samaschools instilled in its students a sense of self as entrepreneurial subjects, updating themselves to fit the demands of a shifting market.[41] One chain connects with the other, ever extending the company's racial politics of care—supporting the Other even while ensuring their integration in a chain of exploitation and dispossession.

Microwork, as represented by Samasource, can be said to be "articulation work," or "work that gets things back 'on track' in the face of the unexpected," work that "modifies action to accommodate unanticipated contingencies."[42] Microwork is the kind of care work that subtends the humming of the imagined futurity made through artificial intelligence and machine learning. The vast supply chain designed and operated by Samasource seeks to keep AI and ML "on track" by validating its data through human labor. This labor is performed by the poor and the working classes of depletion zones—from Kenya and Uganda to San Francisco. Their care work maintains the sociotechnical relations of exploitation at the heart of Big Tech (e.g., Microsoft, Google, Facebook, Uber, Lyft) and some of the richest US logistics companies (e.g., WalMart) who are clients of Samasource. While "sama" means "equal" in Sanskrit, the microwork supply chain that Samasource constructed maintains, reproduces, and expands the differential treatment of workers in depletion zones. These are workers enrolled in curricula for their self-optimization as modern neoliberal subjects that in caring for themselves are made to care for the systems that dispossess and exploit them.

CONCLUSION

Since its founding in 2008, workers at Samasource were enrolled not only to do work for TaskRabbit, Uber, Care, and Lyft, they also maintain and care for the infrastructure upon which all gig workers rely for their work. Microwork keeps digital infrastructures such as image processing, community Q&A queries, and driverless cars running. This kind of work is what Precarity Lab called the *undergig*—invisible work that falls to the background of the digital depletion economy. The emphasis placed on gig workers such as those driving people on Uber or Lyft, as much research, legislation, and policymaking does, while of great importance, can reproduce the invisibility of a wider labor supply chain sustaining global information infrastructures.

Law and policymakers often grapple with how to classify platform work within the umbrella of labor law to regulate, restrict, or provide protection and justice to gig workers.[43] The most notable of these, California Assembly Bill 5 (2019), popularly known as a gig worker bill, sought to define the boundaries of what classified a worker as an independent contractor instead of an app-based employee:

the person was "free from the control and direction" of the hiring company; the person works outside of usual course of company's business; and the person normally works "in an independently established trade, occupation, or business" similar to the work performed. In 2020, the California ballot initiative Proposition 22, backed by gig work platforms like Uber and DoorDash, was passed to reinstate the independent contractor classification to all app-based workers, undoing their status as employees. Though the issue continues to be fought in court,[44] Uber CEO Dara Khosrowshahi argued soon after its approval that Proposition 22 was a model for other states and invited the US federal government to pursue similar legislation.[45] He framed support of the ballot initiative through a racial politics care, given that, in being classified as independent contractors, gig workers would acquire "new benefits and protections with the same flexibility."[46] Preserving the fungibility and expendability of gig work all the while building a façade of care, Proposition 22 constructed app-based "contractors" as a separate class of worker and, in so doing, removed them from existing federal and state labor law protections such as the Fair Labor Standards Act of 1938 or the National Labor Relations Act. The ramifications of Proposition 22 were quickly felt as grocery chains fired their delivery staff to sign contracts with DoorDash, in pursuit of its cheaper labor pool of gig workers. Health care stipends were also reported to cover a small percentage of the overall cost and the labor time required to pay for it was significantly higher than the supposed minimum.[47] The racial politics of care undergirding the classification work of legally defining gig workers solidified the precarity of their everyday.

Efforts at the federal level, such as the Employee Rights Act of 2022 and the Worker Flexibility and Choice Act of 2022, have also revolved around classification work. The former has sought to define the contours of the "future of work" primarily to protect the "successful franchise model and gig economy," as Senator Richard Burr stated in the joint press release with Senator Tim Scott.[48] The bill defines gig workers as independent contractors stating that, "notwithstanding any other provision of law, the fact that an individual accessing work through a digital marketplace company receives retirement or fringe benefits from such digital marketplace company shall not establish, or support the establishment of, an employee and employer relationship between the individual accessing work through a digital marketplace company and the digital marketplace company, respectively."[49] Emphasis on worker access to a market of flexible work arrangements disavows corporate responsibility in drawing up the boundaries for "independent contractors" and in upholding the false choice between flexibility and benefits, between no rights and full rights as an "employee." What Anna Fisher calls the "coercive hospitality" of platforms, enabling access and sharing while hiding their costs to users, is embedded into the classificatory exclusion of gig workers;[50] it absolves companies of the need to pay workers full employee benefits like health care and time off. Furthermore, legal boundaries so often become entangled with the geopolitical boundaries of the state, which precludes understanding transnational labor arrangements that support and make viable industries. Reclassification of gig workers as employees does not undo the differential relations of racial capital, but preserves the distinctions made about whose bodies are deemed extractable and whose labor is exploitable under conditions beneficial for global capital.

We propose the racial politics of care as an analytical lens to grapple with situated and differentiated ambivalences in gig work, in microwork, and in the configuration of neoliberal technologies across enriching and depletion zones. Debates about ethical AI must not be limited to questions of data accuracy and representation, and AI use. Tending to labor through intersectional lenses sheds light on the making and maintenance of interlocking matrices of domination, and its diverse experiences. We examined the plans of Samasource to open the black box of AI development. Yet this chapter only offers insight into the world-view and human-machine configurations constructed by Janah, the Rockefeller Foundation, Samasource, and the state. Future studies of the racial politics of care in microwork supply chains need to also examine them in action, through attentive ethnographic observation of how microworkers understand their participation within these labor supply chains. Doing so further decenters the world-making practices of Silicon Valley and moves us beyond simplified conceptions of exploiter/exploited. More importantly, given our feminist critical race standpoint, it also allows for tending to the desires and aspirations of those whose labor is made invisible by complex sociotechnical relations.

NOTES

From Iván Chaar López: This chapter comes out of the work conducted by the Border Tech Lab around digital labor and racial capitalism. I'd like to thank the members of the BTL for contributing to this project and to my co-author for her sharp curiosity and for pushing us to think microwork supply chains and impact outsourcing. This chapter benefitted from a workshop with the Digital Inequality Lab at the Univ. of Michigan, Ann Arbor. My gratitude to its members for their thoughtful comments and feedback. Lastly, my gratitude to the editors of this volume, Meg Leta Jones and Amanda Lewendowski, for their invitation to be part of the conversation about feminist cyberlaw.

From Victoria Sánchez: First and foremost, I wish to thank Dr. Iván Chaar López, who has been a mentor and supporter of this project since its inception. Thank you for opening your lab to me at a time when it felt hopeless to write, and for your boundless generosity, innovative thinking, and commitment to feminist and antiracist politics. I'd also like to thank the members of the BTL for their fruitful insights, intellectual exchanges, and for making this piece stronger. I feel fortunate to have been surrounded by brilliant women of color thought partners like you. To Meg Leta Jones and Amanda Lewendowski, thank you for continuing to do this work, and for opening a feminist cyberlaw space for all of us to think alongside you. Finally, I wish to dedicate this to all women of color writing and theorizing, especially those in technoscientific worlds.

1. *Partner with Us*, The Next Web (Mar. 15, 2023, 9:38 AM), https://thenextweb.com/partnerships.

2. Samasource was renamed Sama in 2021. Given the company is widely known through its former name, we'll continue using it here. Wendy Gonzalez, *We Are Now Sama: Accurate Data for Ambitious AI*, Sama Blog (Mar. 15, 2023, 9:42 AM), https://www.sama.com/blog/samasource-is-now-sama.

3. Leila Janah (Samasource) *on Transforming the Workplace | TNW Conference 2018*, YOUTUBE (Mar. 15, 2023, 9:43 AM), https://www.youtube.com/watch?v=Re-myC3IvoM.

4. *Our Story*, SAMA (Mar. 15, 2023, 9:44 AM), https://www.sama.com/our-story.

5. *Ethical AI Supply Chain: Purpose Built for Impact*, SAMA (Mar. 15, 2023, 9:45 AM), https://www.sama.com/ethical-ai.

6. Lisa Nakamura's work is critical when thinking about the invisible repair work of women of color online. *Women of Color & the Digital Labor of Repair*, YOUTUBE (Mar. 15, 2023, 10:09 AM), https://www.youtube.com/watch?v=LN9h6ldeVdI.

7. Lilly Irani, *The Cultural Work of Microwork*, 17 NEW MEDIA & SOCIETY 720, 724 (2015).

8. Adrienne Williams, et al., *The Exploited Labor behind Artificial Intelligence*, NOEMA (Oct. 13, 2022), https://www.noemamag.com/the-exploited-labor-behind-artificial-intelligence/.

9. Patricia Hill Collins, BLACK FEMINIST THOUGHT: KNOWLEDGE, CONSCIOUSNESS, & THE POLITICS OF EMPOWERMENT 228–29 (2000) (1990).

10. Jacqui Ayling & Adriane Chapman, *Putting AI Ethics to Work: Are the Tools Fit for Purpose?*, 2 AI & ETHICS 405 (2021); Solon Barocas, et al., FAIRNESS AND MACHINE LEARNING: LIMITATIONS AND OPPORTUNITIES (2021); Montreal AI Ethics Inst., THE STATE OF AI ETHICS REPORT, *Vol. 6* (Feb. 2022).

11. Ruha Benjamin, RACE AFTER TECHNOLOGY: ABOLITIONIST TOOLS FOR THE NEW JIM CODE (2019); Joy Buolamwini & Timnit Gebru, *Gender Shades: Intersectional Accuracy Disparities in Commercial Gender Classification*, 18 PROC. OF MACHINE LEARNING RESEARCH 77 (2018), https://proceedings.mlr.press/v81/buolamwini18a.html; John Cheney-Lippold, *WE ARE DATA: ALGORITHMS & THE MAKING OF OUR DIGITAL SELVES* (2017); Virginia Eubanks, *AUTOMATING INEQUALITY: HOW HIGH-TECH TOOLS PROFILE, POLICE, & PUNISH THE POOR* (2017); Safiya Umoja Noble, *ALGORITHMS OF OPPRESSION: HOW SEARCH ENGINES REINFORCE RACISM* (2018).

12. Jenna Burrell & Marion Fourcade, *The Society of Algorithms*, 47 ANN. REV. OF SOCIOLOGY 213 (2021), https://doi.org/10.1146/annurev-soc-090820-020800. McKenzie Wark, A HACKER MANIFESTO (2004), offers a similar argument through the dialectical couplet of hackers/vectoralists.

13. Aryn Martin, et al., *The Politics of Care in Technoscience*, 45 SOCIAL STUDIES OF SCIENCE 625 (2015); Michelle Murphy, *Unsettling Care: Troubling Transnational Itineraries of Care in Feminist Health Practices*, 45 SOCIAL STUDIES OF SCIENCE 717 (2015); María Puig de la Bellacasa, *Matters of Care in Technoscience: Assembling Neglected Things*, 41 SOCIAL STUDIES OF SCIENCE 85 (Feb. 2011).

14. Martin et al., *supra* note 13, at 629.

15. Puig de la Bellacasa, *supra* note 13, at 86.

16. Martin et al., *supra* note 13, at 627, 632; Murphy, *supra* note 13, at 722.

17. Murphy, *supra* note 13, at 723.

18. Precarity Lab, TECHNOPRECARIOUS (2020).

19. Macarena Gómez-Barris, THE EXTRACTIVE ZONE: SOCIAL ECOLOGIES & DECOLONIAL PERSPECTIVES (2017); Sandro Mezzadra & Brett Nielson, THE OPERATIONS OF CAPITAL: EXCAVATING CONTEMPORARY CAPITALISM (2019); Aihwa Ong, NEOLIBERALISM AS EXCEPTION: MUTATIONS IN CITIZENSHIP & SOVEREIGNTY (2006).

20. Cedric Robinson, BLACK MARXISM: THE MAKING OF THE BLACK RADICAL TRADITION 26–27 (2000) (1983).

21. Rachel Kuo, et al., *Triangulating Race, Capital, & Technology*, in CHI CONF. ON HUMAN FACTORS IN COMPUTING SYS. EXTENDED ABSTRACTS (Apr. 29–May 5, 2022), https://doi.org/10.1145/3491101.3503737.

22. Ong, *supra* note 19.

23. On technology and techno-optimism: Seyram Avle, et al., *Scaling Techno-Optimistic Visions*, Engaging Science, TECHNOLOGY, & SOCIETY 237 (2020); Leo Marx, *Technology: The Emergence of a Hazardous Concept*, 64 SOCIAL RESEARCH 965 (Fall 1997).

24. Mary L. Gray & Siddarth Suri, GHOST WORK: HOW TO STOP SILICON VALLEY FROM BUILDING A NEW GLOBAL UNDERCLASS (2019).

25. Leila Janah, SOCIAL ENTERPRISE FOR IMPACT: RETHINKING OLD MODELS OF CHARITY & BUSINESS, IN PERSPECTIVES ON IMPACT: LEADING VOICES ON MAKING SYSTEMIC CHANGE IN THE TWENTY-FIRST CENTURY 203 (Nina Montgomery ed., 2019).

26. David Atkin, et al., *Evaluating Sama's Training and Job Programs in Nairobi, Kenya*, Sama White Paper (Apr. 6, 2021), https://www.povertyactionlab.org/sites/default/files/research-paper /Samasource%20Evaluation%20Final%20(2)_0.pdf.

27. Janah, *supra* note 3.

28. *A Conversation with Leila Janah*, YOUTUBE (Mar. 15, 2023, 2:31 PM), https://www.youtube.com /watch?v=20mmq3BPmyU.

29. *High-Quality Training Data from Start to Scale*, SAMA (Mar. 15, 2:33 PM) https://www.sama .com/quality-training-data; *Sama Pro*, SAMA ANNOTATE (Mar. 15, 2023, 2:33 PM), https://www.sama .com/sama-pro-manage-data-platform-ai/.

30. Irani, *supra* note 7, at 722. For more see: *Difference and Dependence among Digital Workers: The Case of Amazon Mechanical Turk*, 114 SOUTH ATLANTIC QUARTERLY 225 (2015); Lilly C. Irani and M. Six Silberman, *Turkopticon: Interrupting Worker Invisibility in Amazon Mechanical Turk*, in PROC. OF THE SIGCHI CONF. ON HUMAN FACTORS IN COMPUTING SYSTEMS 611 (2013).

31. Adam Fish and Ramesh Srinivasan, *Digital Labor Is the New Killer App*, 14 NEW MEDIA & SOCIETY 137 (2011); Tarleton Gillespie, CUSTODIANS OF THE INTERNET: PLATFORMS, CONTENT MODERATION, AND THE HIDDEN DECISIONS THAT SHAPE SOCIAL MEDIA 111–40 (2018); Gray and Suri, *supra* note 24; John Horton, *The Condition of the Turking Class: Are Online Employers Fair & Honest*, 111 ECONOMICS LETTERS 10 (2011); Irani, *supra* note 7.

32. On impact sourcing and corporate social responsibility: Ron Babin, *Assessing the Role of CSR in Outsourcing Decisions*, 1 J. OF INFO. SYS. APPLIED RESEARCH (2008), http://jisar.org/1/2/JISAR.1(2) .Babin.pdf; Brian Nicholson, et al. (eds.), SOCIALLY RESPONSIBLE OUTSOURCING: GLOBAL SOURCING WITH SOCIAL IMPACT (2016).

33. Business for Social Responsibility and Rockefeller Foundation, *Global Impact Sourcing Coalition* (n.d.), ROCKEFELLER FOUNDATION, https://www.rockefellerfoundation.org/wp-content/uploads /Global-Impact-Sourcing-Coalition.pdf.

34. Gib Bulloch and Jessica Long (Accenture), *Exploring the Value Proposition for Impact Sourcing*, ROCKEFELLER FOUNDATION (2012), 4, 43. *See also* Avasant, Incentives & Opportunities for Scaling the "Impact Sourcing" Sector, ROCKEFELLER FOUNDATION (Sept. 2012).

35. Ong, *supra* note 19, at 6.

36. Samasource also operates "delivery centers." *A Conversation with Leila Janah*, *supra* note 30.

37. Keith Cunningham-Parmeter, *From Amazon to Uber: Defining Employment in the Modern Economy*, 96 BOSTON UNIV. L. REV. 1673 (2016); Valerio De Stefano, *The Rise of the "Just-in Time Workforce": On Demand Work, Crowdwork, and Labor Protection in the "Gig Economy,"* 37 COMPARATIVE LABOR L. & POL'Y J. 461 (2016); Alexandrea J. Ravenelle, HUSTLE AND GIG: STRUGGLING AND SURVIVING IN THE SHARING ECONOMY (2019); Trebor Scholz, UBERWORKED AND UNDERPAID: HOW WORKERS ARE DISRUPTING THE DIGITAL ECONOMY (2017); Julia Ticona, et al., *Beyond Disruption: How Tech Shapes Labor across Domestic Work & Ridehailing*, DATA & SOC'Y RESEARCH INST. (2018); Kathryn Wells, et al., *The Uber Workplace in D.C.*, KALMANOVITZ INITIATIVE FOR LABOR AND THE WORKING POOR (2019).

38. Lisa Hamilton, *The Future of Workforce Development? Samaschool Is Thinking Gig*, ANNIE E. CASEY FOUNDATION (Mar. 15, 2023, 2:55 PM) https://www.aecf.org/blog/the-future-of-workforce -development-samaschool-is-thinking-gig.

39. Tess Posner, former managing director of Samaschool, helped grow the pilot program in San Francisco to a global reach with 11 sites in the U.S. and East Africa. New America (Mar. 15, 2023, 2:55 PM), https://www.newamerica.org/our-people/tess-posner/.

40. Leila Janah, *Samaschool Launches Online Gig Economy Training Program*, FACEBOOK LIVE STREAM, https://www.facebook.com/leilajanah/videos/samaschool-launches-online-gig-economy -training/1679048622205198/.

41. See description: *Samaschool*, IDEALIST (Mar. 15, 2023, 2:58 PM), https://www.idealist.org/en/nonprofit/11245d7456bb4437a7bd529b89aab9e1-samaschool-san-francisco; Janah, *supra* note 40.

42. Susan Leigh Star & Anselm Strauss, *Layers of Silence, Arenas of Voice: The Ecology of Visible and Invisible Work*, 8 COMPUTER SUPPORTED COOPERATIVE WORK 9, 10 (1999).

43. Emily C. Atmore, *Killing the Goose that Laid the Golden Egg: Outdated Employment Laws Are Destroying the Gig Economy*, 102 MINNESOTA L. REV. 887 (2017); Justin Azar, *Portable Benefits in the Gig Economy: Understanding the Nuances of the Gig Economy*, 27 GEORGETOWN J. ON POVERTY L. & POL'Y 409 (2020); Annette Bernhardt, et al., *The 'Gig Economy' & Independent Contracting: Evidence from California Tax Data*, Working Paper No. 2021–26. California Pol'y Lab (Oct. 2021).

44. Kate Conger, *California's Gig Worker Law Is Unconstitutional, Judge Rules*, NEW YORK TIMES (Aug. 20, 2021), https://www.nytimes.com/2021/08/20/technology/prop-22-california-ruling.html; Veena B. Dubal, *Economic Security & the Regulation of Gig Work in California: From AB5 to Proposition 22*, 13 EUROPEAN LABOUR L. J. 51 (2022).

45. Utah State Senator Daniel McCay introduced bill SB 209 in 2021 to amend the state's labor law and codify gig work as platform-based on-demand labor.

46. Kirsten Korosec, *After Prop 22's Passage, Uber Is Taking Its Lobbying Effort Global*, TECH CRUNCH (Nov. 5, 2020), https://techcrunch.com/2020/11/05/after-prop-22s-passage-uber-is-taking-its-lobbying-effort-global/.

47. Alexander Sammon, *Prop 22 Is Here & It's already Worse than Expected*, AMERICAN PROSPECT (Jan. 15, 2021), https://prospect.org/labor/prop-22-is-here-already-worse-than-expected-california-gig-workers/.

48. *Senator Scott, Colleagues Introduce the Employee Rights Act of 2022*, Senator Tim Scott (Mar. 15, 2023, 3:10 PM), https://www.scott.senate.gov/media-center/press-releases/senator-scott-colleagues-introduce-the-employee-rights-act-of-2022.

49. Employee Rights Act of 2022 (Mar. 15, 2023, 3:09 PM), https://employeerightsact.com/the-bill/.

50. Anna Watkins Fisher, THE PLAY IN THE SYSTEM: THE ART OF PARASITICAL RESISTANCE 51 (2020).

14

Black Feminist Antitrust
for a Safer Internet

Gabrielle M. Rejouis

Intersectionality calls attention to the unique policy needs of Black women. The current content moderation crisis must be addressed through antitrust policies that use a Black feminist framework. While online violence impacts many groups of people, social media platforms' failure to moderate abusive and hateful content puts Black women in disproportionately dangerous positions. Kimberlé Crenshaw created the word "intersectionality" to highlight that Black women have policy needs separate from white women's needs and Black men's needs.[1] The law's omission of Black women sometimes means excluding us from legal protection.[2] Similarly, social media sites, or platforms, do not incorporate policies that reflect Black women's experiences with racism, sexism, and misogynoir. Big Tech reform that does not use a Black feminist framework will fail to move platforms from protecting their own interests.

Policymakers crafted antitrust laws to address these types of power imbalances and to preserve the public interest. Antitrust policies with a Black feminist framework are needed to shift the power dynamics of platforms, foster better content moderation, and make the internet safer. Catherine Knight Steele coined the phrase "digital Black feminism" to describe a school of feminism that "deconstruct[s] white supremacist capitalist patriarchy within digital culture."[3] Designing content moderation policies after incorporating digital Black feminist equities in online governance reform will create better platforms. In this chapter, I will outline the unique ways online attacks impact Black women, describe the power that allows platforms to ignore the content moderation crisis, and conclude with how Black feminist antitrust can tackle this problem. This chapter will focus on online violence as a result of race and gender. I use online violence to describe actual and proposed attacks and harassment made on social media platforms against one person or a group of people. I will refer to the largest and most popular social media companies as dominant platforms because current legal definitions of monopoly have not expanded to include the companies that own Facebook, Instagram, Twitter, also referred to as X, and YouTube.[4]

THE STATUS QUO FOR BLACK WOMEN ONLINE

The current content moderation crisis doubly impacts Black women, reflecting platforms' choices to withhold protections. Platforms maintain an arbitrary requirement to respond to online violence which disregards Black women's needs. This contextual incompetence delays needed intervention putting Black women in avoidable danger. If platforms employed digital Black feminism, they would have mitigated current disinformation and misinformation campaigns.

Technology will preserve existing systems of discrimination without intentional design to the contrary.[5] In a society that discriminates against women and Black people, Black women experience discrimination on multiple fronts.[6] They can be subject to systemic racism; misogyny, or the hatred of women; misogynoir, misogyny rooted in anti-Black racism; or any combination of the three.[7] Black women receive the worst online violence.[8] They are 84 percent more likely to receive an abusive or problematic tweet.[9] For example, a Black woman could receive an online comment with a racial slur, the threat of gendered violence, or a harmful stereotype about Black women. She could also receive a comment with two or three of those phrases. Malicious actors, often referred to as "trolls," a label which can diminish their danger, draw from this broader culture in their attacks.[10] For this reason, the lack of content moderation enforcement largely endangers Black women.

Platforms allowed malicious actors to test the early tools of the online disinformation crisis and the alt-right in campaigns on Black women.[11] Users of 4chan, an anonymous forum website, planned two notable campaigns to attack Black women on Twitter in 2013.[12] These 4chan users seized upon a Twitter conversation in the #SolidarityIsForWhiteWomen Twitter hashtag to divide white and Black feminists.[13] Mikki Kendall, a Black woman, used the #SolidarityIsForWhiteWomen hashtag to start a conversation in response to a male feminist admitting he built his career by opposing Black feminists. The 4chan users sought to derail this conversation by posing as Black women adding bad faith contributions. In a later campaign, 4chan users used those same fake Twitter accounts to launch the Twitter hashtag #EndFathersDay and spread the lie that Black women wanted to end Father's Day.[14] According to the 4chan users, the goal of the #EndFathersDay campaign was to create distrust among Black Twitter users in preparation for a "proper attack."[15] But Shafiqah Hudson and I'Nasah Crockett, Black feminists, identified that the trend's originators were not who they claimed to be. They led two different efforts to combat #EndFathersDay.[16] Hudson created the hashtag #YourSlipIsShowing to catalog suspected accounts pretending to be Black women. Crockett found and shared the 4chan post detailing the campaign on Twitter. Crockett knew first-hand smaller sites like 4chan and Reddit were places for malicious actors to gather and strategize attacks on Black women.[17] Their leadership and contributions from other Twitter users ended this disinformation campaign.

Unfortunately, targets of gendered violence do not always get this level of community support which underscores the impact of platforms' failure to rein in violent conduct. Gendered violence means violence—threats or actual physical, sexual, psychological, and/or economic harm—against a woman because she is a woman.[18] Online gendered violence includes misogynist slurs, death threats, and threats of sexual violence.[19] In addition to women of color, women who are religious minorities and members of the LGBTQ+ community receive the most severe online violence.[20] About half of the women, Black people, and Hispanic people surveyed in a Pew study believe they received online harassment due to their gender, race, or ethnicity.[21]

Platforms will often refuse to respond to online violence unless there are specific threats of or actual physical violence.[22] The distinction between online speech and real-world violence are incompatible with the lived experiences of women.[23] Without intervention, a troll's joke can quickly escalate into strangers sending death threats to one's home. This can quickly accelerate into someone showing up at one's home. In a Pew Research study, more women reported they were "extremely or very upset" by their most recent experience of online violence perhaps because they also reported more experiences with stalking and sexual harassment.[24] One study found 20 percent of women who experienced online violence were also survivors of stalking and physical assault.[25] Women were the victims of 70 percent of the Department of Justice's online stalking cases.[26] The stakes are too high for platforms to forgo moderating content until the violence moves offline.[27] The time from online action to real-world harm is often too short, forcing survivors of online violence to suffer harm while platforms wait for an established connection between the speech and impact.[28]

Platforms have demonstrated that they will fail to respond with the appropriate urgency to online gendered violence if they wait for offline action. In 2014, malicious actors coordinated "Gamergate," the most notable online misogynist campaign. Trolls harassed, doxed, and threatened prominent women in the gaming community.[29] Organizing on 4chan led to mass online attacks and death threats. The physical safety of the women targeted by the Gamergate campaign was endangered by these actions quickly after online mobilization.[30] And platforms were ill-equipped to intervene in time.

Online violence against Black communities takes a different shape than gendered violence. Misinformation is errors in information while disinformation is intentionally misleading information.[31] Malicious actors weaponize misinformation and disinformation to disrupt progress for Black communities.[32] For example, Russian accounts launched a disinformation campaign to suppress the Black vote during the 2016 US presidential election.[33] These accounts heavily targeted Black social media users and posted content to exploit existing racial division.[34] Black voter turnout declined for the first time in twenty years, in some part due to this campaign.[35] If platforms wait for a tangible result from online violence, it will undermine voting rights protections.

Online gendered and racist violence both exacerbates inequalities and punishes those who speak up about concerns. The most active women social media users are more likely to face online violence.[36] Twitter's failure to prevent this abuse discourages women from speaking up against misogyny and sexism.[37] Black communities are often punished for defending themselves from online harassment.[38] This means a Black woman posting about online misogynoir is more likely to face online violence *and* more likely to be penalized by the platform for countering trolls.[39] Platforms do not adequately protect these communities. As a result, online violence drives women and communities of color from platforms.[40] This abuse impedes equal access to platforms and prevents the sharing of anti-racist and feminist content.[41]

Therefore, when we look at the experiences of women and Black people online, we can see that there is a false delineation between online and real-world harm. Online violence bleeds very quickly into tangible and physical impacts.[42] Attempts to categorize online violence in this way hinders timely interventions to the detriment of Black women's safety. To construct solutions to online violence, the experiences of Black women must be met with responsive policies.

The scale of the Gamergate campaign was larger than platforms were prepared to address.[43] But platforms could have prepared for larger campaigns by installing procedures to mitigate violence to Black women or even discourage future misogynist campaigns in response to the smaller #EndFathersDay campaign. In fact, from #EndFathersDay to Gamergate, and from election misinformation to the attack on the Capitol, platforms have demonstrated that they will not act with the necessary urgency to prevent real world violence.[44] This puts Black women in danger of preventable violence.

THE ABUSE OF PLATFORM POWER

Platforms abuse their power to the detriment of Black women. Platforms have either chosen to ignore the harm their sites amplify or developed business models to profit from this violence.[45] They use their insulation to craft vague content moderation policies. These vague policies allow platforms to demonstrate insufficient effort as an attempt against online violence.[46] But their power affords them the choice to ignore violations of civil and human rights.[47] This power imbalance leaves Black women at the mercy of the platform's whims and in danger of misogynoir online.[48]

Platforms make content moderation decisions to preserve their position in the online ecosystem. The architects and current custodians of the internet designed it to benefit those with power.[49] But platforms have too much power which allows them to wield outsized influence over American culture and economy.[50] Dominant platforms expanded their control of the social media market over the last two decades as antitrust enforcers allowed them to acquire other companies.[51] Dominance as the largest or only site performing a particular service, such as microblogging or photo-sharing, insulates platforms from responding to pressure from government regulation and public campaigns.[52] Dominant platforms will continue to allow hate speech and online violence to flourish if this business model goes unchallenged.[53]

Platforms profit by promoting engagement over safety. Twitter thrives on controversy and anger to drive engagement, or to increase the time users spend on the platform scrolling through, posting, or reacting to posts.[54] Facebook allowed hate speech and groups to thrive on its platform rather than make changes that might decrease engagement.[55] Platforms make more money with inflammatory content, which their algorithms promote and moderators selectively ignore.[56] Content moderation that ignores racial and gender violence is part of a larger economy that profits from racism.[57]

Additionally, platforms do not perform content moderation in an equitable way. Current moderation policies do not do enough to punish those targeting Black women.[58] On the other hand, platforms will use their discretion to punish Black users and activists raising racial justice concerns.[59] The enforcement is more likely to be used against Black women than malicious actors.[60] Platforms cannot be trusted to regulate themselves and need external guardrails to protect Black women.[61]

When platforms ignored attacks on Black women, online violence metastasized.[62] The coordinated attacks in the #EndFathersDay hashtag demonstrate how dominant platforms amplify what starts on smaller sites.[63] Black women will be subject to content with misogynoir even if they purposefully avoid certain websites. Malicious actors use the reach of dominant platforms to spread fringe ideologies which increases the scale and possibility of harm to Black women.[64] While we cannot lose hope for improvements, we must acknowledge our current culture of misogynoir. One way to address this reality is to limit the spread of online violence.

To address the broken status quo, Black women need policies that challenge the power that is refraining from content moderation. Despite a majority of Americans labeling online violence a serious matter, platforms are not implementing serious enforcement.[65] Independent developers demonstrate that solutions are feasible to prevent the spread of online violence.[66] While those tools are important, individual actions cannot solve structural problems. We need communal solutions like the ones developed by Black feminists rallying under the #YourSlipIsShowing hashtag.[67] Fixing this failing content moderation system requires restructuring social media to curb violence with Black women in mind.[68]

BLACK FEMINIST ANTITRUST

Antitrust enforcement using a Black feminist framework will redistribute the power withholding content moderation. Antitrust inherently restricts corporate power. But the prevailing theory of antitrust undermines this aim. Antitrust reform needs to reject this theory and address the idiosyncrasies of digital markets. A Black feminist antitrust framework will disrupt the way market power preserves online violence and focus existing antitrust tools on addressing the lived experiences of Black women.

Antitrust policy challenges power imbalances. Antitrust policies naturally restrict corporate power.[69] The first American antitrust law, the Sherman Act, prohibited companies from abusing their power by unfairly raising prices or withholding business.[70] The Clayton Act, the next major American antitrust law, outlawed mergers—the combination of two companies—and acquisitions—the purchase of a company or parts of a company—that would create a monopoly or reduce competition.[71] Historically, antitrust enforcement improved quality of life.[72] Antitrust policies responded to the consolidation of companies during a period of expanding inequality.[73] Congress designed these bills to break up monopolies' undemocratic influence over economics and society. If antitrust ought to equalize society, using it as a tool to advance racial equity is within its purpose.[74]

However, the current interpretation and application of antitrust laws and policies reinforce inequality.[75] The prevailing antitrust theory, the consumer welfare standard, limits enforcement unless the merger between two companies will harm consumers.[76] For example, antitrust regulators can allow two competitors to merge if there is a chance this will reduce costs for consumers. The merger can advance even if it will hurt conditions for workers.[77] Strict application of the consumer welfare standard has led to consolidated markets, fewer small businesses, and poor labor protections.[78] New policies must respond to the impact of monopolies and dominant platforms on more than prices for consumers.[79] Reorienting antitrust policy around restoring "a fair and democratic society" requires a racial equity framework.[80] Making racial equity a goal and providing strong enforcement mechanisms will ensure an online ecosystem that protects Black women from online violence.

Current antitrust law and policies are also insufficient to address the dominance of social media platforms. The legal definition of monopoly has not evolved to encompass the largest social media companies, although their size grants them massive amounts of political and economic influence.[81] A finding of monopoly power, an estimated control of 90 percent of a specific market, is required to trigger antitrust action.[82] However, companies can still act in ways that have historically been considered monopoly power without that much control of the market. Defining a market for social media companies which operate in nontraditional ways presents another hurdle to antitrust case law.[83] It is unlikely that existing antitrust policies can address the power of platforms.[84] Antitrust reform must reflect the ways corporations have evolved since the first anti-monopoly laws.[85]

A Black feminist analysis is crucial to make antitrust policy more responsive to the issues outlined in this chapter. Antitrust reform can shift power and make online spaces more democratic.[86] The power systems that allow online violence are nominally race-neutral. Therefore, race-neutral antitrust policy will not challenge this harm.[87] To ensure antitrust can be a tool for racial and gender justice, changes need to be made to laws and policies.[88] Regulators must apply antitrust laws with the goal of achieving racial equity.[89]

Black feminist antitrust reform uses existing antitrust policies with a racial equity framework. A race-conscious antitrust agenda will challenge platforms' concentrated power and respond to the online violence Black women face. It is crucial that antitrust remains in the toolbox to create better content moderation online.[90] Antitrust laws need to have strong enforcement mechanisms to be effective.[91] Four tools that will be the most effective in restructuring the internet are (1) merger review, (2) structural separation, (3) interoperability, and (4) data portability.

Merger review allows antitrust enforcers to block mergers that will reduce competition in a market.[92] Black feminist merger review would examine how a proposed merger will impact Black communities—including workers and small business owners—and prevent a merger that will likely cause harm.[93] For example, allowing a platform with a lax content moderation policy and a platform with strong policies to merge will likely lead to an overall lax policy that harms Black women. Merger review should also look back at mergers that currently impede competition and consider reversing that merger.[94]

Structural separation, or breakups, bolsters competition by dividing a monopoly into small companies. Platforms argue breakups are too complicated to perform, but breakups are possible and easier than platforms claim.[95] Breaking up a platform like Facebook will reduce the reach of online violence. Larger platforms struggle to manage the volume of content that users upload because they do not invest in moderation.[96] With the right incentives, such as regulation, platforms will innovate ways to scale moderation to the number of users. Smaller platforms with appropriate incentives will facilitate better content moderation. This will prevent online violence from smaller platforms, like 4chan, from being shared to communities that opted out from exposure.

Finally, competition cannot thrive if smaller new platforms cannot interface with dominant ones. Dominant platforms lock in users by making it difficult to try alternatives.[97] Interoperability requires dominant platforms to make certain systems open for third parties, like competitors, to use.[98] Data portability requires dominant platforms to make it easy for users to move their information to other sites.[99] To restructure the internet, new competitors need support to challenge existing platforms. Interoperability and data portability will boost alternatives by reducing the costs of creating a new platform interface or difficulty of moving their online connections to a new platform. We have not experienced robust interoperability or data portability from dominant platforms.[100] Although they provide this option, it is not user-friendly or streamlined. Legislation can lift the arbitrary limits that platforms put on interoperability and data portability and make it easier for users to try new sites. Bolstered interoperability and data portability will support the growth of competitor platforms seeking to create inhospitable spaces for online violence.

Antitrust enforcement under this Black feminist framework will alleviate the harm of online violence. Breaking up dominant platforms will reduce the scale of harm of online violence. Removing market insulation will incentivize dominant platforms to enforce their content moderation policies. Supporting alternatives will give Black women the ability to choose the platform that best aligns with their values. There is no one solution for online violence. But antitrust can create an ecosystem that responds to the needs of Black women.

CONCLUSION

A shift in power is needed for Black women to thrive online. To make the internet a better place for Black women, we must redesign the internet and dismantle white supremacist patriarchal systems. Antitrust with a Black feminist framework is key to curbing rampant online violence. Black feminist ideals can also usher in a key aspect of Black culture—bringing "pleasure and joy" to what was formerly considered "painful."[101]

NOTES

First, I'd like to thank Meg Leta Jones and Amanda Levendowski for organizing this volume with students in mind. Thank you for inviting me to participate. I'm excited for the next generation of feminist policymakers this volume will inspire. Next, I'd like to thank Johnny Mathias, Jade Magnus-Ogunnaike, and Brandi Collins-Dexter for giving me the opportunity to imagine new ways tech reform can protect and advance racial equity. This chapter reflects the policies I crafted and advocated for during my time at Color Of Change. Finally, I'd like to thank my late grandmothers, my mother, and my sister. They model the revolutionary idea of always looking for a solution when faced with a problem.

1. *See* Kimberlé Crenshaw, *Demarginalizing the Intersection of Race and Sex: A Black Feminist Critique of Antidiscrimination Doctrine, Feminist Theory and Antiracist Politics*, UNIV. OF CHI. LEGAL F. 139, 148 (1989).

2. *See id.* at 143.

3. Catherine Knight Steele, DIGITAL BLACK FEMINISM 10 (2021).

4. Spencer Weber Waller, *Antitrust and Social Networking*, 90 N. C. L. REV. 1771, 1775 (2012).

5. *See* Safiya Umoja Noble, Algorithms of Oppression: How Search Engines Reinforce Racism 24 (2018).

6. *See* Steele, *supra* note 3, at 22.

7. Moya Bailey, Misogynoir Transformed: Black Women's Digital Resistance 1 (2021).

8. *See* Steele, *supra* note 3, at 4.

9. Troll Patrol Findings: Using Crowdsourcing, Data Science & Machine Learning to Measure Violence and Abuse against Women on Twitter (2018), https://decoders.amnesty.org/projects/troll-patrol/findings.

10. *See id.; see also* Janet Burns, *Black Women Are Besieged On Social Media, And White Apathy Damns Us All*, Forbes (Dec. 27, 2017), https://www.forbes.com/sites/janetwburns/2017/12/27/black-women-are-besieged-on-social-media-and-white-apathy-damns-us-all/?sh=662d13ce423e.

11. Joan Donovan, *First They Came for the Black Feminists*, N.Y. Times (Aug. 15, 2019), https://www.nytimes.com/interactive/2019/08/15/opinion/gamergate-twitter.html.

12. *Id.*; Caitlin Dewey, *Absolutely Everything You Need to Know to Understand 4chan, the Internet's Own Bogeyman*, Wash. Post (Sept. 25, 2014), https://www.washingtonpost.com/news/the-intersect/wp/2014/09/25/absolutely-everything-you-need-to-know-to-understand-4chan-the-internets-own-bogeyman/.

13. Donovan, *supra* note 11.

14. *Id.*

15. Rachelle Hampton, *The Black Feminists Who Saw the Alt-Right Threat Coming*, Slate (Apr. 23, 2019), https://slate.com/technology/2019/04/black-feminists-alt-right-twitter-gamergate.html.

16. *Id.*

17. *Id.*

18. Twitter Scorecard: Tracking Twitter's Progress in Addressing Violence Against Women Online in the USA 5 (2021), https://www.amnestyusa.org/wp-content/uploads/2021/12/Twitter-Scorecard-Report-2021_FINAL.pdf.

19. *See* Marianna Spring, *I Get Abuse and Threats Online—Why Can't It Be Stopped?*, BBC (Oct. 18, 2021), https://www.bbc.com/news/uk-58924168.

20. Charlotte Jee, *A Feminist Internet Would Be Better for Everyone*, MIT Tech. Rev. (Apr. 1, 2021), https://www.technologyreview.com/2021/04/01/1020478/feminist-internet-culture-activist-harassment-herd-signal; Twitter Scorecard, *supra* note 18, at 3.

21. Emily A. Vogels, *The State of Online Harassment*, Pew Rsch. Ctr. (Jan. 13, 2021), https://www.pewresearch.org/internet/2021/01/13/the-state-of-online-harassment/.

22. Hampton, *supra* note 15.

23. *Id.*

24. Vogels, *supra* note 21.

25. Spring, *supra* note 19.

26. Ultraviolet, Social Media Fails Women: Transforming Social Media Policies For a Feminist Future 9 (Nov. 2021), https://weareultraviolet.org/wp-content/uploads/2021/11/Social-media-fails-women.pdf.

27. *Id.*

28. *See* Brandi Collins-Dexter, Canaries in the Coal Mine: COVID-19 Misinformation and Black Communities 6 (2020), https://shorensteincenter.org/wp-content/uploads/2020/06/Canaries-in-the-Coal-Mine-Shorenstein-Center-June-2020.pdf.

29. Aja Romano, *What We Still Haven't Learned from Gamergate*, Vox (Jan. 7, 2021), https://www.vox.com/culture/2020/1/20/20808875/gamergate-lessons-cultural-impact-changes-harassment-laws.

30. *See* Dewey, *supra* note 12.

31. *See* Collins-Dexter, *supra* note 28, at 7.

32. *Id.* at 6.

33. *See* Scott Shane & Sheera Frenkel, *Russian 2016 Influence Operation Targeted African-Americans on Social Media*, N.Y. TIMES (Dec. 17, 2018), https://www.nytimes.com/2018/12/17/us/politics/russia-2016-influence-campaign.html.

34. *Id.*

35. *Id.*

36. *See* Twitter Scorecard, *supra* note 18, at 10.

37. Troll Patrol Findings, *supra* note 9.

38. Jessica Guynn, *Facebook While Black: Users Call It Getting "Zucked," Say Talking about Racism Is Censored as Hate Speech*, USA TODAY (Apr. 24, 2019), https://www.usatoday.com/story/news/2019/04/24/facebook-while-black-zucked-users-say-they-get-blocked-racism-discussion/2859593002/.

39. *See* Ultraviolet, *supra* note 26, at 15.

40. *See* Twitter Scorecard, *supra* note 18, at 3.

41. *See* Troll Patrol Findings, *supra* note 9.

42. *See* Romano, *supra* note 29.

43. *Id.*

44. *See id.*

45. *See* Noble, *supra* note 5, at 5.

46. *See* Ángel Díaz & Laura Hecht-Felella, DOUBLE STANDARDS IN SOCIAL MEDIA CONTENT MODERATION 8 (2021), https://www.skeyesmedia.org/documents/bo_filemanager/Double_Standards_Content_Moderation.pdf.

47. *See* Twitter Scorecard, *supra* note 18, at 6.

48. *See* Noble, *supra* note 5, at 26.

49. *See id.* at 48.

50. *See* Hal Singer, *Antitrust Can Address Racial Inequalities*, AMERICAN PROSPECT (Feb. 10, 2021), https://prospect.org/economy/antitrust-can-address-racial-inequities/.

51. *See* Rebecca Kelly Slaughter, Commissioner, Fed. Trade Comm'n, GCR Interactive: Women in Antitrust (Nov. 17, 2020), https://www.ftc.gov/system/files/documents/public_statements/1583714/slaughter_remarks_at_gcr_interactive_women_in_antitrust.pdf.

52. *See* Dominic Rushe and agencies, *Mark Zuckerberg: Advertisers' Boycott of Facebook Will End "Soon Enough*, GUARDIAN (July 2, 2020), https://www.theguardian.com/technology/2020/jul/02/mark-zuckerberg-advertisers-boycott-facebook-back-soon-enough.

53. *See* Elizabeth Spiers, *Let's Be Clear about What It's Like to Be Harassed on Twitter*, N.Y. TIMES (Apr. 27, 2022), https://www.nytimes.com/2022/04/27/opinion/elon-musk-twitter-cesspool.html.

54. *See* Twitter Scorecard, *supra* note 18, at 9.

55. Jeff Horowitz & Deepa Seetharaman, *Facebook Executives Shut Down Efforts to Make the Site Less Divisive*, WALL STREET JOURNAL (May 26, 2020), https://www.wsj.com/articles/facebook-knows-it-encourages-division-top-executives-nixed-solutions-11590507499.

56. *See* Jee, *supra* note 20.

57. *See* Jeremie Greer & Solana Rice, ANTI-MONOPOLY ACTIVISM: RECLAIMING POWER THROUGH RACIAL JUSTICE 18 (2021), https://www.liberationinageneration.org/anti-monopoly-activism-reclaiming-power-through-racial-justice (Liberation in a Generation calls this phenomenon the "Oppression Economy" which "uses the racist tools of theft, exclusion, and exploitation to strip wealth from people of color, so that the elite can build their wealth").

58. *See* Ultraviolet, *supra* note 26, at 15.

59. Díaz & Hecht-Felella, *supra* note 46, at 9; Guynn, *supra* note 38.

60. *See* Ultraviolet, *supra* note 26, at 15.

61. *See* Díaz & Hect-Felella, *supra* note 46, at 8 ("For example, an internal Facebook training document from 2017 revealed that out of three groups—female drivers, Black children, and white

men—only white men would be protected under the company's hate speech policy. The rationale was that both race (white) and sex (male) are protected characteristics, whereas the other examples included quasi- or nonprotected characteristics, namely age (in the Black children example) and driving (in the female drivers example)").

62. *See* Donovan, *supra* note 11; *see also* Romano, *supra* note 29.

63. *See* Donovan, *supra* note 11.

64. *See Facebook Ran Recruitment Ads for Militia Groups*, Tech Transparency Project (Oct. 19, 2020), https://www.techtransparencyproject.org/articles/facebook-ran-recruitment-ads-militia -groups.

65. Vogels, *supra* note 21.

66. *Id.*; Amanda Hess, *Twitter Won't Stop Harassment on Its Platform, So Its Users Are Stepping In*, Slate (Aug. 6, 2014), https://slate.com/technology/2014/08/twitter-harassment-user-created-apps -block-together-flaminga-and-the-block-bot-crack-down-on-twitter-abuse.html.

67. *See* Steele, *supra* note 3, at 55.

68. Jee, *supra* note 20.

69. Tim Wu, The Curse of Bigness: Antitrust in the New Gilded Age 54 (2018); *see also* Singer, *supra* note 50.

70. Waller, *supra* note 4, at 1773.

71. *Id.* at 1774.

72. Greer & Rice, *supra* note 57, at 5.

73. *See* Wu, *supra* note 69, at 19.

74. *See* Singer, *supra* note 50.

75. Sandeep Vaheesan, *How Antitrust Perpetuates Structural Racism*, The Appeal (Sept. 16, 2020), https://theappeal.org/how-antitrust-perpetuates-structural-racism/.

76. *See* Singer, *supra* note 50.

77. *See* Wu, *supra* note 69, at 72–73.

78. *See* Slaughter, *supra* note 51, at 5.

79. *See* Greer & Rice, *supra* note 57, at 54.

80. Vaheesan, *supra* note 75.

81. *See* Greer & Rice, *supra* note 57, at 10–11.

82. Waller, *supra* note 4, at 1775.

83. *See id.* at 1792 ("While there are realistic theories under which Facebook already has market power, it is not inevitable that an enforceable agency or court would agree").

84. *See id.* at 1804.

85. *See* Greer & Rice, *supra* note 57, at 47.

86. *See* Jee, *supra* note 20.

87. Greer & Rice, *supra* note 57, at 23, 6.

88. *See* Vaheesan, *supra* note 75.

89. *See* Slaughter, *supra* note 51, at 3.

90. *See* Wu, *supra* note 69, at 23.

91. *See id.* at 48, 50–51.

92. *Id.* at 128.

93. *See* S. 3847, 117th Cong. §4(2) (2022).

94. H.R. 3816, 117th Cong. §2(f)(2)(D) (2021).

95. Wu, *supra* note 69, at 132–33.

96. *See* Gerrit De Vynck & Jeremy Kahn, *Google AI Struggles to Keep Mosque Shooting Clip Off YouTube*, Bloomberg (Mar. 15, 2019), https://www.bloomberg.com/news/articles/2019-03-15/google -s-ai-struggles-to-keep-mosque-shooting-video-off-youtube.

97. Waller, *supra* note 4, at 1790.

98. H.R. 3849, 117th Cong. §4 (2021).

99. *Id.* at §3.

100. Adi Robertson, *How Would Opening Up Facebook Change the Internet?*, The Verge (Oct. 23, 2019), https://www.theverge.com/2019/10/23/20926792/facebook-access-act-interoperability-data-portability-warner-hawley-bill-explainer.

101. Steele, *supra* note 3, at 50–51.

15

Consent (Still) Won't Save Us

Jasmine McNealy

A PROVOCATION AND AN ANALOGY

In late January 2016, the internet came abuzz with news of how one woman was dealing with unwanted attention on social media. Australian model Emily Sears, who at the time had more than 2 million followers on Instagram, had found a solution to men sending unsolicited "dick pics"[1] to her direct messages (DMs).[2] Instead of deleting the photos and simply blocking the accounts sending the DMs, Sears would alert the dick pic sender's romantic partner, after finding their name or account information by searching through the sender's Instagram account. In the alternative, Sears would reply to the sender with a photo of him with his girlfriend.[3] Both contacting their partners and demonstrating that she knew their relationship status would prompt apologies.[4] Sears and her friend Laura Lux, herself with more than six-hundred thousand followers, claimed that they send messages to the romantic partners of these men to fulfill their obligations under "girl code."[5] Lux explained to BuzzFeed:

> So I sent her a message with a screenshot of our conversation telling her that I was really sorry, but I thought she deserved to know how her boyfriend was behaving towards other women. I know if the roles were reversed and it was my boyfriend sending that shit out, I would want to know.[6]

The perils of being a woman online has and continues to receive much needed attention as scholars across many disciplines and the mainstream media examine the impact and implications of internet misogyny.[7] That the sending of dick pics, for example, is not at all abnormal, is deserving of further investigation.

But, although the study of the sending of unsolicited not-safe-for-work (NSFW) photos and other harassment is important, this chapter is not an examination of online sexual harassment or misogyny. Instead, it focuses on the issue of consent.

Both Sears and Lux claim that when they told the men that they would be informing their partners or other listed relatives about the sending of the dick pics, they would quickly receive an apology and sometimes a plea that they not go through with their plan to contact.[8] A question, then, arises as to the expectations these men had for the information, in the form of a photo, sent to these strangers. Even if Sears and Lux had not forwarded the photos, could the men have expected that the shots of their penis would remain between them and the women? Surely, the men had consented to their bits being seen, at least by Sears and Lux. Where does that consent, then, end? On the other hand, by just existing online, or having amassed a following and a touch of celebrity, did Sears and Lux consent to being contacted? Even if they had consented to, perhaps, initial contact, how does one make the inference that they had consented to receiving unwanted or unsolicited photos (data). Finally, have the loved ones of the photo senders consented to being contacted and perhaps embarrassed by the disclosures?

The Sears and Lux anecdote demonstrates an ongoing issue with current data protection and data privacy regimes that focus on individual information control. The usual mechanism for this in data protection is notice and choice,[9] which requires that organizations provide users with information about how their private data might be used and then to choose whether to accept the conditions.[10] Individuals, using their limited understanding of the data ecosystem—what is collected, how it is used, who has access—decide whether to consent. This consent mechanism has proved insufficient for informing us and ensuring that organizations are clear about the expectations users have for their data. This chapter considers the boundaries of consent and the limitations on the continued use of information control as the grounding for data protection regulation, especially with the accelerated use of artificial intelligence and algorithmic decision systems.

ON INDIVIDUAL CONTROL:
CONSENT AND ITS BOUNDARIES

In the West, many trace the foundations of privacy as individual control to Alan Westin's 1967 book *Privacy and Freedom*, in which he defines privacy as "the claim of individuals, groups, or institutions to determine for themselves when, how, and to what extent information about them is communicated to others." This definition is used as a basis for many data protection regulations.[11] Data, information, however, is leaky; "it escapes in unexpected ways, be it through errors, hacks, or whistleblowing."[12] Data is also shared beyond the bounds of what an individual agrees or can possibly imagine. When the government can access this data from third parties like banks or utility companies, it is able to point to the "third-party doctrine," which in general states that law enforcement does not need a warrant to get information about an individual if that information is held by a third-party, as an excuse for why this kind of data access does not violate the 4th Amendment. When private organizations share information commercially, their activities are usually upheld as having been disclosed in the organization's privacy policy or terms of service, to which the individual agreed.

Scholars have written much about the insufficiency of transparency and notice- and -choice architecture online. While transparency is a prerequisite for holding organizations accountable for data collection, usage, and sharing, it places the onus on users to be aware of all the possible ways that organizations might interact with data, of policing those interactions, and to understand the meaning of the organizational disclosures. These requirements are virtually impossible for even the savviest of technology users. Individuals do not have the time or bandwidth to make all the possible choice decisions that might arise in the use of web and app technology.

As further evidence of the reliance of the individual control theory of data protection, a familiar refrain is that those who do not want their information shared should simply not use the technology. This ignores that many technologies are deployed on individuals without their knowledge or consent. Schwartz identified three major problems with the continued use of individual control as privacy: the autonomy trap, the data seclusion deception, and the commodification illusion.[13] In sum, these major problems with individual control illustrate that the individual can never be in total control of their data at all times based on power imbalances between the individual, organizations, and government agencies. Therefore, although choice is looked at as offering power to the individual about how their data might be used, choice does not offer complete control nor supervisory powers.

What does this mean for data interactions in the social media context? The Sears and Lux opening anecdote provides an illustration. Sears and Lux use Instagram, like many others, as a social media platform, a space for garnering attention for their personal brands. With this platform use, they accept interactions with other users. They have "consented" to these social interactions, along with the platform terms. That does not mean, however, that they have consented to all forms of contact, as demonstrated by their responses to receiving unsolicited photos. The problem is that they had no way of proactively controlling the kinds of interactions they would encounter. Consent, then, is both contextual and sociotechnical.

CONSENT AS CONTEXTUAL

The boundaries of consent, whether in personal or business relationships, are based on expectations for disclosure and use of information. This can be demonstrated in the personal realm in cases of invasion of privacy by public disclosure and revenge porn. Some courts have recognized an expectation of privacy in information shared with other people in certain instances in which a special relationship exists.[14] *Miller v. Motorola, Inc.* offers an example of an invasion of privacy case decided based upon the relationship between individuals.[15] Joy Miller sued her employer, Motorola, after the company's resident nurse disclosed her mastectomy surgery to her coworkers. In reversing the lower court's dismissal of the Miller's public disclosure claim, the Illinois appellate court found that Miller had an expectation of privacy in speaking with the medical professional.[16]

No exact calculus exists for determining when courts will find the kind relationship in which an expectation of privacy is present. At least one scholar, however, has called for a consideration of social network theory when examining if a plaintiff had a privacy in information disclosed to others.[17] This would examine not the number of people in a particular group that the information has the potential to reach, but the possibility of the information reaching individuals outside of that group. Therefore, information would be considered private—the person sharing would have an expectation of privacy—even if the group is large, so long as the information remains confined to that group.[18] Lior Strahilevitz enumerates three factors that predict whether information will remain among a particular group: the level of interest the information generates, the group's information sharing norms, and group structure and information flows.[19] Although not expressly decided based upon a social network theory, *Multimedia WMAZ, Inc. v. Kubach* offers an opportunity to consider how a court will consider in group relationships and the impact on the reasonable expectation of privacy.[20]

Kubach was an HIV-positive man who shared his status with around sixty people, including family members, friends, his doctor, and members of a support group. He also appeared on a television show after obtaining assurances from the producers that his identity would be hidden.[21] The show's producers, however, failed to adequately hide his identity and he was recognizable to those in his community who became aware of his HIV-positive status. The court found that despite his having told his status to several people, an expectation of privacy in that information remained because his disclosure was to people who cared about him.[22]

As Helen Nissenbaum argues, expectations related to consent, whether online or off, differ from how consent mechanisms actually behave.[23] The implications of this failure in the data context are particularly significant. Current notice and choices schemes seek to present a measure of control to users. At the same time, to have perfect transparency or notice, organizations would have to inform users of all the ways data are and might be collected, as well as all the ways that data are and might be used, and by whom. Even if this were possible, Nissenbaum points to the transparency paradox or, "transparency of textual meaning and transparency of practice conflict in all but rare instances."[24] Therefore, if organizations make finely detailed disclosures, users may not understand all the ways data are collected and used; if organizations instead choose to make disclosures understandable, the disclosures might not offer enough details so that the user might be adequately informed to consent. Instead, she offers the system of contextual integrity as an alternative.

CONSENT AS SOCIOTECHNICAL

The system of contextual integrity recognizes that consent and privacy are intertwined with human social networks and patterns of communication.[25] Because of the humanity of data disclosure, traditional consent via notice and choice architecture fails to adequately deliver the kind of "control" that is necessary for consent to be at all meaningful. Further, human relationships, depending on the context, can add duties for the recipients of information disclosures. These duties can be related to confidentiality. Both the *Miller* and *Kubach* cases previously mentioned have elements of a less asserted, but related tort claim of breach of confidentiality. Breach of confidentiality, or breach of confidence, arises when the plaintiff can prove that the defendant owed her a duty of keeping information secret, and breached that duty.[26] Such a duty arises between a doctor and her patient,[27] and a lawyer and her client.[28] For such a duty to arise there must be "the assurance of secrecy and the reliance that it evokes," which creates a special relationship between the parties.[29]

Breach of confidence has been asserted outside of the patient/client–specialist, and familial realms. Andrew McClurg argues that intimate partner relationships evoke a similar duty of confidentiality.[30] The basis of such a right can be found in the culture, customs, and laws related to intimate relationships. The legal cases of *Griswold v. Connecticut*,[31] *Eisenstadt v. Baird*,[32] and *Lawrence v. Texas*,[33] according to McClurg, are foundational for the protection of the privacy in intimate relationships.[34]

Breach of confidence has been proposed as a remedy in revenge porn cases.[35] The argument is that, as with privacy, expectations exist about the kind of information that will be kept confidential.[36] This information—including sexual photographs, information about past relationships, kinks, and the like—may be shared with partners based on trust that it will not be revealed to third parties. This trust, according to Ari Waldman, is embedded in the idea of social capital, and relies on the belief that individuals will conform to societal norms.[37] This provides support for the claim that consent has boundaries, and because of this, current consent mechanisms, including notice and choice, do not adequately recognize the limitations and expectations that human information disclosure carry.

BOUNDARIES OF CONSENT

Though perhaps not stated expressly at the time, both Sears and Lux had boundaries about how they would interact with data on Instagram. Although using the social media for their own personal purposes, and thereby consenting to how other users might communicate with them, they did not *de facto* consent to all kinds of communications. Instead, they had limitations on the content of the communications they would accept. In this case, it seems that one boundary was set against other users sharing photos of their genitals. This would seem like a recognizable boundary. Yet, the women reported contacting the loved ones of multiple men who had sent dick pics, demonstrating how boundaries are often ignored and/or how some individuals lack awareness of those boundaries.

Until now, both the opening anecdote and the cases in support of my argument about the insufficiency of the notice and choice consent mechanism have been based on human-to-human information disclosure. Sears and Lux involved social media user interactions; both *Miller* and *Kubach* were cases involving the sharing of sensitive information within close networks. But data disclosure in human-to-organization or human-to-machine schemes follow much the same pattern and are replete with same dangers, if only amplified. Therefore, the current consent schemes in these areas, too, need to be changed. Current controversies in facial recognition technology illustrate the issues with continued reliance on consent.

In June 2022, Google settled a class action lawsuit brought under the Illinois Biometric Information Privacy Act (BIPA) for its use of facial recognition software in connection to its Google Photos product.[38] According to the original claim, Google's facial grouping tool automatically identified users' faces in photos and videos uploaded to Google Photos. The plaintiffs had brought the claim under BIPA, which prohibits the collection and storage of biometric data without informing the user, because the product did not ask for consent in violation of the law. Google agreed to settle the lawsuit for $100 million and to provide notice about the facial grouping tool as required under the law.

Google is not, of course, the only organization that has run afoul of BIPA. Meta—Facebook—has had to field at least two state level lawsuits over its use of facial recognition software. In February 2021, Facebook settled a class action suit claiming its facial recognitions system violated BIPA by not complying with the law's notice and consent requirements.[39] In the settlement, Facebook agreed to pay $650 million. In 2022, the state of Texas sued Meta, Facebook's parent company, for violating the state's privacy law through its repeated use of facial recognition technology.[40] The Texas suit centers Facebook's "tag suggestions" tool that encouraged users to affirm the suggested identity of people in a photo, which would then be connected to the identified person's profile. Facebook ended the use of the tool in 2021, but the lawsuit claims that the company collected data without consent, shared data with third parties, and did not destroy the data in a timely manner.

Perhaps the most recognizable facial recognition lawsuit settlement was that of Clearview AI, another class action lawsuit brought under BIPA. Unlike the Google and Facebook cases in which site users actively use a facial recognition tool, although without notice, in the case of Clearview, the organization was accused of scraping social media data, including photos, in violation of platform rules and without the permission of the data subjects.[41] More than solely collecting and storing this data, Clearview sold access to it voluminous database to many government, corporate, and other organizations.

These cases with "big tech" companies hinge on whether the organizations obtained adequate consent from users, while at the same time failing to recognize that simply consenting to use a site or a site's tools is not blanket permission for the use of personal data for uses beyond the boundaries of the user's imagination or realization. The Google and Facebook settlements leave little to analyze about how courts will consider bounds of consent in these facial recognition cases. The Clearview case demonstrates that even accepted bounds of consent in agreeing to the terms of use for a social media site are not enough to prevent the use and access of personal data by third parties. This should provide further evidence that consent or notice and choice are normative legal constructs that do not provide the kinds of data protection that individuals need against ever emerging ways of collecting, using, and exploiting personal data.

State laws like BIPA and state actions like that of Texas against Facebook may offer a small amount of relief to those in affected classes. But these suits again reflect a focus on individual choice—control of information. Although individual choice is important as a general matter, it does not stop organizations and organizational tools from interacting with personal data in ways that cross personal boundaries. What's needed, instead, is the institution of a regulatory framework that prohibits certain data collection and sharing at the outset of any human–organization or human–machine interaction. Such a framework would assist individuals from being left without recourse if they had offered a measure of consent. Instead, this kind of framework would preclude certain business models and shut off certain kinds of data interactions.

NOTES

1. "Dick pics" are photographs of a human penis. *See, e.g.*, "Dick Pic," UrbanDictionary.com, http://www.urbandictionary.com/define.php?term=dick+pic (accessed, March 20, 2016).

2. Joyce Chen, *Australian Model Emily Sears Is Warning Girls about Guys Who Send Her Penis Pics*, Us WEEKLY (Jan. 29, 2016), http://www.usmagazine.com/celebrity-news/news/australian-model-emily-sears-is-warning-girls-about-guys-who-send-her-penis-pics-w162926; Jay Hathaway, *This Model Deals with Unwanted Dick Pics by Contacting the Dicks' Girlfriends*, NYMag.com (Jan. 29, 2016), http://nymag.com/following/2016/01/how-a-model-deals-with-the-unwanted-dick-pics.html; Madeleine Davies, *Model Responds to Unwelcome Dick Pics By Contacting Senders' Girlfriends*, JEZEBEL (Jan. 29, 2016), http://jezebel.com/model-responds-to-unwelcome-dick-pics-by-contacting-sen-1756022915; Rossalyn Warren, *A Model Is Alerting Girlfriends of the Men Who Send Her Dick Pics*, BUZZFEED (Jan. 29, 2016), http://www.buzzfeed.com/rossalynwarren/a-model-is-alerting-girlfriends-of-the-men-who-send-her-dick.

3. Warren, *supra* note 2; Hathaway, *supra* note 2.

4. *Id.*

5. UrbanDictionary.com defines "Girl Code" as the guidelines that "girls most obey in order not to get kicked out of the community," UrbanDictionary.com, http://www.urbandictionary.com/define.php?term=Girl+Code (accessed, June 17, 2022).

6. Warren, *supra* note 2.

7. Sarah Banet-Weiser & Kate M. Miltner, *#MasculinitySoFragile: Culture, Structure, and Networked Misogyny*, 16 Fem. Media Stud. 171 (2016); Gender Stereotypes, Aggression, and Computer Games: An Online Survey of Women (Feb. 1, 2005), http://online.liebertpub.com/doi/abs/10.1089/cpb.2004.7.714; Jessica Megarry, *Online Incivility or Sexual Harassment? Conceptualising Women's Experiences in the Digital Age*, 47, Part A, Women's Stud. Int. Forum 46 (2014); *Sexual Harassment in Online Gaming Stirs Anger*, New York Times, https://www.nytimes.com/2012/08/02/us/sexual-harassment-in-online -gaming-stirs-anger.html; Jerry Finn & Mary Banach, *Victimization Online: The Downside of Seeking Human Services for Women on the Internet*, 3 Cyberpsychol. Behav. 785 (2000); *Women and the Internet: Promise and Perils* (July 5 2004), http://online.liebertpub.com/doi/pdf/10.1089/10949310050191683.

8. Warren, *supra* note 2; Davies, *supra* note 2.

9. See Robert H. Sloan & Richard Warner, *Beyond Notice and Choice: Privacy, Norms, and Consent*, SSRN Electron. J. (Mar. 27, 2013), http://www.ssrn.com/abstract=2239099.

10. Lorrie Faith Cranor, *Necessary But Not Sufficient: Standardized Mechanisms for Privacy Notice and Choice*, J. Telecomm. and High Tech. L., 10.

11. *Id.*, at 277.

12. Kate Crawford, Kate Miltner & Mary L. Gray, *Critiquing Big Data: Politics, Ethics, Epistemology*, Intl. J. of Commun., *Special Section Introduction*, 10, 1666 (2014).

13. See Paul M. Schwartz, *Internet Privacy and the State*, 32 Conn Rev 821 (2000).

14. *See e.g.*, Y.G. v. Jewish Hospital, 795 S.W.2d 488 (Mo. Ct. App. 1990)(finding an expectation of privacy for a couple receiving in vitro fertility treatments); Multimedia WMAZ, Inc. v. Kubach, 443 S.E.2d 491 (Ga. 1994) (finding an expectation of privacy for a man who had disclosed his HIV-positive status to sixty people).

15. 560 N.E.2d 900 (Ill. App. 1990).

16. *Id.*, at 903–4.

17. See Lior Jacob Strahilevitz, *A Social Networks Theory of Privacy*, 72 U. Chi. L. Rev. 919 (2005).

18. Strahilevitz, *supra* note 34, at 973–980.

19. *Id.* at 970–971.

20. 443 S.E.2d 491 (Ga. 1994).

21. *Id.* at

22. *Id.* at

23. Helen Nissenbaum, *A Contextual Approach to Privacy Online*, 140 Daedalus 32, 35 (2011).

24. *Id.*, at 36.

25. See generally, Helen Nissenbaum, Privacy in Context: Technology, Policy, and the Integrity of Social Life (2009), https://www.degruyter.com/document/doi/10.1515/9780804772891 /html?lang=en.

26. See Alan B. Vickery, *Breach of Confidence: An Emerging Tort*, 82 Colum. L. Rev. 1426 (1982); G. Michael Harvey, *Confidentiality: A Measured Response to the Failure of Privacy*, 140 U. Pa. L. Rev. 2385 (1992); Susan M. Gilles, *Promises Betrayed, Breach of Confidence as a Remedy for Invasion of Privacy*, 43 Buff. L. Rev. 1 (1995); Neil M. Richards & Daniel J. Solove, *Privacy's Other Path: Recovering the Law of Confidentiality*, 96 Geo. L.J. 123 (2007).

27. *See e.g.*, Alsip v. Johnson City Medical Center, 197 S.W.3d 722 (2006); Berger v. Sonneland, M.D., 1 P.3d 1187 (2000).

28. *See e.g.*, Waite, Schneider, Bayless & Chesley Co., LPA v. Davis, 2012 U.S. Dist. Lexis 117634 (S.D. Ohio, Aug. 21, 2012).

29. Vickery, *supra* note 26, at 1428.

30. Andrew J. McClurg, *Kiss and Tell: Protecting Intimate Relationship Privacy through Implied Contracts of Confidentiality*, 74 U. Cin. L. Rev. 887 (2006).

31. 381 U.S. 479 (1965) (finding unconstitutional a ban on the use of contraceptives).

32. 405 U.S. 438 (1971) (holding that the constitutional right to use contraceptives extended to both married and unmarried people).

33. 539 U.S. 558 (2003) (finding unconstitutional a criminal prohibition against homosexual acts).

34. McClurg, *supra* note 30, at 915.

35. See e.g. Justine Mitchell, *Censorship in Cyberspace: Closing the Net on "Revenge Porn,"* 25 Ent. L. Rev. 283 (2014); Janice Richardson, *The Changing Meaning of Privacy, Identity, and Contemporary Feminist Philosophy*, 21 Minds & Mach. 517 (2011); Ari Ezra Waldman, *Breach of Trust: Fighting "Revenge Porn,"* 102 Iowa L. Rev. 709 (2017).

36. Waldman, *supra* note 35, at 713.

37. *Id.*, at 716.

38. Dan Avery, *Last Day to File a Claim for Google's $100 Million Privacy Settlement*, CNET (Sept. 24, 2022), https://www.cnet.com/personal-finance/googles-100-million-facial-recognition-lawsuit-who-can-claim-money-from-the-settlement/; Jim Hagerty, *Google Settles Lawsuit with Illinois Residents for $100M after Photo App Privacy Concerns*, USA TODAY (June 3, 2022), https://www.usatoday.com/story/tech/2022/06/03/google-pay-illinois-settlement-photo-privacy/7495827001/; Emma Roth, *Google to Pay $100 Million to Illinois Residents for Photos' Face Grouping Feature*, The Verge (June 6, 2022), https://www.theverge.com/2022/6/6/23156198/google-class-action-face-grouping-biometric-information-illinois-privacy-act.

39. Torsten Kracht, Lisa Sotto & Bennett Sooy, *Facebook Pivots from Facial Recognition System Following Biometric Privacy Suit*, Reuters (Jan. 26, 2022), https://www.reuters.com/legal/legalindustry/facebook-pivots-facial-recognition-system-following-biometric-privacy-suit-2022-01-26/.

40. Peter Granitz, *Texas Sues Meta, Saying It Misused Facial Recognition Data*, NPR (Feb. 15, 2022), https://www.npr.org/2022/02/15/1080769555/texas-sues-meta-for-misusing-facial-recognition-data; Cecilia Kang, *Texas Sues Facebook's Parent, Saying It Collected Facial Recognition Data without Consent*, New York Times (Feb. 14, 2022), https://www.nytimes.com/2022/02/14/technology/texas-facebook-facial-recognition-lawsuit.html.

41. Adi Robertson, *Clearview AI Agrees to Permanent Ban on Selling Facial Recognition to Private Companies*, The Verge (May 9, 2022), https://www.theverge.com/2022/5/9/23063952/clearview-ai-aclu-settlement-illinois-bipa-injunction-private-companies; Nick Statt, *ACLU Sues Facial Recognition Firm Clearview AI, Calling It a "Nightmare Scenario" for Privacy*, The Verge (May 28, 2020), https://www.theverge.com/2020/5/28/21273388/aclu-clearview-ai-lawsuit-facial-recognition-database-illinois-biometric-laws.

16

Revisioning Algorithms
as a Black Feminist Project

Ngozi Okidegbe

We live in an age of predictive algorithms.[1] Jurisdictions across the country are utilizing algorithms to make or influence life-altering decisions in a host of governmental decision-making processes—criminal justice, education, and social assistance to name a few.[2] One justification given for this algorithmic turn concerns redressing historical and current inequalities within governmental decision-making.[3] The hope is that the predictions produced by these predictive systems can correct this problem by providing decision-makers with the information needed to make fairer, more accurate, and consistent decisions.[4] For instance, jurisdictions claim that their turn to risk assessment algorithms in bail, sentencing, and parole is in order to de-bias decisions made in these areas. However, this hope has not borne out in practice. Rather than de-biasing decision-making, algorithms have tended to operate to reinforce it.[5] A primary reason is that these systems tend to produce disparate predictions that track existing social inequities and facilitate harmful outcomes for marginalized communities, particularly racially and otherwise politically oppressed communities.[6] To compound the issue, since these systems tend to be applied to an entire sector, the predictions produced operate to maintain existing inequities, social hierarchies, and the resulting political, economic, and social oppression of our current moment.[7] Professor Safiya Umoja Noble's work has provided us with a language and a framework to understand this state of affairs. She employs the term "algorithmic oppression," which she uses to refer to how algorithms "serv[e] up deleterious information about people" and resultingly "reinforce oppressive social and economic relations."[8] By cementing existing political, social, and economic hierarchies, these algorithmic systems—as Professor Dorothy Roberts explains—exacerbate marginalized communities' vulnerability to state-sanctioned violence, resource deprivation, and other precarious outcomes that hamper their ability to exercise full citizenship in this country.[9]

When viewed in tandem, the multifaceted effects of algorithmic oppression threaten to "lock in" our unequal status quo into the future.[10]

The stakes are high. Resisting and counteracting how algorithms lock in the structural inequalities and violence produced and mediated by our institutions, legal structures, and laws is imperative. This is particularly so given how algorithms continue to proliferate and the ideology that sustains their usage continues to deepen. Yet, as we contend with how to approach algorithmic oppression, Black Feminists provide us with a useful starting point. Their work reveals how algorithmic oppression is a system design stemming from the interests, attitudes, and values of those in charge of adopting, constructing, implementing, and overseeing algorithmic systems.[11] As Professor Roberts reminds us, "the outcomes of [algorithmic systems] depend on the particular ideologies, aims, and methods that govern [their] use."[12] Given this, algorithmic systems are not predisposed to this function. It is possible to reenvision the paradigm governing the use of algorithmic systems in order to orient them toward more equitable, democratic, and just ends.

My scholarship in the field of law and technology coalesces around revealing and contesting how various dimensions of the paradigm governing algorithmic systems are incongruent with justice. My work seeks to orient this paradigm toward the liberatory ideologies and epistemologies of the oppressed communities working to reform or dismantle and reconstitute the institutions, the systems, and laws responsible for their oppression. Reflecting on the theme of this book, my work has been a Black Feminist project. Informed by Black Feminist praxis and theory, my work aims to put forth a set of democratic and epistemic practices around algorithms that can bring about the kind of algorithms that could aid racial justice, gender justice, class justice, and other justice-seeking efforts. In that spirit, this chapter explores how applying a Black Feminist approach to the paradigm governing algorithmic systems could blunt algorithmic oppression and produce the conditions needed for creating algorithms designed to challenge and contest unequal systems that subordinate politically oppressed people in our country. Using the example of criminal legal algorithms, it sketches out possible orientations for how to envision this shift. In so doing, this chapter is in community with a growing set of thought and praxis devoted to dismantling oppression in our reality and in our imaginaries. The chapter will proceed in two parts. The first half will provide background on the use of criminal legal algorithms. The second half will explore the implications of taking a Black Feminist approach.

CRIMINAL LEGAL ALGORITHMS

My work focuses on *criminal legal algorithms*, a term that encompasses risk assessment algorithms used in policing, bail, sentencing, and other areas of criminal administration.[13] These predictions are used by police, judges, and other system actors to inform the decisions around the use or nonuse of criminal legal resources. As Professor Jessica Eaglin explains, enacting jurisdictions theorize that the predictions produced by these algorithms will shape and rationalize system actors' decision-making toward outcomes consistent with protecting public safety.[14]

The proliferation of algorithmic systems has generated significant criticism. Algorithm critics worry that algorithmic systems will maintain or further exacerbate existing inequalities within criminal administration.[15] In practice, criminal legal algorithms have not dismantled the racial and class dimension of how policing, surveillance, incarceration, or other criminal law resources are deployed.[16] One reason is that, as Professor Erin Collins's work shows, the reliance on algorithmic systems has operated to prevent a critical interrogation of the ideological commitments that concentrate criminal law resources on racially marginalized and other politically oppressed bodies and communities in the first place.[17] As it currently stands, criminal legal algorithmic systems aid, rather than reduce, the subordinative effect of the criminal legal system on marginalized communities.

Attending to how algorithms support the subordinative function of the criminal legal system requires more than what is offered by technocratic-based reform efforts. These efforts tend to point in the direction of making algorithms and the paradigm governing them more participatory, more transparent, more accurate, or more subject to oversight regimes.[18] As I have suggested in prior work, these reforms are worth pursuing, since their actualization would reduce algorithmic oppression on the margins.[19] The problem is that these efforts are insufficient because they sidestep the democratic and epistemic dimensions of algorithm oppression and resultingly keep it in place. In the following subsections, I will briefly lay out these dimensions as they will set us up for understanding how a Black Feminist paradigm could usher in more equitable algorithms.

Democratic Dimension

The democratic dimension of algorithmic oppression concerns the fact that the paradigm governing algorithms is democratically exclusionary to racially and otherwise politically marginalized communities. In *The Democratizing Potential of Algorithms?*, I discuss how marginalized communities are excluded from the construction, implementation, and oversight of algorithmic systems.[20] The democratic exclusion experienced by marginalized communities within the paradigm governing criminal legal algorithms is not unique. It is consistent with the democratic exclusion that these communities experience in our society more generally. As Professor Jocelyn Simonson has forcefully argued in the criminal legal arena, criminal legal institutions democratically exclude the marginalized people that are the most likely to be subjected to state-based regulation and violence.[21] Instead, these institutions tend to be responsive to those who benefit from the status quo, which helps explain why our criminal legal system concentrates state violence on marginalized bodies and the political, economic, democratic, and social consequences of that violence in marginalized communities.

When understood in this light, the problem is not that the paradigm governing criminal legal algorithms is not designed to facilitate the participation of marginalized communities within it—though that is an issue. The problem is that the democratic exclusion within this paradigm maps onto and exacerbates the democratic exclusion that these marginalized communities already experience in criminal law governance. In so doing, it operates as an additional barrier to attempts by marginalized communities to contest and overcome the harmful ways in which the criminal legal system has operated in their neighborhoods. To provide context, marginalized communities have developed a body of resistance tactics in the face of exponential rates of incarceration, police violence, and surveillance.[22] The current paradigm governing algorithms undermines this critical work, since resistance tactics are powerless against decisions predicated on the result of an algorithmic prediction.[23] At the same time, the democratic exclusion of marginalized communities within the paradigm means that these communities cannot stop algorithmic predictions from hampering their on-the-ground racial justice efforts. The result is that algorithmic systems and the paradigm that governs them operate as an additional barrier to attempts by marginalized communities to reform or abolish and reconstitute the criminal legal system.

Epistemic Dimension

The epistemic dimension of algorithmic oppression concerns the fact that the paradigm governing algorithms is epistemically exclusionary to marginalized communities. In *Discredited Data*, I focus on how this epistemic exclusion plays out in algorithmic construction.[24] As a starting point, algorithmic construction refers to the steps that developers take to build and train algorithmic systems. During this stage, developers are tasked with making critical decisions around problem formulation as well as data collection and data utilization. The choice of data has emerged as an important focal point for how algorithmic oppression occurs. As researchers Kristian Lum and William Isaac have raised, one reason for which algorithmic systems produce disparate results is the data used to construct and train them.[25] Because the data used in algorithmic construction is shaped by social hierarchies in our society, the predictions produced reflect these hierarchies. In other words, bias in, bias out.[26] However, as I have explained in prior work, biased data is not the only epistemic problem impacting algorithmic construction.[27] Another epistemic problem is that developers exclusively rely on a certain set of knowledge sources to obtain their data.[28] In the criminal law realm, these sources are criminal legal institutions, such as the police, pretrial service agencies, courts, and parole boards.[29] This reliance on what I term "carceral knowledge sources" occurs despite the fact that the data derived from the knowledge produced by these knowledge sources are well-known to be inaccurate, incomplete, and biased in regard to racially and otherwise politically marginalized people.[30]

The exclusive reliance on carceral knowledge sources comes at the expense of obscuring different knowledge sources, particularly knowledge sources tethered to marginalized communities (which I term "community knowledge sources"). Community knowledge sources are routinely ignored and discredited by developers.[31] This discrediting cannot be explained by a preference for quantitative data, since developers also utilize the qualitive data produced by carceral knowledge sources within algorithmic construction.[32] The cause of this exclusion is epistemic oppression. Coined by Professor Miranda Fricker, epistemic oppression refers to the exclusion of subjugated communities from dominant knowledge production and validation processes.[33] The harm of this epistemic oppression is that it ensures that powerful groups "have some sort of unfair advantage in 'structuring' our *understandings* of the social world."[34] As I have argued in prior work, this unfair influence distorts the range of possibilities achievable through algorithms, because it tethers algorithms to the status quo, even though other ways of knowing could generate better outcomes than currently exist.[35] The result is that algorithms reinforce the epistemic oppression that has and continues to hamper efforts by marginalized communities to shift the epistemes, imaginaries, and ideologies that keep inequality in place in our current time.

WHEN BLACK FEMINISM ENTERS THE FRAME

I have laid out the democratic and epistemic dimension of algorithmic oppression using the example of criminal legal algorithms and the paradigm that governs their utilization. The rest of the chapter explores the implications of applying a Black Feminist lens. As a first step, it is necessary to define Black Feminism. Although there is no single answer, Black Feminism is premised on resisting and countering oppressive structures and the violent ways of knowing and being that support them. The project of Black Feminism is to create a political movement against capitalism, racism, gender hierarchy, heteropatriarchy, and other systems that subordinate Black women.[36] It also seeks, as Professor Ula Y. Taylor notes "to develop institutions to protect what the dominant culture has little respect and value for [which is] black women's minds and bodies."[37] Though originating from the distinct experience of Black women,[38] Black Feminism shares space and is in conversation with Critical Race Theory, QueerCrit, TribalCrit, Afrofuturism, Indigenous futurism, and other liberatory imaginaries.

Defining the Black Feminist tradition is difficult given the diversity of perspectives taken by Black Feminists. However, there are at least four common themes that unify Black Feminist theory. First, there is no common or universal form of oppression. As Professor bell hooks explains, each oppressed community experiences oppression differently.[39] Black Women experience a distinct form of oppression that endows them with a particular standpoint and perspective about it and how to resist it.[40] At the same time, as Professor Patricia Hill Collins reminds us, the diversity of identities among Black women results in different expressions of this standpoint.[41]

Second, resisting oppression requires naming and rejecting the ways of knowing and being that support and naturalize oppressive outcomes in society. As Professor Collins notes, social institutions produce knowledge that reinforces existing inequalities in service of white supremacy.[42] This understanding enables a dismantling of the privileged position that knowledge produced by institutions hold in shaping our reality. Third, Black Feminists recognize knowledge is positional.[43] Objective knowledge does not exist. All knowledge is reflective of the perspectives of those who produce it.[44] Finally, Black women alongside all subjugated people are credible, reliable, and legible epistemic agents.[45] They are knowers of their own oppression, despite attempts by dominant knowledge production and validation processes to discount and discredit their knowledge.[46]

Applying these themes to the paradigm governing algorithms provides us with an important starting point for a reorientation.

The paradigm governing algorithms must account for differently situated oppression: An important theme of Black Feminism is that there is no common oppression. This means that the paradigm governing algorithms must be made to account for difference. No one group can stand in for another. This lesson is important given how technology companies have often engaged in tokenism as a stand-in for transformative change. Diversity for diversity sake, as Professor Ruha Benjamin points out, cannot address algorithmic oppression.[47] This is particularly so given that diversity schemes tend to be intentionally designed to privilege the most privileged members of an oppressed group.[48] A Black Feminist approach would aim for the inclusion of all oppressed people at every stage of the paradigm governing algorithms with a particular focus on those oppressed on various axes.

The paradigm governing algorithms must reject violent ways of knowing and being: Another important theme connected to Black Feminism is that oppression shapes every aspect of the paradigm governing algorithms. This thinking has manifested itself in the makeup of those in control of algorithmic adoption, design, implementation, and oversight, which is primarily white, affluent cisgendered men.[49] While this makeup can be attributed to the lack of educational opportunities afforded to oppressed communities, it is also the result of a white, male, capitalistic, and otherwise oppressive way of thinking about algorithms. A Black Feminist approach would upend this approach. One mechanism to accomplish this feat would be to adopt a power-shifting model to the paradigm governing algorithms which I have raised in past work.[50] Power-shifting, a concept theorized by Professors Jocelyn Simonson and K. Sabeel Rahman, seeks to use institutional design as one tool among many to redress racial and other power imbalances created by substantive and procedural inequities.[51] In the arena of algorithms, adopting a power-shifting approach would mean ceasing complete or substantive control over algorithmic systems to the communities that have been most harmed by it.

The paradigm governing algorithms must turn to subjugated knowledge: Black Feminists call for a turn to subjugated knowledge. They push for the disruption of dominant knowledge production practices that have oriented our society toward anti-Black and otherwise subordinative outcomes. A Black Feminist approach requires us to epistemically disinvest from courts, institutions, and other knowledge production sites that have been critical in structuring the current crises impacting marginalized people.[52] Beyond the knowledge produced by Black women, the move also invites engagement with the knowledge of those most affected by state violence, surveillance, and containment practices. This call for engagement with the epistemes of those subordinated within racialized, classed, and gendered hierarchies follows the traditions of critical theories that ask us to "look to the bottom"[53] as a method to not only destabilize existing social hierarchies, but also to rebuild our society on more equitable and democratic terms.[54] This turn is not a simple process. In regard to the paradigm governing algorithms, it requires us to create new institutions designed to promote subjugated knowledge. Moreover, it means disrupting hierarchical knowledge production practices within marginalized communities[55] that have epistemically oppressed those traditionally unable to actualize full membership in these communities.[56] As I have suggested in prior work, one concrete way to accomplish this feat would be to develop a community jury system "in which community members task themselves with the obligation to present their own knowledge . . . at various intervals during the year while being compensated for their labor."[57]

CONCLUSION

The creation of algorithms informed by Black Feminism would be revolutionary—perhaps too radical for our current system, given this society's current commitment to white supremacy and other violent ways of being. However, as I have noted in past work, even if these algorithms are never used by system actors, they would still constitute a statement by marginalized people that the system is out of line with their values, views, and pursuit of freedom—a fact that beneficiaries of the system need to be reminded of.[58] Moreover, such algorithms would not function to maintain social oppression. That being said, imagine if such algorithms were used. They could act as a democratic check on unequal laws and legal processes if accounted for by system actors. When combined with resistance efforts underway by marginalized communities, such algorithms could present a path toward meaningfully reforming or dismantling the criminal legal system and other unequal systems. This is the power of tapping into Black Feminism and other subjugated ways of knowing. They allow us to imagine how to build a more equitable future. Maybe algorithms and other currently oppressive technological systems could become vehicles of liberation. Unlocking that potential requires turning to the ways of knowing and being of those in the fight for more a just world.

NOTES

This chapter builds off the insights developed in my prior work. I owe thanks to Amanda Levendowski and Meg Leta Jones for inviting me to contribute this chapter. I appreciate the helpful feedback and support I received from Erin R. Collins, Nicole McConlogue, Jamelia Morgan, and I. India Thusi.

1. *See* Danielle Keats Citron, *Technological Due Process*, 85 Wash. U. L. Rev. 1249, 1253, 1276–77 (2008); Ryan Calo & Danielle Keats Citron, *The Automated Administrative State: A Crisis of Legitimacy*, 70 Emory L.J. 797, 800 (2021).

2. *See* Dorothy E. Roberts, *Digitizing the Carceral State*, 132 Harv. L. Rev. 1695, 1695 (2019) (reviewing Virginia Eubanks, Automating Inequality: How High-Tech Tools Profile, Police, and Punish the Poor [2018]).

3. *See id.*, at 1696.

4. Ben Green, *The Flaws of Policies Requiring Human Oversight of Government Algorithms*, 45 Comput. L. & Sec. Rev. 1, 1 (2022).

5. *See* Roberts, *supra* note 2, at 1713 ("Moreover, [these algorithms'] forecasts of the future are based on data that were produced by existing racial discrimination in systems such as policing, housing, education, health care, and public assistance. The future predicted by today's algorithms, therefore, is predetermined to correspond to past racial inequality").

6. *See* Sonia K. Katyal, *Private Accountability in the Age of Artificial Intelligence*, 66 UCLA L. Rev. 54, 69 (2019).

7. *See id.*

8. Safiya Umoja Noble, Algorithms of Oppression: How Search Engines Reinforce Racism 4, 10 (2018).

9. *See* Roberts, *supra* note 2, at 1699, 1708, 1713–14.

10. *See* Rebecca Crootof, *"Cyborg Justice" and the Risk of Technological-Legal Lock-In*, 119 Colum. L. Rev. F. 233, 235 (2019).

11. *See* Noble, *supra* note 8, at 4–7.

12. Roberts, *supra* note 2, at 1697.

13. *See id.*, at 1716. For clarity, the term *risk assessment algorithms* refers to algorithms that employ a statistical method and use information about an individual or location to produce a prediction about that individual or location in the future.

14. Jessica M. Eaglin, *Technologically Distorted Conceptions of Punishment*, 97 Wash. U. L. Rev. 483, 504 (2019).

15. *See* Bernard E. Harcourt, *Risk as a Proxy for Race: The Dangers of Risk Assessment*, 27 Fed. Sent'g Rep. 237, 237 (2015) (warning that "risk today has collapsed into prior criminal history, and prior criminal history has become a proxy for race").

16. *See generally* Jessica M. Eaglin, *Racializing Algorithms*, 111 Calif. L. Rev. (June 2023).

17. *See generally* Erin R. Collins, *Abolishing the Evidence-Based Paradigm*, 48 BYU L. Rev. (2022). But another reason concerns the biased reaction that system actors have toward algorithmic predictions. As the work of Megan Stevenson explains, system actors tend to have an unprincipled approach to applying algorithmic predictions, particularly where those predictions would lead to less racially coercive results, such as the release of a marginalized defendant. *See, e.g.*, Megan T. Stevenson & Jennifer L. Doleac, *Algorithmic Risk Assessment in the Hands of Humans* 24–31 (IZA Inst. of Lab. Econ., IZA DP No. 12853, 2019), https://www.econstor.eu/bitstream/10419/215249/1/dp12853.pdf (exploring the role of judicial discretion in following or ignoring algorithmic predictions).

18. *See for example* Barry Friedman & Maria Ponomarenko, *Democratic Policing*, 90 N.Y.U. L. Rev. 1827 (2015) (problematizing the lack of democratic input around police use of surveillance technologies); Andrew Guthrie Ferguson, *Surveillance and the Tyrant Test*, 110 Geo. L.J. 205 (2021) (advocating for a multifaced approach to oversight of algorithmic systems).

19. Ngozi Okidegbe, *Abolitionist Democracy for the Data Driven Age* (work in progress).

20. *See generally* Ngozi Okidegbe, *The Democratizing Potential of Algorithms?*, 53 CONN. L. REV. 739 (2022) [hereinafter Okidegbe, *Democratizing Potential*].

21. *See* Jocelyn Simonson, *Democratizing Criminal Justice through Contestation and Resistance*, 111 NW. U. L. REV. 1609, 1617–21 (2017).

22. *Id.*

23. Ngozi Okidegbe, *Of Afrofuturism, of Algorithms*, 9 CRITICAL ANALYSIS L. 35, 41 (2022) [hereinafter Okidegbe, *Of Afrofuturism*].

24. *See generally* Ngozi Okidegbe, *Discredited Data*, 107 CORNELL L. REV. (forthcoming 2022) [hereinafter Okidegbe, *Discredited Data*].

25. *See* Kristian Lum & William Isaac, *To Predict and Serve?*, SIGNIFICANCE (Oct. 2016), at 14, 16, 18 (describing and demonstrating how algorithmic outputs reinforce bias); *see also* Sandra G. Mayson, *Bias in, Bias out*, 128 YALE L.J. 2218, 2224 (2019).

26. Mayson, *supra* note 25, at 2224.

27. *See generally* Okidegbe, *supra* note 24.

28. *See id.*, at 4–6 (introducing the "data source selection problem").

29. *See id.*, at 15–22 (discussing these carceral knowledge sources in depth).

30. *See id.*, at 22–23 (explaining why exclusive reliance on carceral knowledge sources is an important component to the problem of algorithmic discrimination).

31. *Id.*, at 37.

32. *Id.*, at 37–38 ("Developers often formally and informally consult institutional actors such as judges, prosecutors, and defense lawyers").

33. Miranda Fricker, *Epistemic Oppression and Epistemic Privilege*, 25 CANADIAN J. PHIL. 191, 191 (1999) (theorizing about epistemic oppression's impact on knowledge production processes).

34. *Id.*

35. Okidegbe, *supra* note 24, at 39. This point is informed by Briana Toole, *From Standpoint Epistemology to Epistemic Oppression*, 34 HYPATIA 598, 611 (2019).

36. *See* Ula Y. Taylor, *Making Waves: The Theory and Practice of Black Feminism*, 28 BLACK SCHOLAR 18, 18–19 (1998).

37. *Id.*

38. *See generally* Patricia Hill Collins, *Learning from the Outsider Within: The Sociological Significance of Black Feminist Thought*, 33 SOC. PROBS. S14 (1986).

39. *See* BELL HOOKS, FEMINIST THEORY: FROM MARGIN TO CENTER 4–9 (2015).

40. Collins, *supra* note 38, at S16.

41. *Id.*

42. *See* PATRICIA HILL COLLINS, *Black Feminist Epistemology, in* BLACK FEMINIST THOUGHT: KNOWLEDGE, CONSCIOUSNESS, AND THE POLITICS OF EMPOWERMENT 251, 251 (2nd ed., 2000) (noting that knowledge production practices are not neutral and instead are shaped by the intersecting privilege or oppression that the producer experiences in society).

43. *See id.*

44. *See id.*

45. *See* Collins, *supra* note 38, at S16–18.

46. *See id.*

47. Ruha Benjamin, RACE AFTER TECHNOLOGY: ABOLITIONIST TOOLS FOR THE NEW JIM CODE 15 (2019) ("Just having a more diverse team is an inadequate solution to discriminatory design practices that grow out of the interplay of racism and capitalism"). *See also*, Leila Marie Hampton, BLACK FEMINIST MUSINGS ON ALGORITHMIC OPPRESSION 2 (2021) (accompanying remarks at the 2021 ACM Conference on Fairness, Accountability, & Transparency [FAccT '21]).

48. Olúfẹmi O. Táíwò, *Being-in-the-Room Privilege: Elite Capture and Epistemic Deference*, 108 THE PHILOSOPHER (2020) (discussing the fact that the viewpoints of the most privileged members of

an oppressed group are afforded deference and epistemic privilege in comparison to the viewpoints held by the most marginalized members of an oppressed group), https://www.thephilosopher1923.org /essay-taiwo.

49. *See* Kate Crawford, *Artificial Intelligence's White Guy Problem*, NEW YORK TIMES (June 25, 2016), https://www.nytimes.com/2016/06/26/opinion/sunday/artificial-intelligences-white-guy -problem.html.

50. *See generally* Okidegbe, *supra* note 20.

51. *See* K. Sabeel Rahman & Jocelyn Simonson, *The Institutional Design of Community Control*, 108 CALIF. L. REV. 679, 699–719 (2020) (advocating for endowing oppressed communities with control over governmental institutions implicating in racial and class subordination).

52. *See* Amna A. Akbar, Sameer M. Ashar & Jocelyn Simonson, *Movement Law*, 73 STAN. L. REV. 821, 859–65 (2021).

53. Mari J. Matsuda, *Looking to the Bottom: Critical Legal Studies and Reparations*, 22 HARV. C.R.-C.L. L. REV. 323, 324–26 (1987).

54. *See* Akbar, Ashar & Simonson, *supra* note 52, at 859–65.

55. *See* Olúfẹ́mi Táíwò, *Being-in-the-Room Privilege: Elite Capture and Epistemic Deference*, THE PHILOSOPHER, https://www.thephilosopher1923.org/essay-taiwo (accessed Sept. 8, 2022).

56. *See* Okidegbe, *supra* note 23, at 47–48 ("One could also imagine that the idea of data itself would be expanded to take into account ways of knowing about public safety that are inclusive of all people, even those at the periphery of marginalized communities, such as people living with psychological disabilities, transient people, and other people who have traditionally been unable to actualize their full membership within a community").

57. *Id.*, at 47.

58. *Id.*, at 48.

Conclusion

Toward a Feminist Cyberlaw A-Ha

Kate Darling

Revolution is not a one time event.
—AUDRE LORDE

When I was a doctoral student in intellectual property law & economics, I had a Post-it note above my desk. On it, I had scribbled a John Perry Barlow quote: "Intellectual property is an oxymoron." Barlow and other early pioneers of cyberlaw inspired me to critically examine the assumptions behind copyright and patent law, and I was enamored with the concept of the free flow of ideas.

While I was finishing my doctorate, I moved to Boston and began working as an IP advisor to MIT's Media Lab, advocating for more of what we called "openness." At the Media Lab, we refused to grant exclusive licenses to our patents, made an open-source default for code-based projects, and created an IP pledge for workshop and hackathon participants: they had to promise to make any of the work they did under our roof freely available to society.

One day, I was asked to join a conference call. The request came from an organizer of a Media Lab hackathon called "Make The Breast Pump Not Suck," an event that would bring together designers, developers, and parents from all over the country to innovate around a very outdated piece of technology: the breast pump. One of the teams that had registered for the event wanted to talk to me about the IP pledge. When I dialed into the call, the participant expressed some concerns about not retaining ownership of their hackathon work, especially given the presence of sponsor companies at the event. Could the companies steal the project if it was made freely available?

I had fielded this question many times from the MIT community and was confident in my answer. I told them that our hackathons were about collaboration and sharing. That we believed everyone should have access to the results of the joint creative process in the room. Don't worry, I said, many hackathon teams had gone on to create successful businesses in the past, even after open-sourcing their first idea or prototype. "In my experience," I said, "the companies that participate in our hackathons want to collaborate. They are not here to take ideas from you. Instead, they often end up funding projects or offering to bring you, the innovators, on board to help further develop the work."

The conference call went silent for a moment. Then, the hackathon organizer spoke up. She explained that the participant was part of a team of Black women from Detroit who were bringing their local project to the event. She gently urged me to consider the participant's concerns within the historical context of Black people being denied credit or having their work stolen.

US American culture and history has long erased Black women's work and contributions. I currently work at the intersection of robotics, AI, and society, where I can see the erasure still happening. For example, landmark research by scientists Joy Buolamwini, Timnit Gebru, and Deborah Raji first brought attention to algorithmic bias in facial recognition, but when the CBS news broadcast *60 Minutes* ran a segment about it with multiple expert interviews, they neglected to mention any of the Black female pioneers (despite spending hours gathering information from Buolamwini herself.) It's no accident that Black women have been continuously denied credit for activist movements, or have seen others appropriate their ideas and inventions, and that, as Nina Srejovic and Blake E. Reid demonstrate in their chapters, some groups of people have not been regarded as inventors at all.

The moment I was challenged to think about the hackathon policy through this lens, my "sharing ideas" evangelism came tumbling down. While I didn't exactly become a copyright or patent advocate, it made me understand that "ownership" has a different meaning and importance depending on who you are, and that the IP rebellion I had romanticized often came from a place of great academic height and privilege. With unequal power structures in place, not everyone benefits from the same rules. As Amanda Levendowski, Alexandra J. Roberts, and others express in their chapters a "fair" rule can be an inequitable one, and they urge us not only to see this, but also to consider creative ways of leveraging existing institutions to redistribute power to marginalized groups.

Even the most well-meaning work can be oblivious to the ways it might create or uphold systems of oppression. As Hannah Bloch-Wehba argues in her piece, cyberlaw's early anti-regulatory ideals of free speech paved the way for harm and civil rights abuse online, leading to corporate control mechanisms that are themselves discriminatory. Just as Ngozi Okidegbe warns in her chapter that algorithms can "lock in" our unequal status quo into the future, we must be wary of "locking in" a cyberlaw dogma, or a certain kind of voice. The way we do that is by continuing to broaden our frames of reference.

Feminist Cyberlaw is needed, because we need different perspectives. This collection challenges dominant narratives, exposing some of the hidden interplay of technology, law, and power structures (and is not afraid to use flower metaphors.) Whether it's a Black Feminist approach to criminal legal algorithms or antitrust, exploring Section 230 from an abolitionist viewpoint, or rethinking privacy and security for reproductive rights in the wake of *Dobbs*, the chapters in this book are gulps of fresh air. Like that hackathon conversation years ago, this collection of work created many "a-ha" moments for me, and I hope it did for you, too.

These "a-ha" moments are incredibly valuable, not only because they expose us to new ideas, but because they prompt us to ask what else we are missing. When I was schooled on that call, it was uncomfortable, because I felt like I should have known. How had I never realized the inequity of making everyone play by the same rules when they don't have the same power? The discomfort helped me grow more aware of other blind spots to historical and cultural context, and especially to power dynamics. (For example, how social norms like being "nice" are rules, and enforcing them equally can be inequitable, as well.) My work needed to be more thoughtful, and more critical of the legal, technical, and economic systems I looked to as solutions in the past.

I have a request, if I may. Or perhaps even a call to action. If any part of this book inspired an "a-ha" moment for you, please consider carrying it forward. Many of the chapters create a road map to do so. This conclusion is supposed to speak to the future of feminist cyberlaw (or as some might call it: cyberlaw). All I can say is that this book makes me incredibly hopeful for the future of scholarship in this area. Rather than simply put forth (valid and important) feminist critiques of existing technology, legal institutions, and ways of thinking, much of the work here provides new frameworks to examine our challenges, as well as creative ideas to address them, outlining bold, constructive paths toward change.

And, as Meg Leta Jones writes in the introduction, this is only the beginning. Like her, I've received many an email with "helpful" advice from people who are concerned about the way I speak on the radio. May this book pave the way for more voices in cyberlaw, voices with upspeak and vocal fry, androgenous voices, voices that do or don't code-switch, voices that have something new to say, in a way that we haven't heard before.

I hope one of them will be your voice. Thank you for reading.

ABOUT THE CONTRIBUTORS

KENDRA ALBERT is a public interest technology lawyer, who works as a clinical instructor at the Cyberlaw Clinic at Harvard Law School and as the director of the Initiative for a Representative First Amendment. They hold a BHA. in History and Lighting Design from Carnegie Mellon University and a JD from Harvard Law School. Kendra serves on the board of the ACLU of Massachusetts and as the chair of the board of the Tor Project.

ESHA BHANDARI is deputy director of the ACLU Speech, Privacy, and Technology Project, where she works on litigation and advocacy to protect freedom of expression and privacy rights in the digital age. She focuses on the impact of big data and artificial intelligence on civil liberties. Esha is also an adjunct professor of Clinical Law at New York University School of Law, where she co-teaches the Technology, Law, and Policy Clinic.

HANNAH BLOCH-WEHBA is an associate professor at Texas A&M University School of Law. Her teaching and research focus on privacy, free expression, and technology. She is also an affiliated fellow at Yale Law School's Information Society Project, NYU School of Law's Policing Project, and the Center for Democracy and Technology.

IVÁN CHAAR LÓPEZ is an assistant professor in the Department of American Studies at the University of Texas at Austin. He is the principal investigator of the Border Tech Lab, and his work appears in *American Quarterly, Social Studies of Science, Critical Ethnic Studies, The Guardian*, and *Interactions* (ACM).

CYNTHIA H. CONTI-COOK is an expert on the legal and digital technologies of criminalization. She is a civil rights attorney and strategist who has participated in coalitions at the forefront of campaigns against police secrecy (Repeal50-A in NYS) and for NYPD accountability. In 2022, Cynthia was featured on CNN, MSNBC, and interviewed by Michael Moore about her observations on existing technology threats to bodily autonomy.

LEAH CHAN GRINVALD is the dean and Richard J. Morgan Professor of Law at the William S. Boyd School of Law at the University of Nevada, Las Vegas. Her research and writing focus on the enforcement of intellectual property laws, both domestically and internationally. Prior to entering academia, Leah was the Global Corporate Counsel for Taylor Made Golf Company, Inc. (formerly a subsidiary of adidas), and prior to her in-house role, an associate at the law firms of Latham & Watkins and Clifford Chance LLP.

KATE DARLING is a research scientist at the MIT Media Lab and the author of *The New Breed: What Our History with Animals Reveals about Our Future with Robots*. Her work examines the intersections of robotics, law, ethics, and society.

ELIZABETH E. JOH is a professor of law at the University of California, Davis School of Law. Professor Joh is a leading expert on the intersection of policing, technology, and privacy. Her writing has appeared in leading law reviews as well as in major publications for general audiences.

MEG LETA JONES is Provost's Distinguished Associate Professor in the Communication, Culture & Technology program at Georgetown University where she researches rules and technological change with a focus on privacy and automation. She's also a core faculty member of the Science, Technology, and International Affairs program in Georgetown's School of Foreign Service, a faculty affiliate with the Institute for Technology Law & Policy at Georgetown Law Center, and a faculty fellow at the Georgetown Ethics Lab.

AMANDA LEVENDOWSKI is an associate professor of law and the founding director of the Intellectual Property and Information Policy Clinic at Georgetown Law. Her scholarship and clinical work use intellectual property, privacy, and cyberlaws to shape better technologies. She also creates art through her Cyberspace and Technology (CAT) Lab. She lives in Washington, DC, with her husband and her cat, Waffles.

KAREN LEVY is an associate professor in the Department of Information Science at Cornell University and associated faculty at Cornell Law School. She researches the legal, social, and ethical dimensions of data-intensive technologies. Levy is a New America National Fellow and a Fellow of the Canadian Institute for Advanced Research, and is the author of *Data Driven: Truckers, Technology, and the New Workplace Surveillance*.

JASMINE MCNEALY is an associate professor in the Department of Media Production, Management, and Technology in the College of Journalism and Communications at the University of Florida.

MICHELA MEISTER is a PhD candidate in computer science at Cornell University. She studies algorithms, networks, and recommender systems. Before starting her PhD, she worked as a software engineer at Google Research.

NGOZI OKIDEGBE is a Moorman-Simon Interdisciplinary Career Development Associate Professor of Law and assistant professor of Computing & Data Sciences. Her focus is in the areas of law and technology, criminal procedure, and racial justice. Her work examines how the use of predictive technologies in the criminal justice system impacts racially marginalized communities. Professor Okidegbe's articles have been published or are forthcoming in the *Critical Analysis of Law, Connecticut Law Review, UCLA Law Review, Cornell Law Review*, and *Michigan Law Review*.

BLAKE E. REID writes, teaches, and practices at the intersection of law, policy, and technology. He is an associate professor of law at Colorado Law, where he serves as the (outgoing) director of the Samuelson-Glushko Technology Law & Policy Clinic (TLPC) and as the faculty director of the Telecom and Platforms Initiative at the Silicon Flatirons Center. Before joining the faculty at Colorado Law, he was a staff attorney and graduate fellow in First Amendment and media law at the Institute for Public Representation at Georgetown Law and a law clerk for Justice Nancy E. Rice on the Colorado Supreme Court.

GABRIELLE M. REJOUIS (she/her) is a legal fellow at United for Respect (UFR) and the Athena Coalition, where she advocates against worker surveillance and the use of technology to erode workers' rights. Prior to joining UFR, she managed the federal tech and antitrust policy portfolio at Color Of Change and co-organized the Color of Surveillance: Monitoring Poor and Working People conference for the Center on Privacy & Technology at Georgetown Law. She earned her JD from Georgetown Law and BA from the New Jersey Institute of Technology.

ALEXANDRA J. ROBERTS is professor of law & media at Northeastern University School of Law and Northeastern University College of Arts, Media & Design. She teaches and writes about intellectual property, trademarks, entertainment law, and false advertising.

VICTORIA SÁNCHEZ is a visiting researcher at the Border Tech Lab, The University of Texas at Austin. Her research interests include feminist STS, the racial politics of care, and Latinx Studies. She is also a gamer, and currently works on the Diversity & Inclusion team at Riot Games.

NINA SREJOVIC is a visiting professor at Georgetown University Law Center. Professor Srejovic's research tackles the intersection of new technologies and intellectual property and examines root causes for the underrepresentation of women in the innovation narrative. Professor Srejovic is a graduate of the University of Michigan Law School and Stanford University.

OFER TUR-SINAI is a senior lecturer at Ono Academic College in Israel, where he teaches IP law, private international law, and legal aspects of high-tech entrepreneurship. Ofer holds an LLB (summa cum laude) from Hebrew University of Jerusalem, LLM (Kent Scholar) from Columbia University, and an LLD: Doctor of Laws from Hebrew University. Prior to becoming a full time law professor, Ofer clerked for the honorable Justice Dorit Beinisch of the Israeli Supreme Court and worked as a transactional lawyer in prominent law firms both in New York and in Israel. Ofer's writing focuses on IP law and innovation theory.

ANJALI VATS is an associate professor of law at the University of Pittsburgh with a secondary appointment in communication. Her book, *The Color of Creatorship: Intellectual Property, Race and the Making of Americans* (Stanford UP, 2020), examines how intellectual property law is shaped by race, colonialism, and nationalism.

INDEX

Founded in 1893,
UNIVERSITY OF CALIFORNIA PRESS
publishes bold, progressive books and journals
on topics in the arts, humanities, social sciences,
and natural sciences—with a focus on social
justice issues—that inspire thought and action
among readers worldwide.

The UC PRESS FOUNDATION
raises funds to uphold the press's vital role
as an independent, nonprofit publisher, and
receives philanthropic support from a wide
range of individuals and institutions—and from
committed readers like you. To learn more, visit
ucpress.edu/supportus.